J

Xmas - 74.

Narvik

SEA BATTLES IN CLOSE-UP · 9

Narvik
BATTLES IN THE FJORDS

CAPT PETER DICKENS
DSO MBE DSC Royal Navy

LONDON

IAN ALLAN LTD

First published 1974

ISBN 0 7110 0484 6

All rights reserved. No part of this book may be reproduced or transmitted in any form or by any means, electronic or mechanical, including photo-copying, recording or by any information storage and retrieval system, without permission from the Publisher in writing.

© Peter Dickens 1974

Published by Ian Allan Ltd, Shepperton, Surrey and printed in the United Kingdom by Morrison and Gibb Ltd, London and Edinburgh

Contents

Preface   9

1. Norway 1940   13
2. The Forces Gather   21
3. April 9th and the Occupation of Narvik   34
4. The First Battle of Narvik   48
      Narvik Harbour   59
      The Battle in the Fjord   74
5. The Vortex of the Storm   97
6. The Second Battle   112
7. Afterthoughts   156

Appendix 1—Ships and Senior Officers   160
Appendix 2—Weapons   166
Appendix 3—Casualties   171

Bibliography   173
Index   175

Maps and Plans

General Map—The German Approach (1)	15
The German Approach (2)	26
Approaches to Narvik, Evening April 9th	45
Ofotfjord—The 2nd British Destroyer Flotilla Approach	53
Violation of Narvik Harbour, 0430 April 10th	59
Narvik Harbour 0450	64
The *Diether von Roeder*'s Torpedoes	69
Battle in Ofotfjord	75
Wolff Turns West	83
Collision	85
The Rescue	86
April 13th—The Second Battle	
1230–1300	122
1300–1330	127
1330–1400	130
1400–1500	139

Preface

I had thought in my innocence that all was known about the Naval Battles of Narvik that needed to be known in order to write their story, but I was very wrong. New facts kept coming to light, and as the scope of my enquiries grew I found I had undertaken twice the amount of work I had bargained for; fortunately, pleasure and excitement grew in like proportion.

The interplay of the main German and British forces outside Vestfjord, before the invasion of Norway, which so nearly resulted in a momentous confrontation; the narrowness of the margin by which Warburton-Lee was not reinforced by a cruiser and four large destroyers before the first battle; the potentially decisive effect of five U-Boats in the fjords; the catastrophic results of the German torpedo's failure; the impotence of the gun at the ranges for which it had been designed; and tactical details outside the scope of studies concerning the Norwegian campaign as a whole; all these I believe need to be brought out for a proper understanding of what happened. There is fresh drama too, but alas gaps remain in my research which I have been quite unable to fill; I apologise for these, and for any mistakes I have unwittingly made in reconstructing events from the known facts.

I have tried to tell the story from the viewpoints of both sides equally, with no moral or political bias, and to strike a mean between over-dramatisation and dry-as-dust factual narrative; the one is tedious, the other unreal because what people do in action is only comprehensible against a background of barely tolerable tension.

Whether those who come after think that these battles were exciting or not, they were certainly among the most traumatic experiences in the lives of those who took part. Many prayers were said by those lapsed in the practice; clean underclothes were sheepishly donned, to minimise contamination of possible wounds; warm, enticing messdecks and cabins were but lingeringly abandoned for the frozen decks; well-loved photographs were scrutinised with new and perhaps final intensity; one officer went below and wept when he believed a wrong decision to have been timidly taken. The future was a blank; all assurance of security had vanished and could only be brought back by mighty exertions, but even so someone had to lose. Criticism must be sensitive and sympathetic to be valid.

Narvik has enlarged and enriched my circle of acquaintance considerably, and to my great pleasure and advantage because everyone has been wonderfully interested and helpful; I cannot begin to thank them enough. I was very lucky to meet or be in touch with so many survivors of the battles:

British
First Battle

Captain H. F. H. Layman DSO★	HMS *Hotspur*, in command.
Mr G. Watling	HMS *Hotspur*, Leading Seaman.
Captain J. P. Wright DSO★ OBE	HMS *Hostile*, in command.
Captain J. G. Little OBE	HMS *Hostile*, Engineer Officer.
Captain G. H. Stanning DSO	HMS *Hardy*, Captain's Secretary.
Lieutenant Commander G. R. Heppel DSO	HMS *Hardy*, Flotilla Torpedo Officer.
Mr C. E. Cope	HMS *Hardy*, Leading Seaman.
Captain F. L. Millns CBE DSC	HMS *Havock*, Gunner (T).
Commander J. B. Burfield MVO DSC★	HMS *Havock*, Torpedo Control Officer.
Commander H. A. Stuart-Menteth DSC	HMS *Hunter*, First Lieutenant.
Captain A. G. Reid OBE	HMS *Hunter*, Engineer Officer.
Captain Charles Evans	SS *North Cornwall*, Master.

Second Battle

Rear Admiral St J. A. Micklethwait CB DSO★★	HMS *Eskimo*, in command.
Captain R. D. Ritchie CBE MVO	HMS *Eskimo*, Gunnery Officer.
Rear Admiral R. A. Currie CB DSC★	HMS *Warspite* and *Renown*, Staff Officer Operations to Admiral Whitworth.
Captain W. L. M. Brown DSO OBE DSC	HMS *Warspite*, Observer.
Lieut Commander F. C. Rice DSM	HMS *Warspite*, Pilot.

Mr M. Pacey	HMS *Warspite*, Telegraphist Air Gunner.
Vice Admiral Sir Hilary Biggs KBE CB DSO*	HMS *Hero*, in command.
Mr F. Smith	HMS *Hero* and *Furious*, Telegraphist Air Gunner.
Captain G. H. Peters DSC	HMS *Foxhound*, in command.
Commander E. B. Tancock OBE DSC*	HMS *Forester*, in command.
Captain I. G. H. Garnett DSC	HMS *Bedouin*, Gunnery Officer.
Lieutenant Commander R. C. Henley	HMS *Bedouin*, Torpedo Control Officer.
Commander D. P. Willan DSC	HMS *Icarus*.
Commander V. C. F. Clark DSC*	HMS *Punjabi*, First Lieutenant.
Vice Admiral Sir Peter Gretton KCB DSO* OBE DSC	HMS *Cossack*, First Lieutenant.

German

Konteradmiral K. Smidt	*Erich Giese*, in command.
Fl Admiral M-E. Wolff	*Georg Thiele*, in command.
Kapitän zur See C. Rechel	*Bernd von Arnim*, in command.
Kapitän zur See H. Friedrichs	*Hans Lüdemann*, in command.
Kapitän zur See F. Böhme	*Anton Schmitt*, in command.
Kapitän zur See K. T. Raeder	*Erich Giese*, Junior Officer.
Kapitän zur See H. Dehnert	*Diether von Roeder*, Junior Officer.

I am also extremely indebted to: Mr J. D. Lawson, Rear Admiral P. N. Buckley CB DSO and all the staff of the Naval Historical Branch, Ministry of Defence; Mrs Sutherland (formerly Mrs Warburton-Lee), Mrs Robert Sherbrooke, Mrs Trevor Lean, Messrs A. G. Mallis and C. J. Susans of the Weapons Museum, RN Armament Depot, Priddy's Hard, Captain S. W. Roskill CBE DSC, Captain B. H. Kent of HMS *Mercury*, Dr J. Rohwer of the Bibliothek für Zeitgeschichte Weltkriegbücherie, Stuttgart, and the British War Graves Commission.

Lastly, the manuscript has been read critically by Admiral Micklethwait, Admiral Wolff, Captain Layman, Commander Burfield and Lieutenant Commander Heppel to whom the reader and I owe much gratitude, their considerable efforts having ensured the greatest possible degree of accuracy.

CHAPTER ONE

Norway 1940

'The war is going to start properly soon, and I'm going to start it.' So wrote Captain Bernard Warburton-Lee, Captain (D) Second British Destroyer Flotilla, to his wife on April 5th, 1940. When she received the letter the war had started indeed, and her husband had earned its first Victoria Cross, posthumously.

It is often said that the period between the outbreak of hostilities and the Germany invasion of Norway was far from 'Phoney' at sea. Already over 400 allied merchant ships had been sunk, at a cost to the Germans of 17 U-Boats; the *Royal Oak*, the *Courageous*, six destroyers and three British submarines had gone; the Battle of the River Plate had been fought and the *Graf Spee* lost. More had happened besides, and both the British Fleet and the German U-Boats and raiders had spent an exhausting winter at full stretch, yet the psychological atmosphere was still one of unreality. No armies had moved, and it has to be admitted by even the most ardent exponents of Sea and Air Power that a campaign or war must usually be judged to be won or lost by the answer to the question: whose soldiers are standing where?

There was an air of expectancy; men wondered how they personally would react to real war, fighting to the last ounce of their strength, killing and being killed: disturbing questions that each can only answer, by experience, for himself. But at the same time, the 'phoney' attitude on the British side still led many to think it possible that no one would get killed; that if they just held on the war would solve itself; and that all that really mattered to the British Home Fleet was to prevent the Germans breaking out into the Atlantic in strength. That would be serious indeed.

Throughout the winter Norway's strategic importance became increasingly clear to both belligerents and was much discussed in high places. The greater part of Germany's iron ore, on which her war economy depended absolutely, was mined in North Sweden and normally shipped from Lulea on the Baltic; but when that port froze it had to be sent through Narvik in Norway. From there the freighters would have been vulnerable to British attack had it not been for the unique configuration of the Norwegian coast, the Inner Leads making it possible to remain in territorial waters protected from seaward for the major part of the passage. Ships other than ore-carriers had also sought safety in the Leads: blockade runners; even naval auxiliaries such as the *Altmark*, which had been armed and carried prisoners of war; and who could tell whether Germany would not use them for warships and U-Boats, exerting pressure on a Norway too weak to resist, to overlook such infringements of her neutrality. And the British; what might they not do?

British and German Plans

The First Lord of the Admiralty, Winston Churchill, found the logic of these facts to lead inexorably towards action to stop the enemy's Norwegian coastal trade, and by the spring he had his way. The plan was simple and on a deceptively small scale: at three places where the route was not protected by off-lying islands it was to be mined, thus forcing traffic out of territorial waters and into the arms of the contraband control service, who would seize enemy ships and allow neutrals to pass freely. Since, however, the enemy could be expected to react violently to this blow to his vital interests, a military expedition was prepared in case he should go so far as to land in Norway.

In Germany, Admiral Raeder's thinking ran on similar lines. His country must have the ore at all costs, and great strategic advantage was to be had from the free use of Norwegian coastal waters, and even bases. The British would inevitably try to stop the traffic but must not be allowed to succeed. For Germany there was no cheap and easy solution to the problem such as laying a few minefields: indeed there was only one solution, the occupation of Norway up to and including Narvik. The end link of this remorseless chain of logic was the need for complete surprise; a wholly airborne invasion was impracticable, and there was no hope of traversing the sea to Northern Norway in the face of an alerted Home Fleet. The operation had, therefore, to be planned and mounted as a set piece; this would take time, and it was as early as March 1st that Raeder persuaded Hitler to order the occupation of Norway and Denmark for early April, when the Danish Belts would be free of ice, daylight

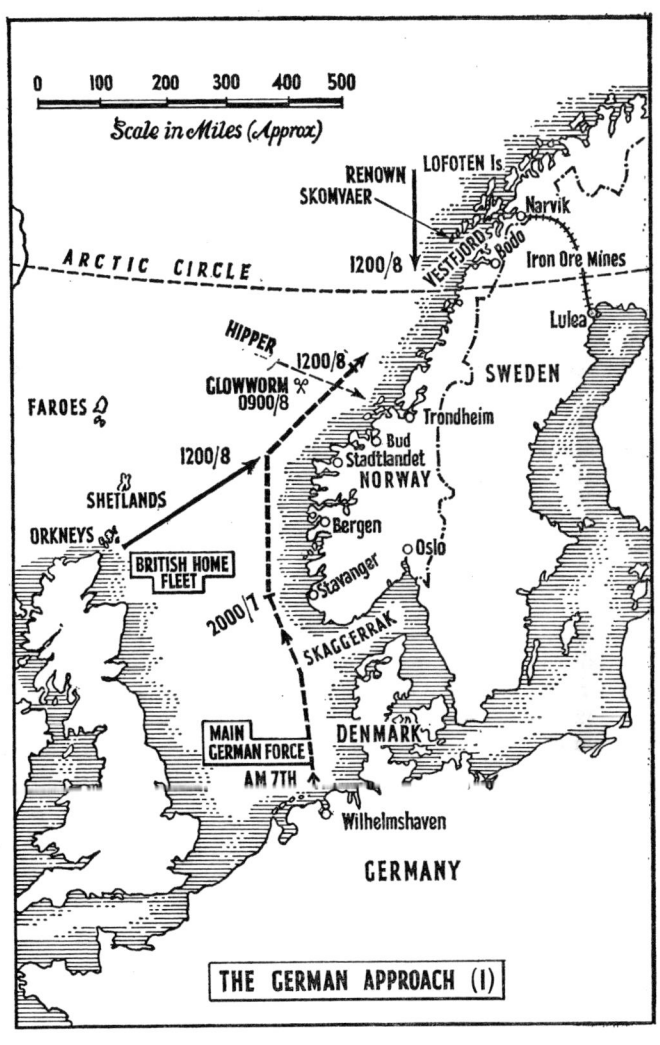

General Map—The German Approach (1)

would have come to the Arctic circle and, hopefully, spring weather would assist the sea voyages.

The Germans got wind of the British plan, were determined not to be forestalled, and it so happened that the two undertakings coincided. When Warburton-Lee wrote of starting the war properly he referred to his assignment of escorting the northernmost force of minelayers. He may well have anticipated a consequential naval battle, for the Germans would surely react; but neither he nor any British commander apparently guessed what they were really up to. The minelaying operation having been mounted with the utmost secrecy, the British assumed that the enemy knew nothing about it; and when large German forces were found to be at sea off the Norwegian coast, they took it for a most unlucky chance. What could be the explanation? Surely that the dreaded Atlantic break-out was beginning.

Both tradition and current doctrine in the Royal Navy demanded that a major threat to the trade routes be countered by maximum effort. If this is understood, the British reactions to the German moves become easier to apprehend than when they are viewed with the unfair clarity of hindsight.

German Operation Weserübung

Surprise, ruthless determination and unrestrained vigour were the keynotes of the orders. The risks were well understood, but the imperative need to secure Norway was so great that success was considered to justify the loss of no less than half the entire surface fleet if necessary. Thus what to the free world appeared as the brutal violation of a peaceful, innocent and undefended neutral, the Germans believed to be vital for the defence of their homeland against the remorseless and inhuman British blockade. By such stuff are men's hearts stirred to battle.

Troops were to be landed, mainly from warships, in the early hours of April 9th at Narvik, Trondheim, Bergen, Kristiansand and Oslo. Surprise demanded that the assaults be simultaneous and consequently the forces sailed from Germany at varying times. Having landed their troops, the warships were to return at the earliest possible moment; for the sooner they could sail, the less would be the risk of meeting superior British forces. Both outward and homeward voyages were to be covered by the battlecruisers *Gneisenau* and *Scharnhorst* under Vice-Admiral Lütjens, and in overall command of naval operations would be Admiral Saalwechter, Marinegruppenkommando West (Group West) near Wilhelmshaven.

U-Boat Command would assist to the full, and independently routed merchant ships, posing as innocent traders and using the Leads as necessary, were to provide the soldiers with their heavy weapons, ammunition, transport and stores, and the warships with fuel for their return journeys.

The Air Force was to be used extensively for combat and transport; Narvik, however, was out of reach, and operations there must of necessity be entirely naval and military. It is well known that the British were shocked and dismayed by the decisive impact of air power on their hitherto unassailable Navy, but it seems that the Germans also underestimated its importance in thinking they could capture and hold Narvik without it; that place was the prime objective, the apex of a great pyramid built up towards it, yet its seizure was planned as a long-odds gamble.

The Destroyers

No fewer than 10 of Germany's 22 large, modern ships were to comprise the Narvik force. Each would embark 200 mountain troops with light weapons, and such equipment as mountain guns and motor cycles as could be lashed on deck. The British were later much concerned at the danger from mines in the fjords, but none were taken.

The leadership of this force fell naturally on to the shoulders of the Kommodore Destroyers, Kommodore Friedrich Bonte. An experienced destroyer officer and a man of moral standards, he nevertheless leaves the impression of lacking in decisiveness; a worrier who found it hard to judge between conflicting arguments. When a sailor fell overboard from the *Von der Tann* in 1917 there had been no mental dilemma and Bonte had jumped instantly; but believing as he did that Hitler and National Socialism were inherently bad, he suffered as he yet served them. That is not to say he was half-hearted about the operation, far from it, but his distress can perhaps be read between the lines of this order to his men:

'New tasks await us; we will carry them out. We have sworn it to the Führer. Whoever swears on the flag of the Führer has no longer any individual rights. Long live the Führer!'

Bonte's leader was the *Wilhelm Heidkamp* (Korvettenkapitän Hans Erdmenger) of the brand new Diether von Roeder class, which was an improvement on the earlier Leberecht Maass class, though carrying the same main armament. (See Appendix 1.)

Also belonging to the new class were the ships of the Third Flotilla, led by Fregattenkapitän Hans-Joachim Gadow in the *Hans Lüdemann* (Korvettenkapitän Herbert Friedrichs), with the *Hermann Künne* (Korvettenkapitän Kothe), *Diether von Roeder* (Korvettenkapitän Erich Holtorf), and *Anton Schmitt* (Korvettenkapitän Friedrich Böhme).

The Fourth Flotilla was equipped with the older class of destroyer, albeit none were completed earlier than 1937. It was led by Fregattenkapitän Erich Bey in the *Wolfgang Zenker* (Fregattenkapitän Gottfried Pönitz), with the *Bernd von Arnim* (Korvettenkapitän Curt Rechel), *Erich Giese* (Korvettenkapitän Karl Smidt), and *Erich Koellner* (Fregattenkapitän Alfred Schultze-Hinrichs).

Last but certainly not least was a single ship of the First Flotilla, the *Georg Thiele* (Leberecht Maass class) commanded by Korvettenkapitän Max-Eckart Wolff, with the Flotilla Commander, Fregattenkapitän Berger also embarked.

From the North German ports, where the forces assembled, to Narvik is about 1,020 nautical miles, and the time of arrival, 0415 on 9th April, was mandatory. Prudent navigation, and the probability of set-backs such as breakdowns and bad weather, indicated a moderate speed giving plenty of time in hand; but the longer the time at sea, the greater the chance of interception, and an average speed of over 20 knots was chosen. This could be expected to impose great strain on hulls, machinery and men, and might well result in some ships failing to arrive, but these risks were accepted in the overriding interest of surprise. Sailing time thus became early on 7th.

Bonte's force was to sail with the *Gneisenau* and *Scharnhorst* as far as the entrance to Vestfjord (see map. p. 15), and the force destined for Trondheim, consisting of the heavy cruiser *Hipper* and four destroyers, would also be in company for much of the voyage.

The U-Boats

U-Boat Command was ordered to support the operation with every available submarine, but Admiral Dönitz went further, stopping all training and fitting out his six instructional boats for active service. His first task was to protect the surface forces from enemy attack while they were in the fjords, and to this end he decided to station a group of U-Boats outside the ports with orders to follow the warships into narrow waters. Secondly he had to be prepared for enemy counter-landings, but since he could not guess where these might take place he would hold other groups to seaward ready for redeployment. For the Narvik operation he allowed four boats, which were to be on station in the outer Vestfjord when the destroyers arrived; these were the *U51* (Kapitänleutnant Knorr), *U25* (Korvettenkapitän Schütze), *U46* (Kapitänleutnant Sohler), and *U64* (Kapitänleutnant Schulz). The last named did not arrive for the opening phase.

Dönitz was not altogether sanguine about his boats' chances of success in confined waters; navigation would be difficult, it would not be easy to charge batteries undetected, and there would be constant risk of being sighted from the shore or by enemy patrols. On the other hand the enemy was bound to come to them, if he wished to thwart the invasion; and they were equipped with the modern G7e electric, trackless torpedo, whose warhead was detonated by the Pi.G7a magnetic pistol which, exploding underneath its target, was expected to inflict considerably greater damage than the impact type.

A further drawback, which did not appear in advance, was the absence of direct communication between U-Boats and surface ships, or indeed of much mutual understanding of each other's problems. In the German Fleet, as in the British, the Submarine arm tended to be something of a private navy controlled by its own Headquarters, and although it was fortunate that this was sited adjacent to Group West outside Wilhelmshaven, every signal from a U-Boat that concerned the destroyers had to be de-coded at U-Boat Headquarters, passed to Group West, re-coded, and re-transmitted. To operate destroyers and U-Boats in the same narrow waters being unconventional, it would seem that unconventional communications should also have been instituted.

The Trojan Horses

Essential supplies for Narvik would be carried in the freighters *Alster*, motor transport and military stores, *Rauenfels*, army weapons and ammunition, and the tankers *Kattegat* and *Jan Wellem*, fuel and naval stores for the destroyers and U-Boats. The first three of these were to sail from Germany; the last, a converted whale factory ship, was happily at Murmansk so that her voyage to Narvik would be both shorter and less conspicuous. Pains were taken to make the ships appear as innocent as possible to both external and internal inspection;

the *Alster*, for instance, was given a layer of coke over her main cargo.

British Operation Wilfrid

Mines were to be laid in the morning of April 8th off the southern shore of Vestfjord and near Statlandet, together with a dummy minefield off Bud. (See map p. 15.) The northern group of mine-laying destroyers would comprise the *Esk*, *Impulsive*, *Icarus*, and *Ivanhoe*, two of those main armament guns and both torpedo tube mountings were to be removed to compensate for the extra topweight of the mines; this weakening of their fighting capability was to prove significant later. The minelayers were to be escorted by four ships of the Second Destroyer Flotilla: the *Hardy* (Captain Warburton-Lee), *Hotspur* (Commander Herbert Layman), *Havock* (Lieutenant Commander Rafe Courage), and *Hunter* (Lieutenant Commander Lindsay de Villiers).

The dummy minefield off Bud was to be simulated by two destroyers of which one, the *Hero* (Commander Hilary Biggs), also belonged to the Second Flotilla. The whole force was to sail to the area in company with, and under the orders of, Vice-Admiral Jock Whitworth in the battlecrusier *Renown*, whose screen comprised the *Greyhound* and *Glowworm*.

When the mines had been laid the minelayers were to return to base, while their escorts would remain on patrol to warn shipping and arrest any enemy ships that might be forced out of territorial waters; a small detachment of Royal Marines was embarked in each ship for this latter purpose. It is unnecessary to go into further details of Operation Wilfrid because, in the event, the minefields' potential effect was nullified by the German invasion. What matters is that British and German forces were coincidentally at sea in the same area.

CHAPTER TWO

The Forces Gather

The support ships *Alster*, *Rauenfels* and *Kattegat* sailed from Germany on April 3rd for their crucial voyages. They must arrive on time or the troops and destroyers would be out on a limb indeed, but they must not be unmasked or the operation could end in total disaster, if it was able even to begin. 'Softly softly catchee monkey', they slipped into the Leads and virtually vanished from friend and foe alike. Some time later the *Jan Wellem* left Murmansk for Narvik; she was of course subject to the same compulsions but her task was a great deal easier.

Admiral Whitworth sailed from Scapa Flow in the *Renown* on April 5th and steered northeast for Operation Wilfrid, collecting the minelayers and their escorts as he went. His speed was moderate; there was no need to hurry, for the Northern Ocean was virtually a British lake, and it was important to preserve the minelayers from weather damage.

Only one apparently minor incident marred the even progress of the passage. On the morning of the 6th the *Glowworm* lost a man overboard and turned back to search; the visibility being low she was lost to sight immediately, and Whitworth could not tell her of a forthcoming course alteration, wireless silence being rigidly enforced. Roope, the *Glowworm*'s Captain, had not yet been told the orders and did not know where to go, so when Whitworth detached two destroyers to the Shetlands for fuel in accordance with the plan, he told them to try and find the *Glowworm* and tell her to rejoin at a rendezvous off Vestfjord the next day; if they missed her they were to pass the order by coded signal on arrival in harbour. Neither expedient succeeded and the *Glowworm* remained lost. Otherwise the 6th was a peaceful day with the weather not too bad; it was to be the last such for many days.

Although nothing actually happened to the British force on the

7th, anxiety and doubt began to assail senior officers when aircraft sighting reports were received of unusual enemy activity to the west of Denmark. These culminated in a remarkably accurate description of the main German force which had sailed on time: one battlecruiser, one pocket battleship, three cruisers and 12 destroyers, course northwest off the entrance to the Skaggerak at about 1325. The information was delayed and did not become available until 1730.

This was a threat, and more than a threat; but to what? A clue had been given in an Admiralty message to the Commander-in-Chief, Home Fleet, Admiral Sir Charles Forbes:

'Recent reports suggest that German expedition is being prepared. Hitler is reported from Copenhagen to have ordered unostentatious movement of one division in ten ships by night to land in Narvik. Simultaneous occupation of Jutland. Sweden to be left alone. Moderates said to be opposing the plan. Date given for arrival in Narvik 8th.'

Why then was there any doubt? Because the second paragraph read:

'All these reports are of doubtful value and may well be only a further move in the war of nerves= 1259/7th.' (Time of origin.)

Nevertheless the Fleet sailed from Scapa at 2015 on the 7th.

Admiral Whitworth was not sent this latter signal, but did receive the enemy reports on which to ponder during the night of the 7th. At 2000 he reached a position southwest of the tip of the Lofoten Islands, Skomvaer, where he detached the minelayers and escorts. The cruiser *Birmingham* and two destroyers were supposed to meet him there but did not, and they, with the *Glowworm*'s continuing absence, gave him cause for nagging concern. He took the *Renown* with her only remaining escort, the *Greyhound*, to patrol 30 miles west of Skomvaer and await events.

The Germans' Stormy Passage

The weather worsened. When, only yesterday, the mountain troops had embarked in the German destroyers all had been gay and exciting. Men from the Tyrol, Styria, Carinthia and the Voralberg, in the very heart of Europe, met ships and sailors for the first time; their boots clattered on steel decks, they slipped down ladders and fiddled like children with valves and switches to the alarm of their hosts. Where were they going? To Scotland perhaps, there were mountains there; yes, it must be Scotland, and why not? Whisky is good.

They were dreadfully overcrowded to be sure, but the voyage would not be long.

Now, as darkness closed in on the evening of the 7th, they knew they had come to hell. Emasculated by nausea they found themselves hurled from one unyielding bulkhead to another, only to be catapulted back whence they had come; where they sought to put their feet the deck forestalled them by plunging downwards, and they only met it again on the upthrust which jarried their ankles but failed to stop their stomachs. There were many broken limbs and countless abrasions, and in their minds fear strove for mastery with resigned despair. No wonder some felt they must breathe fresh air at any cost, even to the extent of disobeying the most rigid order to stay below; and no wonder the swirling, cascading masses of water that were wrenching boats, stores, guns and motor cycles from their lashings, seized them too and swept them into the black void astern.

Ten men were lost that night, but there was no going back for them; even if time had permitted it would not have been practicable. The gale was in the southwest, on the port quarter, and every destroyer officer knows how nearly impossible it is to keep a ship on a steady course while at high speed in such conditions. Each comber lifts the stern and hurls it violently to starboard; the rudder is then in thin water, or perhaps none at all, and unless a starboard correction has been applied in anticipation by a helmsman highly skilled in his art, the ship will take matters out of his hands, complete the turn, and lie over on her starboard beam-ends, broached to. The *Hans Lüdemann* did so, missing another ship by feet as she yawed, and it may be supposed that the Captains were unhappier even than the soldiers for they knew the dangers to be real. Speed could not be slackened, and yet the 17 ships must stay in tight formation for the visibility was low and it would be so easy to lose touch. The *Wilhelm Heidkamp* and *Anton Schmitt* nearly collided; the *Wolfgang Zenker* and *Bernd von Arnim* suffered partial steering failures, and weather damage was universal. The newer Diether von Roeder class, with higher freeboard and greater buoyancy forward, put up a better showing than the others, whose design for seakeeping was afterwards judged officially to be poor. Nevertheless the successful completion of the passage was a fine achievement, especially allowing for the German Fleet's strategic position which did not allow it the experience of almost continuous sea-time in all weathers of its British opponent.

Admiral Raeder had demanded the greatest possible tenacity and determination, and he got them.

The dawn of the 8th was wild, and revealed the formation to be in similar case. The *Erich Giese* indeed was nowhere to be seen and neither could she see any other ship; her gyro room was flooded and she was doing her best to steer by a madly swinging magnetic compass. The *Bernd von Arnim* retained only a tenuous link with the force through the blurred vision of one other destroyer. The *Hans Lüdemann*, too, was on her own until just before 0800 when her Captain, Friedrichs, and the Third Flotilla Leader, Gadow, were reassured to sight another ship; but their relief was only momentary for a second look revealed her to be foreign, probably British. She was of course the *Glowworm*.

The Glowworm Epic

Gadow judged the enemy to be unready for action, and soon great gouts of smoke clearly indicated that she was struggling to raise steam in all three boilers. At first he thought it his duty to close and sink her before she could make an enemy report, but then he realised that the chances of a successful gun action in that weather were small, though it was by no means impossible that an unlucky hit on the *Hans Lüdemann* might prejudice his overriding aim of delivering his troops safely at Narvik. He therefore ordered Friedrichs and the *Bernd von Arnim*, who had by now also stumbled into the fray, to evade.

That seems to have been easier said than done, probably because Roope rightly saw his duty as the traditional one of keeping touch with and reporting the enemy, and the three ships were engaged for nearly an hour. They pitched, rolled and turned, their guns blazing but without any recorded hits. That was to be expected; in such weather the gunnery of those days tended to be full of sound and fury, signifying very little. The ship most at risk was the *Bernd von Arnim* of the older class who had twice to stop to right herself after particularly vicious rolls at full speed, her bridge having scooped up half a metre of water from the sea. Her Captain, Rechel, compared her design most unfavourably with that of his opponent, 800 tons lighter.

But then the *Hipper* returned from the north to help the German destroyers. The range, dictated by the visibility, was short; the cruiser's steadier motion enabled her to hit the *Glowworm* time and time again with 8in shells and Roope, seeing the end, closed to fire torpedoes, which the *Hipper* avoided, and retired behind smoke to give the impression that he was trying to escape. The *Hipper*, following, emerged from the smoke to see the *Glowworm* on a closing course at full speed, too near to avoid. She crashed into the big cruiser's starboard side and all guns fell silent, perhaps through awe for when she drifted astern they did not re-start. The Germans took pains to rescue all the survivors they could, but there were only 38 and Roope was not among them. His was the first VC to be earned, though it could not be awarded until his deed became known much later.

The *Hipper*'s damage was severe but did not prevent her from carrying out her mission at Trondheim. More important were the *Glowworm*'s enemy reports which she transmitted regularly while in contact with the enemy, at first specifying two destroyers and finally 'one unknown warship'. Her signals at last faded and ceased, leaving all who received them in no doubt that she had been overwhelmed by a heavy ship. Her glorious sacrifice, like that of Grenville's *Revenge*, will never be forgotten in the Royal Navy; but had the information she died to obtain been properly interpreted, she could have been the instrument of saving Norway, no less, and her name would have been honoured by the world.

As it was, all remained obscure to the British who felt there was no option but to dispatch forces to the scene of action, even though the enemy was more likely to have moved on by the time they arrived. From the south, the Commander-in-Chief sent the battle-cruiser *Repulse* (Captain E. J. Spooner DSO) with two cruisers and four destroyers, while Whitworth took the *Renown* and *Greyhound* southwards, all at their best speeds.

The Plot Thickens

Admiral Whitworth started to puzzle out the enemy's most likely intention, and what he ought to do about it; this proved to be a thankless task. In the first place he was not helped by the *Renown*'s port bulge peeling away from the ship's side as a result of her thrusting into the gale, so that speed had to be reduced. Then, at 1045, he received an Admiralty signal ordering the minelaying destroyers and escorts to join him; no reason was given and he could only presume the Admiralty wanted a concentration of force to seaward to guard against a German break-out to the north. But half an hour later the Admiralty signalled that it seemed possible that the German forces

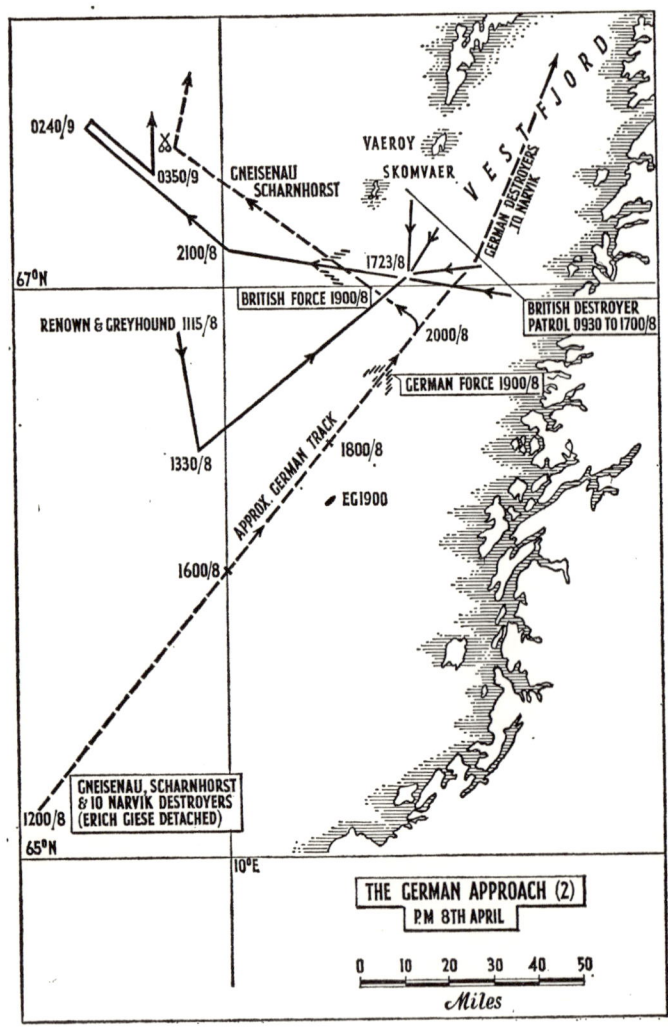

The German Approach (2)

were on their way to Narvik, so he altered course for a point on their probable line of advance, and well ahead of them. (See map p. 26.) When he reached it, however, at 1330, the visibility was down to two or three miles and he realised he would have little chance of intercepting with only the *Greyhound* in company. He may also have reasoned that his fighting strength was hardly a match for the massive enemy force previously reported, and on both counts it became clearly desirable to obey the Admiralty and join the destroyers, which had not been possible while he was chasing to the south. He therefore set course to the northeast towards the entrance of Vestfjord, and ordered Warburton-Lee to sweep towards him.

The Germans were now about 50 miles astern of the *Renown*, on approximately the same track.

Admiral Whitworth continued to size up the situation. So far he had had no instructions, merely imprecise information and some tentative guesswork; and since the indications were that his seniors were as much in the dark as he, he found himself in the classic position of the commander on the spot who must try to interpret his seniors' wishes when they themselves have not formed any, and then be prepared to accept the blame for anything that might go wrong. The task was made no easier by the mass of signals with which the air was cluttered, at which the coding staff worked at high pressure to present their Admiral with rapidly accumulating detail, much of it irrelevant to his problem but all having to be read carefully just the same. Furthermore the weather was rough and getting rougher, always an inhibiting environment for intense and critical thought.

Nevertheless it might have been thought, during the afternoon of the 8th with the information then available, that Narvik was the key. Apart from the immediate tactical position, strategy might also be expected to influence a senior admiral placed as was Whitworth, if only to help him anticipate his seniors' wishes. If Narvik was in any danger of German occupation, questions arose, such as: Iron ore—is Britain to have it, or Germany? What about the rest of the important trade with Scandinavia with which regular convoys were even then running? What would be the effect of German naval bases in North Norway? It is even perhaps fair to mention the vital North Russian convoys later in the war, though only in the sense that, for the very reason that one cannot foretell the future, it may well pay handsomely to hold on to what one has or at least deny it to the enemy.

A German naval foray into the Atlantic would indeed be serious but would not last the length of the war; the loss of a friendly neutral and potential ally might well do so. And the *Renown* with her destroyers were already in the right place at the right time to save Narvik at least.

Whitworth knew, however, that by giving priority to a break-out he would be echoing his seniors' thoughts. He therefore listed the enemy's likely moves in the order:

1 Return to his base at once. (The *Glowworm*'s last signal had given the *Hipper*'s course as south.)
2 Make for Iceland. (Iceland was certainly vital to the allies, but it is hard to imagine Hitler landing a force there and maintaining it from bases in Germany. Later, using Norway as a springboard, a descent became more practicable and the allies took precautions accordingly.)
3 Make for Murmansk where it was possible a tanker was waiting with fuel.
4 Proceed to Narvik.

Not only was Narvik placed last, but two out of the four possible courses of action indicated an enemy course west of the Lofotens, and it is hardly surprising that the Admiral decided to patrol there after collecting the destroyers.

To the south a patrolling aircraft sighted and reported the *Hipper*'s force at 1430, not so very far from where it had sunk the *Glowworm*, and steering west. The *Repulse* raced to intercept, and was followed by the Commander-in-Chief with his slower battleships, but nothing was sighted, the *Hipper*'s westerly course being merely to delay arrival at Trondheim until dawn the next day. Admiral Forbes received one indication after another of great enemy activity to the south of Norway, and became convinced at about this time that that country was about to be invaded; but of the large force last reported off the Skaggerak as long ago as 1330 the day before there was no sign—none.

German Progress
The Narvik force pressed on steadily and in formation again, except for the *Erich Giese* who was, however, following, and in no trouble after one unnerving experience. Through the scudding mist an easily

recognisable British destroyer passed on opposite courses and vanished again as soon as seen. Just possibly this was the *Hero*, patrolling her dummy minefield. "There I was," says Biggs, "All by my little self, and I only discovered afterwards that the German Fleet must have passed a few miles to seaward. Nobody told me anything."

During the afternoon one of the *Erich Giese*'s mountaineers fell overboard, but the gale easing temporarily Smidt was able to manoeuvre the ship to pick him up, accepting that she would fall even further astern in consequence.

At Narvik itself the *Jan Wellem*, flying the German ensign, steamed majestically into harbour looking huge beside the ore-carrying tramp steamers. A Customs Officer inspected her and found nothing suspicious, though she had exceptionally large food stocks including, strangely, live pigs and poultry. He wondered why she had come, for she could not carry ore; perhaps she had been driven in by the British.

Hide and Seek

The *Renown* first met the minelaying destroyers, who were already on their way south; and then, at 1715 in position 23 miles south of Skomvaer, at the very centre of the entrance to Vestfjord, the *Hotspur* sighted her.

As soon as the force was formed, Admiral Whitworth set course to seaward according to his plan—away from the track of the oncoming Germans. Shortly afterwards, at 1752, he received an Admiralty message addressed to him:

'As aircraft only sighted part of the enemy force, it is possible that the undetected part is still making for Narvik.= 1724/7th'

He noted that the undetected part consisted apparently of two cruisers and 12 destroyers, but took no action; neither did the Commander-in-Chief issue any orders or guidance to him.

The Admiralty's part in these events has often been criticised for over-interference with the men on the spot, which naval history has shown to be often ill-advised, but this time sympathy is surely due. As might be expected, the Germans' intention to occupy Norway became clearer more quickly in London where all information was concentrated, and although the men on the spot had been given a broad hint, they had not reacted. How long should the Admiralty have waited for such a reaction when every moment counted and a vital issue was at stake? Interference or not they deemed it their duty to make the position clear beyond all doubt:

'To Vice-Admiral Commanding Battlecruisers, repeated to Commander-in-Chief. Most Immediate. The force under your orders is to concentrate on preventing any German force proceeding to Narvik. May enter territorial waters as necessary.=1850/8th'

Admiral Whitworth was shown this signal very soon, at 1915. It was not just an indication of the Admiralty's wishes, but an order in the most direct terms, the words 'is to' making it so according to hallowed and well-understood naval usage. He nearly, so nearly, obeyed; but let him speak for himself:

'On receipt of this signal I calculated that the enemy had had ample time to reach my vicinity if they were proceeding direct to Narvik. Assuming that they had not yet passed me I decided to proceed up Vestfjord with the object of placing myself between the enemy and his objective. There were two objections to this course of action; One was the possibility of being brought to action by a superior force (four of my destroyers had no torpedoes and only two guns). The other was the navigational danger of approaching a dangerous coast in low visibility without having been able to fix the ship's position for three days.

'The weather at this time showed signs of improving and I decided to disregard both these objections. But the improvement proved to be only a lull and it came on to blow with great force from the north-west, accompanied by rain and snow squalls with prolonged periods of bad visibility. This sudden deterioration in the weather decided me to change my plans, because I felt that the enemy would make little progress and not try to make Vestfjord during the dark, and would probably stand to seaward during the dark hours, so I decided to do the same.'

What might have happened if the *Renown*'s force had turned back into Vestfjord? The map on p. 26 shows the best possible reconstruction of the situation but should not be considered accurate since records are sparse, largely because no ship on either side knew precisely where she was. The Germans had been quite unmolested since the *Glowworm* incident in the morning, and had only to contend with the weather which they had beaten. At 2000, on schedule, they reached a position which cannot have been far from where the *Renown* had met Warburton-Lee two hours earlier. There, with a 'Good luck!' to Bonte and his destroyers, Admiral Lütjens turned the battlecruisers away to the northwest. His next task was to break north to the Arctic; an admirable move if it was intended to mislead the British, who had already largely misled themselves along these very lines.

The *Gneisenau* and *Scharnhorst* were again following the *Renown* along roughly the same track, perhaps 20 to 30 miles apart. Speeds were slow and getting slower as the wind rose steadily to storm force; experienced sailors who were at sea that night had never met anything like it; the cold was numbing and the visibility negligible. Had the *Renown* turned, she might have encountered the German battlecruisers. It is of course futile to speculate on the probable outcome of the ensuing battle, necessarily fought at point-blank range, except to say that British attention would probably have been diverted from the German destroyers. However, the certain presence of German warships in such an incriminating position might well have had the effect of alerting Norway to her danger six or so hours before the deadline.

Had the *Renown* missed the battlecruisers, her chances of intercepting the destroyers in Vestfjord were good. In either event 'The Battle of Narvik' would have had quite a different meaning from the one we know.

The *Repulse*'s force had spent the dog-watches vainly searching for the *Hipper*, but at 2000/8th the Commander-in-Chief sent it north to reinforce Admiral Whitworth for he was by now clearly seized with the prime importance of Narvik. The destroyers of this force were to play a prominent part in the events of the next few days and should be introduced: the *Bedouin* (Commander J. A. 'Bes' McCoy), *Punjabi* (Commander Trevor Lean), *Eskimo* (Commander St J. A. Micklethwait), and *Kimberley* (Lieutenant Commander Richard Knowling). The first three named were of the large Tribal class, with eight 4.7in guns and four torpedoes, while the *Kimberley* had six guns and ten torpedoes; they were all new and good matches for the big German destroyers, which could not be said for the much smaller 'H' and similar classes.

At 2014/8th Admiral Whitworth told his force of nine destroyers:
'Our object is to prevent German forces reaching Narvik. My present intention is to alter course at 2100 to 280 degrees, and to turn 180 degrees to starboard in succession at midnight. Enemy heavy ships and light forces have been reported off Norwegian coast.'

If it should be asked how the Admiral would defend Narvik by steering directly away from it, the answer would be the weather, which had now worked itself into such a fury that the destroyers could merely butt into it at slow speed, virtually hove to.

The Germans Slip Through

At 2100 Kommodore Bonte considered that he should be abreast of Skomvaer and entering Vestfjord. The only positive indication of his position was a single radio beacon, though that was not identified with certainty, and he relied mainly on dead-reckoning. Given the highest navigational skill it was still a courageous act to press on into ever more confined waters, and Bonte's heart must have been in his mouth. How could he be sure that the right allowances had been made for factors such as leeway, increased distance travelled when the gale had been astern and a reduction now that it was on the port bow and the ships were straining into it? There would also have been inaccuracies in steering and engine revolutions that were unavoidable in heavy weather and incalculable. Nevertheless he made for the entrance, as the British, in no more difficult circumstances, did not.

Slowly, at first barely perceptibly, the ships' movements became less fierce and Bonte knew they were in a lee. But for him one achievement led on to the next trial; the final test must be a sure fix of the land, and heaven send that this should not be achieved by striking one of the myriad rocky islets. A light was sighted to starboard but not identified, then a cliff nearly ahead that caused a violent evasive turn to port; torpedoes were nearly fired as the rocks looked like an enemy ship, which it would have been no surprise to find. There was also the British minefield to worry about.

Gradually the navigational clues fitted with one another and the force was on track; but where was the *Erich Giese*? Had she met with disaster and, if so, had she given the show away? In fact no. Although some 50 miles astern she continued to follow gamely, though scarcely happily. As night fell and the full strength of the northwesterly gale hit her, Smidt was confronted by his Engineer Officer who reported gloomily, "Herr Kapitän, we have water in the fuel tanks and the engines will soon stop." But needs must when the devil, and the Captain, drive; on further investigation the fault was found to be the pumps partially losing suction owing to the ship's violent rolling and this could be corrected. Later in the night a rock loomed ahead and Smidt ordered, "Hard-a-starboard", in the nick of time; having missed it by 100 yards it proved a blessing in disguise for it was identified on the chart, and from there onwards the passage was plane sailing. That the lighthouse was not operating was to be expected as the German forces had been told that the Norwegian Government, uneasy at last, had ordered all navigational lights to be extinguished. It was a half measure that had no effect on events, especially as many lights were unmanned and could not be switched off.

Don't Look Round Now!

Out at sea the storm was at its height and at 2200 Warburton-Lee reported to his Admiral that the destroyers were unmanageable. Course was therefore altered to 310°, directly into the weather, and speed reduced to eight knots. There was no longer any pretence of a tactical formation and the destroyers trailed astern of the *Renown*, striving merely to retain their fighting trim and, indeed, to stay afloat. The *Gneisenau* and *Scharnhorst*, themselves tender in a head sea, came down to seven knots and unwittingly took station on the *Renown*'s starboard quarter. The formation generated a massive difference of potential that needed only near approach to strike an arc.

CHAPTER THREE

April 9th and the Occupation of Narvik

Admiral Whitworth waited for the first glimmer of daylight to lead his destroyers in the difficult manoeuvre of turning 180° in those frightening seas. The moment came at 0230/9th, the alteration was achieved safely, albeit slowly, and the force headed back to guard Vestfjord.

At 0300 Kommodore Bonte rounded Baroy Island with nine ships and started his final dash through the narrows of Ofotfjord at 27 knots. (See map p. 53.)

Battlecruiser Action
At 0337 a snow-trimmed Father Christmas of a signalman literally blew into the Admiral's chartroom on board the *Renown* and asked Commander Bob Currie, the Staff Officer Operations, to step outside for a moment. "Look sir!"

"Call the Admiral—press the alarm!" The weather was just as bad as it had been, but the growing light revealed that the snow and rain storms were separated from each other with clear patches between. In one of these, ten miles on the port bow, were the two German battlecruisers, instantly recognised as enemies, but thought to be one *Scharnhorst* and one *Hipper* class. This was an understandable mistake when the silhouettes are compared, but there may also have been an element of the *idée fixe* about it, for it will be remembered that only one battlecruiser had been reported by the original sighting aircraft. The mistake may be thought minor, yet it could have helped Admiral Whitworth decide to engage. It is also of interest as an illustration of many instances during these operations, on both sides, when men saw what they expected to see and failed to see what they did not, even though it was there.

Turning the ponderous *Renown* into the ponderous seas to a northerly course took time, but that hardly explains the prolonged

34

pause, half an hour less a minute, between sighting and opening fire at nine miles range. Nevertheless it was bravely done and the Germans, hindered by tricks of the light and also, doubtless, by not expecting the unexpected, remained oblivious of the British approach and did not reply for a further six minutes. Then the battle raged; the *Renown* hit the *Gneisenau* three times, destroying her fire-control, and was herself hit twice, though harmlessly.

The British destroyers followed gamely and the 2nd Flotilla carried out a 'Divisional Concentration Shoot', a somewhat grand description of a gallant achievement in maintaining an output of fire at all from the little 1,400 ton ships that were being tossed, buffeted and sluiced over by the great Arctic breakers. Warburton-Lee's Secretary, Paymaster Lieutenant Geoffrey Stanning, thought he was the only man on the *Hardy*'s bridge who could see the enemy because, wearing glasses and prudently having two pairs with him, which he wiped rapidly in succession, he could at least catch momentary glimpses through the spume; everyone else's normally perfect eyes were 'gummed up with icy salt'. It may be remarked that Stanning was in the Navy for his love of ships and ship-handling, which he was debarred from practising owing to his short sight.

The *Hotspur*'s foremost gun was under water much of the time and its Captain, Leading Seaman Watling, had several times to rescue members of his crew who were swept off their feet while carrying heavy shells and cartridges. One man who became wedged under the guardrail with his legs over the side, still tried desperately to roll his shell up the canted deck towards the gun. "We fired about one salvo in three"; a fine achievement, and Warburton-Lee signalled later to his team: 'Our first divisional concentration appeared to go well. Enemy bolted.'

Well yes! But it cannot in all honesty be reported that the Germans actually noticed the destroyers' fall of shot, though they did see a line of gunflashes astern of their big enemy, and that certainly influenced Admiral Lütjens' decision to turn away to the north-eastwards. There were other factors too; the German Navy's strategic inferiority led then, as always, to commanders afloat being instructed to preserve its few heavy ships intact, and now this must have seemed all the more desirable so that they could fulfil the second aim of the operation, to cover the invasion forces' return to Germany. Unfortunately there is no record of whether the Admiral considered using the greatly superior fighting power of his two modern ships to overwhelm the old *Renown*, and then to dominate the Lofoten area for perhaps the next 24 critical hours during which his destroyers were due to re-emerge, and thus achieve the aim even more surely. Had he done so there could have been no first Battle of Narvik; but as it was he fled and the British crowed, unaware as yet that they were being led on a wild goose chase away from what really mattered.

The *Renown* slowly drew astern of her enemies which were eventually lost to sight, but long before that the British destroyers were forced out of the fight by the weather. Admiral Whitworth told them to go and patrol Vestfjord, a gallant act for it left him quite alone in the presence of a superior enemy.

Narvik—The Germans Arrive

Surprise was complete, and the German forces reaped the due reward for their boldness and determination; but the events of this day at Narvik, a sombre one in Norwegian history, will only be described in outline in so far as they set the scene for the morrow's battle.

Snow storms scudded across the fjord and helped preserve surprise as Bonte led his force up the last straight. He detached ships for previously allotted tasks as he went: first the *Diether von Roeder* to patrol the entrance near Baroy where she could also give a helping hand to the *Erich Giese*, whom he still hoped would turn up. Next, the *Hans Lüdemann* and *Anton Schmitt* landed their troops at Ramnes and Hamnes to seize the gun batteries that were believed to be there. This little operation was both trying and fruitless because the ships' boats had been damaged by the heavy weather at sea, the snow on the mountainside was six feet deep, and there finally proved to be no batteries anyway, only gun-emplacements which had misled both the German and British Intelligence Services. The former were disappointed since heavy coastal guns would have served their purposes well; the latter continued to believe in their existence.

Further to the east the three ships of the 4th Flotilla forked left for Herjangsfjord, at the head of which lay Elvegaardsmoen with its Army training camp and depot. The place was overwhelmed by the German mountain troops and fell without resistance.

The Kommodore arrived off Narvik itself at 0415, as planned, with the *Wilhelm Heidkamp*, *Bernd von Arnim*, and *Georg Thiele*. (See map p. 59.) The visibility was thicker than ever as the *Bernd von Arnim* went ahead to land the first assault troops at the Post Pier. On her depended the success of the operation and Rechel had been ordered to ignore all opposition in achieving it; he therefore sailed past the old Norwegian Coast Defence Ship *Eidsvold*, which was lost to view again before she could take any action, and threaded his way through a mass of merchant shipping in the harbour. Crews tumbled up from below in great confusion, to greet him in different ways as their nationalities suggested. "Are you English?" anxiously by the British sailors, and "Deutschland über alles" with gusto by the German. Then a snowsquall blotted out everything, including his own forecastle.

Bonte meanwhile was dealing with the *Eidsvold*, who had fired a live round across his bows and ordered him to stop. His orders were to present the operation to the Norwegians as a friendly move to protect them from the British, and on no account was he to fire first. The Norwegian ship was very old but she was also powerful at close range; she had been warned by a patrol vessel of the Germans' approach; her crew were at action stations and her Captain, Willoch, had been ordered to resist any German attack. But unwilling as he was, or perhaps morally unable, to break the peace that had blessed Norway for so many years in one short moment, he allowed the *Wilhelm Heidkamp*'s boat to bring a negotiating officer, who demanded instant and complete surrender. Willoch radioed his Senior Officer, Captain Askim of the *Eidsvold*'s sister ship *Norge*, for last minute instructions, and was told to fight. Still not being able to grasp the stark reality of the crisis even as he looked down the grim muzzles of the *Wilhelm Heidkamp*'s guns and torpedo tubes, he passed this message excitedly to the German officer who clicked his heels, returned to his boat and, when clear of the ship, fired a red Verey light. Encouraged by the Army Commander, General Dietl, to do everything possible to expedite the landing of his troops, Kommodore Bonte ordered the *Eidsvold* to be sunk. Four torpedoes were fired of which two hit; the old ship disappeared in a few seconds and there were only eight survivors.

This story is not concerned with Germany's moral justification for invading Norway. That having been said, it is hard to see what else Bonte could have done; the *Eidsvold*'s guns were pointing at him, the two ships were declared enemies, and it was merely a question of who was to fire the first shot. Nevertheless he hated the act, both because it outraged his sense of honour and might well stiffen Norwegian resistance, to such an extent that he became quite distracted for the rest of the day, and even his judgement may have been affected.

The young Mayor of Narvik, Theodor Broch, awakened by the explosions, threw open the windows of his house on Framnes. He thought it must be the Ore Company blasting, but it was a strange time, 0445, to do so.

Inside the harbour the next ship Rechel saw was the *Norge*, and as he watched, her heavy guns started to train. The *Bernd von Arnim* was of course at action stations, but sailors and soldiers were also massed on the upper deck, the former to secure the ship alongside, the latter to jump ashore. But there was as yet nowhere to jump, nor anything in sight to indicate where the Post Pier might be. In that moment of extreme tension and danger, and with the full weight of responsibility on his junior shoulders, Rechel showed outstanding tenacity of purpose and rigid self-discipline. He edged his ship towards a German tramp and hailed her for directions, but she could not help; he therefore moved north between the ships and finally sighted the loom of the Ore Quay. He then turned his bows eastward and, with impressive nerve, stopped, so as to allow the northwesterly wind to drift him towards where he now knew the Post Pier must be. He gave his Gunnery, Torpedo and Close Range Weapons Officers permission to engage the moment the Norwegian did so, without further orders.

On board the *Norge* Captain Askim was as slow to react as his brother Captain, even though he knew from Willoch that the attacking force was German and had heard the explosions of the *Eidsvold*'s last moments. At last, when he saw the *Bernd von Arnim* slip alongside the Post Pier, he opened fire at 900 metres range. But the first crucial salvo fell short, and when the German replied with all guns the Norwegian shooting became wild, and the remaining shots went over the target into the town. The battle continued for some minutes as the *Norge* dodged behind two merchant ships and fouled her enemy's range. Rechel was fighting a naval action on his port side and a military one to starboard; the latter had priority, and he edged his ship ahead to a place where the soldiers could land.

Guns are unmistakable and the Mayor was now in no doubt what he was hearing; he could see the flashes too, but could not yet deduce who might be shooting.

Rechel saw an opportunity to fire torpedoes and did so, but something went very wrong for the first five missed, even at that close range. The sixth malfunctioned to the extent of running on the surface, but it hit and exploded, as did the seventh, and the *Norge* rolled over and sank. 97 men survived. From Framnes the fog looked like a sea of flame.

The torpedo failures were attributed to those technical causes which seemed most probable at the time: shallow water (about ten fathoms), icing-up of tube mechanisms, too close range for attainment of set running depth after initial dive, and so on. Subsequently, however, Rechel met the Master of a German merchant ship which had been anchored some 500 yards from the *Bernd von Arnim*, who told him that one of the torpedoes had run underneath where he was standing at the time. The ship drew seven metres, the torpedo had been set to two, and the failure was inexplicable because the range was ample for the torpedo to have levelled off in depth. It is hardly surprising that the right deduction was not drawn as a result of this one incident; but the calamitous truth was that the depth-keeping mechanism of the G7a torpedo was almost completely ineffective against medium or shallow draught targets.

The *Bernd von Arnim*'s troops were landed, and were soon backed up by those from the *Georg Thiele*. The British freighter *North Cornwall* was anchored in the centre of the harbour awaiting her turn to load, and her Master, Captain Charles Evans, had been anxiously watching the *Norge*'s last agony without being clear who had brought it about. Now he saw the second German destroyer appear from behind another British ship which was anchored in the harbour entrance, the *Blythmoor*, recognised the Swastika in the growing light, and ordered all confidential documents to be destroyed.

The Master of the German *Bockenheim* was not so level headed. Having been briefed by the German Consul, in company with all the other German Captains, on what to do if the harbour were to be attacked by the British, he took counsel of his fears and, without waiting for positive identification, ran his ship aground on Ankenes and set her alight.

With the *Wilhelm Heidkamp*'s troops came General Dietl. The Norwegian Garrison Commander surrendered instantly, as the Germans had known he would, and when Mayor Broch had dressed hastily and run the half-mile into the town a Swastika flew over the City Hall, and Narvik was part of the new Greater German Reich. It took the Mayor less than five minutes to realise he did not like it.

Now What?

The operation's success was neatly rounded off by the *Erich Giese*'s safe arrival, and Bonte was also extremely pleased to see the *Jan Wellem*, even though there was as yet no sign of the other tanker, *Kattegat*, or of the Army Support Ships *Rauenfels* and *Alster*. On further investigation, however, problems revealed themselves, and the more Bonte considered them the more serious they seemed.

The *Jan Wellem*'s cargo consisted both of furnace fuel oil for the destroyers and diesel oil for U-Boats, and there was insufficient of the former to top up all the ships. It was however possible to mix these fuels without a great loss of efficiency, but far more inhibiting was the whaler's slow pumping capacity; it would take at least seven hours to fill two destroyers, one on each side, and there was therefore no question of the force being able to leave Narvik together that night. The Kommodore decided to wait 24 hours; he could have sent his ships in groups as they finished fuelling, but felt that would lessen their chances of breaking through the British opposition which was now to be expected. For the same reason he decided that the *Kattegat* must be written off for practical planning purposes.

General Dietl was worried too, wondering how he was going to hold Narvik against growing Norwegian resistance and whatever the allies might do, with no anti-aircraft or field guns, and no reserves of stores and ammunition; even the mountain guns he had started with were lost, wrenched from their lashings during the gale. He asked, and Bonte agreed, to leave him two destroyers.

All ships settled down to repair weather damage, rest their crews and above all to fuel. The officers and men of the five British merchant ships present were confined on board the *Jan Wellem*, and prize crews took over their ships. Captain Evans made the best of his predicament by getting to know his host Captain, whom he found to be courteous and helpful.

There was no German press announcement but rumours were rife in Wilhelmshaven. Frau Böhme, wife of the *Anton Schmitt*'s Captain, found out what she could from Headquarters and then toured the naval town on her bicycle to comfort and reassure the ship's company's families. The price of a good Captain's wife is above rubies and blessed is the ship with one. Irene Courage of the *Havock* was another such, among many, and a great favourite of officers and men. But there was no bicycling for her; she was ill and would not live to see her men again. Her loss would shake them more than the battle.

The British at Sea

The Home Fleet knew nothing of events at Narvik, but the Commander-in-Chief had been told quite a lot about what was happening to Norway. All through the night reports came in of great activity, and at 0446 he heard that German warships were approaching Oslo, Bergen, Stavanger and Trondheim. He concluded then, without any doubt, that Germany was invading Norway, but is not recorded as taking the next step in logical reasoning, namely that the probable German aim in so doing was to secure Narvik and the iron ore. Nor did he evidently ask himself what must have happened to the 12 missing enemy destroyers, for they had clearly not been in company with the battlecruisers during the *Renown*'s action. He was told by the Admiralty:

'Narvik must be watched to prevent enemy forces landing=0845/9th'

In the north the *Renown* had chased the enemy until he was out of sight, and then returned to the area west of Skomvaer. The *Repulse* and her four destroyers had hurried north during the night, and then put on a spurt to try and join the action but to no avail. Captain Warburton-Lee had led his nine destroyers back to the entrance of Vestfjord, and established a patrol across it at 0930 when he reported the fact.

It is hard to suppress the irreverent notion that all the senior officers retired to their sea-cabins after a particularly trying night for a spruce-up and breakfast, and to ponder their next moves, for they all made signals at nearly the same moment:

Repulse to her force: 'Am proceeding to Vestfjord to prevent any German forces entering Narvik and to join Captain (D) 2=0931/9th'

Commander-in-Chief to Warburton-Lee: 'Send some destroyers up to Narvik to make certain no enemy troops land there. Norway is at war with Germany=0952'

Admiral Whitworth to Warburton-Lee: 'Join me at 1800 in position 50 miles southwest of Skomvaer=0957'

Warburton-Lee thus stepped to the centre of the stage. The Commander-in-Chief's order was after his own heart, and it was convenient that the latter's overriding seniority allowed him to ignore Admiral Whitworth's order to retire.

Captain Spooner's signal is a good example of an officer breaking away from his assigned task to do what he considers to be right, and it was eminently so. The message also shows that a very strong force was available on the spot, and further proof that this was so is given by the *Hotspur* who made visual contact with the *Repulse* just as the Second Flotilla turned to enter the fjord. There were present, in addition to the *Repulse*, the light cruiser *Penelope*, four 'H' class destroyers, the *Greyhound*, three Tribals, the *Kimberley*, and the four half-armed minelayers.

Indeed there was one more destroyer, the *Hostile*, a significant ship belonging to the 2nd Flotilla and commanded by Commander J. P. 'Willy' Wright. She had been in the area as part of a small independent operation with the cruiser *Birmingham* to round up enemy fishing trawlers. Detached to take a prize to the Orkneys, Wright found himself within 40 miles of the *Glowworm*'s action and steered straight for the spot. He found nothing, luckily; and then hearing on the wireless that 'all this hoo-ha was blowing up', he deemed it his duty to take part but could not at first make out where the various forces were and which would be the most rewarding one to join. He sighted the outline of a heavy ship on a northwesterly course in the afternoon of the 8th and steered to close. Then the visibility shut down and he forebore to press in, not wishing to become another *Glowworm* should the ship turn out not to be, as he thought, the *Renown*. His instinct was sound; the *Renown* was at least 100 miles to the northeast, and although the *Repulse* was nearer, the ship is much more likely to have been the *Hipper*.

As the signalled situation clarified, Wright realised that he was closer to the *Renown* than to the Commander-in-Chief and steered for Vestfjord. During the night he fell in with the *Repulse*'s force, and on arrival off Vestfjord at 1130/9th Captain Spooner thoughtfully told him that his Captain (D) was going up to Narvik and suggested he might like to go too. He would, and he went.

The Admiralty Takes Charge

To Warburton-Lee from Admiralty:

'Press report states one German ship has arrived Narvik and landed a small force. Proceed Narvik and sink or harass enemy ship. It is at your discretion to land force and capture Narvik from enemy present. Try to get possession of battery if not already in enemy hands= 1200/9th'

This was followed an hour later by:

'Battery at Narvik reported to consist of three 12 or 18 pounders mounted on Framnes and facing northwest. Guns 4inch or less may be in position on both sides Ofotfjord near Ramnes.'

Four comments should be made. Firstly, there were no guns at Ramnes as the Germans had discovered, and they had been further annoyed to find that the Norwegians had spiked those on Framnes. Secondly, the Admiralty had given a direct order to a junior commander, thereby overriding the authority of both the Commander-in-Chief and Admiral Whitworth, and effectively inhibiting them from using their initiative in future. Thirdly, the directive was unnecessary as it did not materially change the one previously given by the Commander-in-Chief.

Fourthly, the Admiralty's willingness to initiate such a small-scale operation on the basis of just one press report, taken at its full face value without question, is hard to understand. Narvik being the ultimate in Norway, as Mr Churchill well knew and it is his signature that shows clearly between the lines of this and later signals, the Germans were surely likely to make sure of it by using greater force than needed rather than less. Had the British taken the same line there was nothing to lose and everything, that is Narvik, to gain. Perhaps the Admiralty did not know that stronger forces were readily available, for there will always be much that the Admiralty cannot know from their lofty distance; but what they did know and might have reiterated was that Narvik was vital, and left the men on the spot to interpret that in practical terms.

Tranoy

Captain Warburton-Lee, as the man thrust forward to bear the brunt both of action and for any possible failure, felt his mind to be concentrated wonderfully and resolved to do some investigating on his own account. There was a Pilot Station at Tranoy in the upper Vestfjord where it seemed likely that information might be obtained, and there he stopped off. On the way he ordered his ships to prepare shells for shore bombardment and to organise landing parties, one platoon from each.

It fell to Stanning, who spoke German, and Lieutenant George Heppel the Flotilla Torpedo Officer, to land and find out what they could. Their mission was highly charged, yet the setting was Gilbertian; they stood in a group of men and boys, and struggled to converse in a mixture of German and English amplified by gestures and pictures drawn in the snow. They definitely established that certain German destroyers had gone up the fjord, but there seemed to be some disagreement among the Norwegians as to whether there were four or five. They settled in the end for six, but long afterwards Stanning lived through the scene again and wondered agonisingly whether they were trying to say that there were two groups, of four and five respectively. Strangely enough, other and apparently more subtle messages were conveyed with comparative ease: one submarine had also been seen; the narrows were probably mined; Narvik was strongly held; the German destroyers were much bigger than the British ones and the latter would be well-advised not to attack until they had twice as many ships. This counsel came from a small boy wise beyond his years; but nobody listens to small boys.

As their boat took Heppel and Stanning back to the *Hardy*, the *Hostile* rounded the point. She was very welcome.

Council of War

Warburton-Lee gathered his staff around him in the charthouse as was his custom. They were as fine a team of dedicated and competent young officers as could be found in the Royal Navy, for the 2nd Flotilla under Warburton-Lee was regarded as rather special and was allowed the cream: Clark (Gunnery), Gordon-Smith (Navigation), Cross (Signals), Heppel and Stanning. The last-named describes the discussion.

'It was the most thorny situation. We had been told to attack Narvik and must therefore do so unless there were urgent and strong reasons against it. The Admiralty had obviously no idea how strong the enemy forces were, and to ask for further instructions would be delaying the operation to an unreasonable extent; and we also had a feeling that our operation at Narvik had been timed to fit in with some other undertaking further down the coast, and any delay on our part might possibly prejudice someone else's success, or even safety. But whether the Admiralty would consider the extremely grave risk to five modern destroyers justifiable in view of the new information seemed doubtful. On the other hand our information was not necessarily reliable, and as the Admiralty had given us specific information it was reasonable to suppose they knew better.

'Captain (D) was in a quandary; if he decided to attack the place and failed, perhaps with the loss of several ships, he'd be told by the Admiralty that he was mad to go in when he knew there was considerable opposition. If on the other hand he decided to withdraw

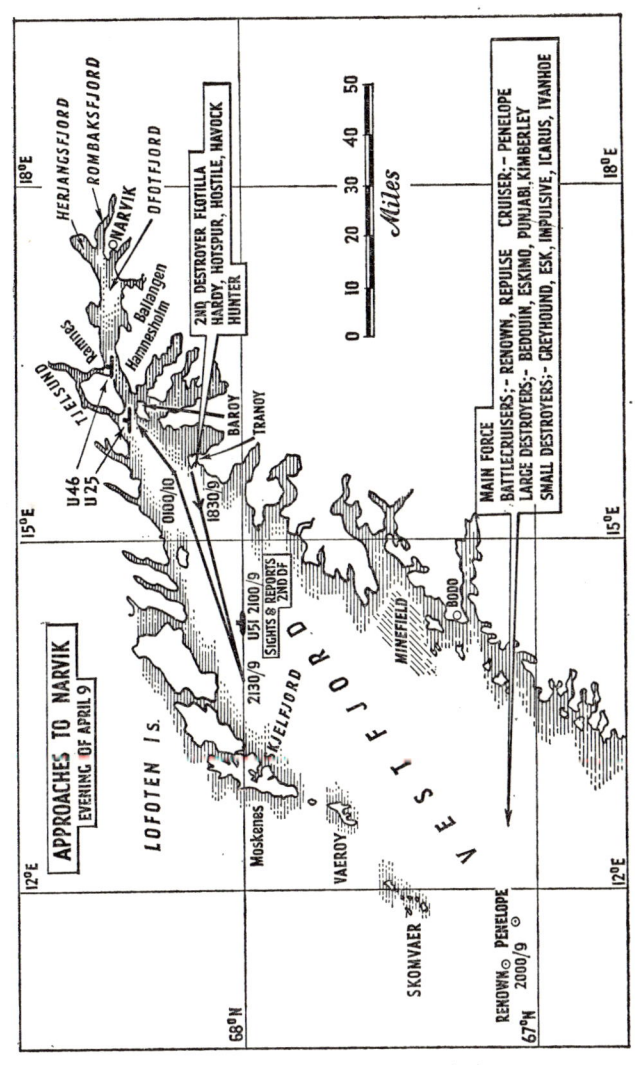

Approaches to Narvik, Evening April 9th

he would be asked why he did so on the unreliable information of small boys, when the Admiralty had given him specific intelligence which he should have had no reason to doubt.

'After the conference he spent a most unhappy half hour by himself in which, to my mind, he more than earned his VC. We all waited about, quite unable to help him as it was a decision he alone could take, and that without encouragement or advice from us. He decided, as we had been hoping, to go on with the operation, and I went straight away to cypher a message to the Admiralty.' The message read:

'Norwegians report Germans holding Narvik in force, also six destroyers and one U-Boat are there and channel is possibly mined. Intend attacking at dawn high water = 1751/9th'

Although there would still have been time to reach Narvik before dark that evening, dawn offered a far better chance of achieving surprise, and high water, fortuitously coinciding in time, should lift the ships over any mines there might be. The naval meaning of 'intend' when used by a junior officer to a senior, is that the action will be carried out unless otherwise ordered; it does not demand a reply, but its irrevocability depends on whether time permits one. That is official naval usage; naval custom exhorts, 'Never "propose" when you can "intend", and never, never ask for guidance.'

'If it be a sin to covet honour, I am the most offending soul alive'

More than bare facts and logic went into the making of the signal, since enshrined into Royal Naval tradition, that cost Warburton-Lee such agony and bloody sweat. He now knew that the enemy's strength was superior to his, and although this disadvantage could be mitigated by the bold exploitation of surprise it would clearly be far better were he to be reinforced; but his character almost dictated that he should not ask for any lest he be thought timid. He was a man of integrity, honour and ambition; a dedicated man, intensely professional, and although an excellent games-player, somewhat aloof and single-minded. Some thought him too dedicated, though these also admired and respected him; but to those close to him, such as his staff and the crew of the *Hardy*, he could intersperse his untiring drive for greater and greater efficiency with moments of unbending, and they warmed to him. Would it have been possible for him to add a paragraph, 'Request reinforcements if available.'? Or might a subconscious conflict between integrity and ambition have whispered that the commander of such reinforcements might be senior to him and either purloin his glory or bungle the operation? Or that the least hint of uncertainty in his tone might cause his seniors to doubt his competence and to cancel the project? No! The only concession he could make to his well-grounded fears was to allow his seniors time to take the proper action. He must have hoped beyond hope that they would.

The signal reached the outside world at 1830. The Commander-in-Chief considered that no further action was needed by him, the Admiralty having taken matters out of his hands. The Admiralty, presumably realising that this was so and that they must now assume responsibility for the detailed conduct of a far-off operation, replied:

'During dark hours your force is to patrol to the east of Ramnes to prevent destroyers escaping by channels to the north. Attack at dawn all good luck=2059/9th'

This Warburton-Lee contemptuously ignored. To have spent the night so near his objective would have severely risked forfeiting surprise, his only tactical asset apart from boldness and the fighting efficiency of his ships.

Admiral Whitworth, also a man of integrity and dedication, was plunged by Warburton-Lee's signal into a state of real concern. Had it not been for the Admiralty's intervention, responsibility for the operation would have been his; to what extent should he now assume it? He knew for sure that reinforcements were available, indeed every ship of his augmented force could reach Narvik by dawn; but should he act, might not his orders conflict with the Admiralty's next pronouncement and make matters worse? Nevertheless he made this signal:

'To *Penelope*, repeated to Warburton-Lee. Take *Bedouin*, *Punjabi*, *Eskimo*, *Kimberley* under your orders and proceed in support of Captain (D) 2 in dawn attack on Narvik as directed by him. Unless otherwise ordered by him you should pass through position 20 miles southwest of Tranoy at 0100 tomorrow, 10th=1959/9th'

This order which, had it been implemented, posterity would have acclaimed as inspired, was sent visually to the ships in company; but before it could be coded and transmitted by W/T, doubt prevailed:

'Cancel my 1959=2038'

CHAPTER FOUR

The First Battle of Narvik

So was the die cast. Warburton-Lee led his five ships down the fjord to the southwest; having decided to arrive at Narvik at dawn, he had to lose time before entering Ofotfjord and could thus afford an attempt to mislead any watchers. He was also allowed leisure to turn his mind from the great decision to his tactical plan, and the thorough briefing of those who would carry it out. His orders were sent as a series of signals: (See maps pp. 45–53.)

1 Ships are to be at action stations from 0030. When passing Skredneset *Hardy* will pass close to shore and order a fine line of bearing. Thereafter ships are to maintain narrow quarterline to starboard so that fire from all ships is effective ahead.

2 Germans may have several destroyers and a submarine in vicinity, some probably on patrol. Ships are to engage all ship targets immediately and keep a particular lookout for enemy who may be berthed in inlets.

On approaching Narvik, *Hardy*, *Hunter* and *Havock* engage enemy ships or shipping inside harbour with guns and torpedoes.

Hotspur engage ships to northwest of Framnes, and the Framnes battery if firing. *Hostile* assist on either target. Prepare to make smoke for cover and to tow disabled ships.

3 If opposition is silenced, landing parties from all ships except *Hotspur* make for Ore Quay unless otherwise ordered. *Hardy*'s First Lieutenant in charge.

4 Details of batteries as in Admiralty message on pp. 42, 43.

5 Ships are to operate Asdics whenever possible and attack any submarine.

6 Additional signal to withdraw will be one Red and one Green Verey light from *Hardy*.

7 Half outfit of torpedoes (four) to be fired unless target warrants

more. Destroyer depth settings to be used. (6ft and 8ft, alternate torpedoes.)

8 In order to relieve congestion of movements all ships when turning to fire torpedoes or opening are to keep turning to port if possible. Watch adjacent ships, keep moderate speed.

9 Additional communications. Set watch on:

(a) 2800kc/s on remote control. (British destroyers unlike their opponents had not yet been fitted with voice radio. This circuit was operated by a morse key on the bridges, and used for rapid manoeuvring and action signals, usually in the form of groups from the Fleet Signal Book.)

(b) Fire Control Wave. (For concentration firing; not used.)

These orders were clearly admirable for the assault on Narvik Harbour, containing neither too much information nor too little; but in the light of hindsight two omissions may perhaps be thought strange. Was the destruction of merchant ships inside the harbour to have equal tactical priority with that of enemy warships? And what was to be done if the Flotilla were attacked by unexpected forces from unexpected directions? The trained staff officer may also wonder why paragraph 1 did not state the aim unequivocally; but Layman, Wright, Courage and de Villiers did not have to be told that their object was the total destruction of the enemy.

Having despatched his plans and his supper, Warburton-Lee sent for his Secretary and, he hoped, reassurance. What would the Admiralty think of his taking such a risk? Or of his delay in attacking? Or if he should call the whole thing off? This was no vacillation, but it was intensely human. We do our heroes ill-service by assuming that they always know instantly what to do and how to do it, like a Western film star. Rather should we see them as ordinary men who make themselves remarkable by accepting great responsibility on our behalf in circumstances where they can know but little of the whole truth, cannot therefore be sure they are right yet are ready to be absolutely decisive; and our gratitude to them should be all the more devout.

Stanning understood this well, and knew there was no real chance of the operation being cancelled; he said, truly, that the ship's company was enthusiastic and would be bitterly disappointed if it were. He could not have been more comforting to his lonely Captain, for nothing is more inspiring than the men's full-hearted support, as every officer knows.

Shortly afterwards at 2100, Kapitänleutnant Knorr in *U51* sighted the Flotilla still heading southwestward. He reported it and its course, and the British were lucky that the signal was received by Bonte without delay. Only half an hour later Warburton-Lee altered back for his final approach, but Knorr did not see the ships again.

In the *Hardy*, Heppel assembled all men off watch and told them their fate; at which they unmistakably demonstrated that enthusiasm of which Stanning had spoken by sucking their teeth with true British phlegm. Melodrama was provided only by the messdeck loud-speaker which, turned on as Heppel left, declaimed, "it's a lovely day tomorrow".

German Preparations

As Captain Warburton-Lee sized up the situation and prepared his plan, his opponent was doing the same in the Captain's cabin of the *Weilhelm Heidkamp*. Kommodore Bonte's instructions were quite clear, he was to take his force of destroyers home to Germany intact, but forced by lack of fuel to stay at Narvik for at least one night, he had to decide what to do with his ships in the meantime.

Clearly, the refuelling operation must continue as rapidly as the *Jan Wellem*'s slow pumps would allow, and without any pause between one destroyer and the next. That meant four ships in the harbour at any one time, vulnerable to air or surface attack. The rest could either be dispersed at anchor in neighbouring bays or stationed on patrol in the approaches; but a ship under way would use more fuel than one at anchor, and it would not be surprising if Bonte also considered it important to allow his officers and men, particularly his Captains, a good night's rest after their rigorous exertions and before embarking on a new, and probably even more trying, endeavour. There is nothing to indicate that he considered whether there was anything his ships might do to help the three lost support ships over their last lap.

Bonte's decision hinged on the degree of probability of an enemy attack. To help him decide, Group West had passed him some extremely interesting information culled from intercepted British signals. The Royal Navy would certainly have been appalled to realise the insecurity of its high-grade cyphers in the hands of the Germans' brilliant signal intelligence organisation. By 1900 Bonte knew that a large force, probably the main body of the Home Fleet, consisting of heavy ships and numerous destroyers was on its way north; that the force already off Lofoten probably included two battlecruisers; and that one destroyer flotilla had been ordered to attack a so far unidentified objective.

It is hardly strange therefore that Bonte acknowledged the possibility of a naval counter attack; but then he went on to argue that the three U-Boats already on station could be relied upon to give him all the early warning he needed, especially as he had particularly requested Group West to impress them with the importance of doing so. *U51*'s misleading report strongly reinforced this view; and he could reasonably expect even surer results from *U25* off Baroy and *U46* at Ramnes, for here the fjord was so narrow that they must certainly detect every ship that passed. Bonte was also sanguine that the U-Boats would inflict serious damage on an incoming enemy.

What Bonte thought when the visibility and weather worsened drastically is not recorded. He was probably confirmed in his feeling of security, deeming that navigation up the fjord had become virtually impossible, but not considering that the U-Boats would be equally handicapped.

Such might have been Bonte's logical reasoning; but the commander is unwise who neglects the psychological element when appreciating his enemy's probable course of action. That very morning Germany had affronted the Royal Navy's *amour propre* to an insupportable degree, and a grim determination to retrieve its honour should surely have been anticipated. Furthermore, penetrations into enemy harbours such as Cadiz (1587), Quiberon Bay (1759), Zeebrugge (1918), carried out with such boldness and ferocity that the defenders are both astonished and confounded, were a cherished part of its much vaunted tradition. It is true that only exceptional leaders will succeed in such ventures and they are rare, but Bonte would have been well-advised to be ready, both in his mind and in his dispositions, to meet a Drake, Hawke, Keyes, or Warburton-Lee.

As it was, Bonte's preparations for the coming night showed every sign of emanating from a desperately tired man; he was also unhappy, the *Eidsvold*'s sinking continuing to trouble him inordinately. Only one mobile patrol was ordered, mainly against enemy submarines and only just outside the harbour; the ships not refuelling or waiting to do so were to disperse to Herjangsfjord and Ballangen Bay; his own leader, the *Wilhelm Heidkamp*, had fuelled and he wanted to join the others outside, but allowed himself to be persuaded by the General to stay for mutual consultation. He had even offered the latter the use of his cabin, but that had been refused on the grounds that the position ashore was as yet far from stable. All these things reveal Bonte's feeling that his force was safe during the night and in the early morning, and it is therefore logical that no instructions were given about what to do should an attack take place, nor provision made for co-ordinating the three separate forces. Neither, of course, was the aim in such an event made clear, and this was to matter, for each Captain needed to be absolutely clear whether he was to engage a raiding force aggressively, or so as to preserve his ship from damage. Finally, there was no recognition of the importance of dawn, qua dawn.

Bonte left it to Fregattenkapitän Gadow of the 3rd Flotilla to organise the patrol and fuel his ships during the night; and thus it came about that the five super-destroyers of the new class, *Wilhelm Heidkamp*, *Hans Lüdemann*, *Hermann Künne*, *Diether von Roeder*, and *Anton Schmitt*, were all in the harbour area at daybreak. The 4th Flotilla, *Wolfgang Zenker*, *Erich Giese*, and *Erich Koellner*, were to anchor at the head of Herjangsfjord, and the *Georg Thiele* (limited to 27 knots by a minor defect) and *Bernd von Arnim* in Ballangen Bay. These movements took place at intervals during the night.

In Narrow Waters

The *Hermann Künne* sailed for the first patrol at 1900, and Kothe interpreted the orders to allow him freedom to cruise between Ramnes and Bogen Bay; we may admire his initiative. At midnight Böhme took the *Anton Schmitt* out of harbour to relieve him, while the British 2nd Flotilla steamed up Vestfjord, still south of Tranoy. Both found the weather unpleasant and frustrating to an inordinate degree; bitter cold would have sapped the resolution but for the constant exercise of will-power, and continuous snowstorms reduced visibility to never more than 400 yards, and often less, so that Böhme could only check his position by an occasional glimpse of the burning *Bockenheim* on Ankenes, and British skill at navigation and station-keeping were tested to the limit. A fully lit merchant ship charged through their line, probably between the *Hotspur* and *Hostile*, and as likely as not without even being aware of them. Quick witted and experienced, Wright swerved away, but could not then find his friends again. He had, however, already shown that he intended to get his ship into the battle come what may and he found his own way up to Narvik.

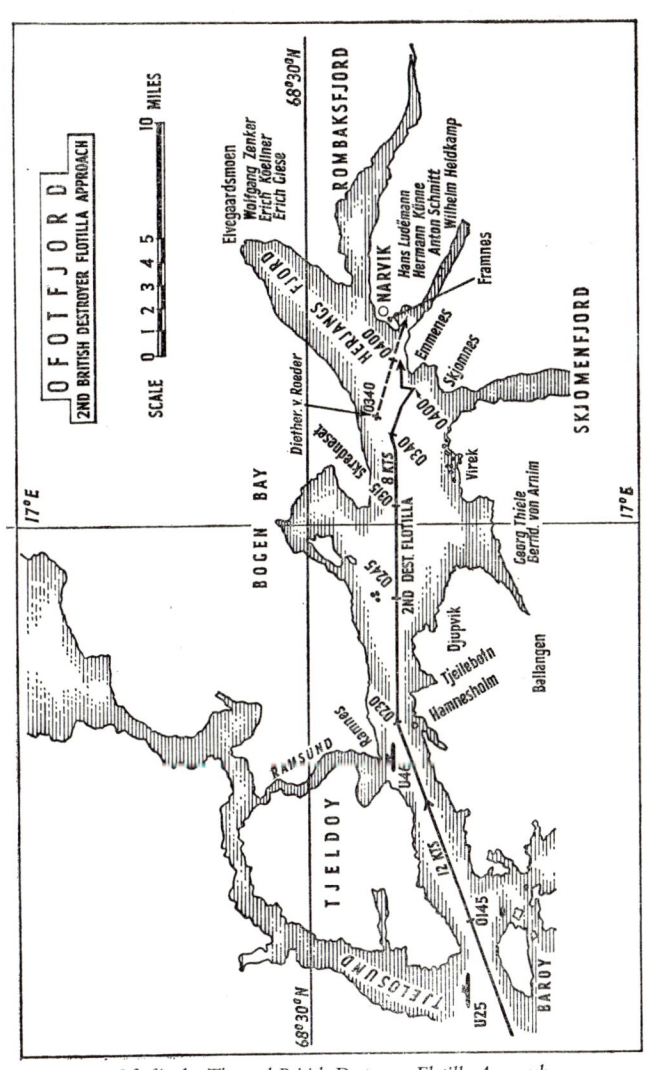

Ofotfjord—The 2nd British Destroyer Flotilla Approach

Lieutenant Commander 'Rusty' Gordon-Smith, the Flotilla Navigator, sighted Tranoy Light at 0030/10th and took his departure on a voyage that must surely be judged epic in the records of his art. Extreme accuracy was not achieved, but the courage with which he had pressed for the undertaking and now saw it through was both remarkable and a tactical factor of the first importance; for Bonte, lulled into security by the awful weather, had gone to bed.

The fjord above Tranoy is still as much as five miles wide and Warburton-Lee put on a burst at 20 knots, clearly so as to give time in hand for later contingencies. Officers of the Watch peered through the driving snow at the ghostly outline of the next ahead and hung on grimly; sometimes they would lose her and increase speed, only to find themselves riding up alarmingly and having to sheer off. Disaster could happen fast at that speed, but their destroyer training had fitted them well for the test and there are worse things than snow; hard-driven spray or heavy rain batter the eyeballs, so that looking becomes a feat of will, whereas snow is light and passes overhead, deflected by the bridge structure. But it was very thick.

Baroy was probably sighted, for at 0130 the turn into Ofotfjord was made without slackening speed. Here lay the *U25* but she heard nothing and saw less; had Schütze too decided in his mind that there was no danger of a British attack? It was not until 0145, when off the tip of Tjeldoy where the fjord narrows to $1\frac{1}{2}$ miles, that Warburton-Lee reduced speed to 12 knots. Tension mounted in the white darkness and sounds were muffled, but Gordon-Smith retained his navigator's professional calm, so maddening in normal circumstances, so reassuring in time of stress. To aid his dead-reckoning he used his echo-sounder to the full, but that was limited in value since the mountains plunge nearly vertically from the sky to the sea-bed at 300 fathoms so that there is little shoaling to give warning of danger. The Asdic however could return a sharp echo from such a coast and indicate its distance, a very useful property.

The Admiralty sent a signal to Warburton-Lee:

'Reported that German garrison arrived Narvik in apparently empty ore ships which may still have stores on board and are to be sunk if possible. Endeavour to ascertain strength of Germans landed, what guns and whether Norwegian batteries are in German hands= 0104/10th'

The tension in London, and the urge to do or say something, can be imagined. Nevertheless the first part of the signal confirmed a totally erroneous misconception and distracted Warburton-Lee from his proper aim of destroying German warships, while the second merely evoked snorts of irritation. 'Why does not Nelson stop making signals,' snapped Collingwood before Trafalgar. 'We all know what we have to do!'

At 0210 the snow blackened ahead and Gordon-Smith ordered, 'Hard-a-starboard' on the instant. The line was thrown into confusion, but all followed somehow and no ships hit anything. In the *Havock* they thought it was land—'you could have thrown a heaving-line on to it!' But in the *Hardy* they could not be sure, floating ice perhaps; but even that should have returned an Asdic echo which this did not. Whatever it was the *Hotspur* lost sight of the *Hunter*, whereupon the following signals were exchanged between her and Warburton-Lee in plain language wireless telegraphy:

'From (D)2. Are you all right?=0214'
'From *Hotspur*. Yes, you are just out of sight=0216'
'From (D)2. My course and speed 075 degrees, 12 knots =0217'
'From (D)2. I am about to pass Hamnesholm abeam to starboard =0225'
'From (D)2. Hamnesholm abeam=0228'
'From *Hotspur*. In touch=0230'

The Germans having thus been gratuitously informed that a force of British ships would arrive off Narvik at 0400, its aim and precise composition was then clarified for them:

'From (D)2. Good luck, let them have it=0240'
'From (D)2. Make your callsigns if in touch=0246' Callsigns were immediately made by all ships.

It is clear from the wording of these signals that Warburton-Lee and his professionally competent staff were not in any way concerned that they might give anything away; for there was surely no need to be quite so explicit even if they did think it essential to confirm that the Flotilla was still in company. Neither were German telegraphists anxiously searching their frequency dials for the first sign of an enemy transmission close at hand. It is hard to comment justly from the age of Electronic Warfare, when few if any enemy detections are made without the aid of one of its agencies; yet it is a fact that although long distance messages had been intercepted and de-cyphered by both sides from World War I onwards, no one had apparently thought of doing the same in the tactical sphere.

'And Pilate took water, and washed his hands before the multitude.'
(Matthew 27—24)

Stanning had been busy de-cyphering another Admiralty message:

'Norwegian defence ships *Eidsvold* and *Norge* may be in German hands. You alone can judge whether in these circumstances attack should be made. We shall support whatever decision you take =0136'

The *Hostile* passed Hamnesholm at 0248 and reported the fact. She thus did *U46*'s job for her, since the latter was also there but blind in the snow. At 0300 the *Diether von Roeder* relieved the *Anton Schmitt* on patrol, closed up at full action stations, and steered a west-northwesterly course into a blank wall of snow. Her orders, received from Gadow by voice radio, were:

'Patrol against submarines in front of the harbour entrance until daylight.'

Böhme anchored the *Anton Schmitt* just to the south of the *Jan Wellem* to await the next fuelling vacancy alongside. He went aft to the grateful warmth of his cabin and turned in, albeit fully clothed and with his life-jacket over his head. Although only a junior commanding officer he was acutely conscious of danger, whether from air or sea, and wisely so. Other similar instances are recorded; in the *Erich Giese* a young officer was seen by a senior to be putting on his pyjamas and was told, "You must be mad! Sleep in your clothes so that you're ready for anything." Kommodore Bonte's inactivity and lack of concern became less and less understandable.

This was the time of night when human vitality is always at its lowest ebb, and the unconsciousness of utter exhaustion had descended on the German destroyers. The British force was no more than ten miles away and progressing so well that its speed could be reduced to eight knots. Skredneset Light was not sighted but Gordon-Smith altered course to 080 degrees at 0329 on dead-reckoning, so as to keep close to the north shore as the orders required.

Close Quarters

Gordon-Smith of the *Hardy*, and the Navigating Officer of the *Diether von Roeder*, both advised their Captains to turn towards Narvik Harbour having calculated that they were in *exactly the same position at exactly the same time*, 0340. The *Hardy*, however, was somewhat to the south and west of her dead-reckoning position, perhaps owing to an over-correction for the flood stream and some leeway from the now northeasterly wind. The two ships turned to course 110 degrees and kept perfect station on one another, at the most 1½ miles apart and probably less, totally unaware of the fact.

While in this formation Warburton-Lee told his team:
'I am steering for the entrance of Narvik Harbour=0343'
This was doubtless to ensure that all ships were on the top line and to convey a sense of drama entirely appropriate to the circumstances. Had the Germans been listening, or had the transmission broken through to even an unalerted operator, it may be assumed that they would have been similarly stimulated.

Daylight was slow to appear and Warburton-Lee reduced speed to six knots at 0348 to give it a chance. Heppel, as Flotilla Torpedo Officer, had been studying the chart and advised his Captain to enter harbour as near to the southwest shore as he dared. Although it was possible to 'angle' a torpedo to run on a course other than the direction in which the tube was pointing, this could not be done as a method of last minute control as was normal in the German ships. The British tubes had to be locked in the beam position before firing, and the course of the torpedo was determined by firing at the right moment as the ship turned. Knowing therefore that the destroyers would have to swing when inside the harbour, Heppel urged that plenty of room should be allowed for doing so. It seems likely that a 20 degree turn together to starboard at 0350 was intended to achieve this aim; it incidentally caused the Flotilla to draw slowly away from the *Diether von Roeder*.

The *Hostile* rejoined the tail of the line and the *Hotspur* reported her presence at 0353. She had 'pinged' her way up on her Asdic with only one 'hard over' to avoid some menacing blackness, whether substance or shadow Wright could not say, and had arrived on time. At 0400 Gordon-Smith made a final course adjustment to 100 degrees. 'Stand by!' Eyes strained but the snow blanketed everything, even the already quiet hum of boiler fans; the hush in the men's hearts was absolute.

'Stop engines=0403'
The visibility lifted slightly, and simultaneously land appeared on the port bow. Was it Framnes? No, for very soon the coast ahead was seen to be continuous and Warburton-Lee's perplexity is well pictured by a rapid fire of manoeuvring signals: 'Speed 10 knots, turn 40 degrees to port together—stop engines—go astern—stop

engines.' Then Gordon-Smith was satisfied that he was off the bay south of Emmenes, and turned north at ten knots; dawn's arrival was still tardy however, and at 0412 speed was again reduced to six knots.

Having made his landfall Warburton-Lee was determined not to lose touch again, and altered course to due east at 0415. At that moment, $1\frac{1}{2}$ miles ahead of the *Hardy* on her new course, Holtorf decided unlike Warburton-Lee that daylight had come, and took the *Diether von Roeder* into harbour a matter of minutes before mutual sighting would have been certain. The god of war seemed to lust for battle, and manipulate the affairs of men to ensure his satisfaction.

For six minutes the British crept along the coast, slightly light-headed from prolonged tension. Heppel and Stanning were re-questioned about what they had been told at Tranoy; had they misunderstood the number of German destroyers? If there were really as many as six why was there no patrol? Perhaps it would be possible to secure the town with their landing parties after all. Stanning suddenly remembered it to be his birthday, but Warburton-Lee regretted that to send below for a bottle of champagne just at that moment would be inappropriate.

The visibility improved slowly but constantly. The real Framnes appeared fine on the port bow, and then the harbour entrance opened to reveal a solid mass of shipping which made the raiders gasp with astonishment; but no enemy was yet to be seen and all was eerily still. 'There was such a tide as moving seemed asleep,' quoted Stanning to himself, and everyone looked at each other, puzzled and unsure. You couldn't really start a battle when everybody's sound asleep, they thought.

Stations for Entering Harbour

There is no indication that Warburton-Lee allowed himself the luxury of romantic scruples. The operation itself and the nightmare trip up the fjords had been undertaken only on the assumption that surprise could be achieved. He had won it brilliantly, favoured by little more than that degree of fortune which the brave usually command; the initiative could still be lost and he pressed forward at 12 knots to cover the remaining mile without delay. The *Hotspur* and *Hostile* were detached on their supporting mission to the north-east; the *Hunter* and *Havock* were told to wait their turn; and the *Hardy* entered harbour, alone.

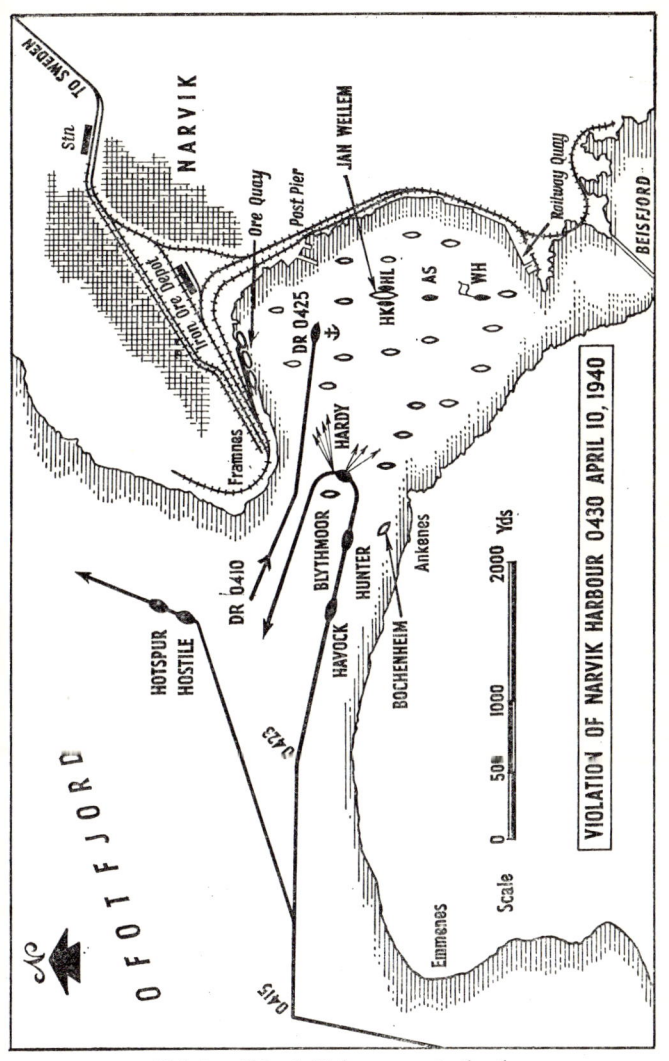

Violation of Narvik Harbour, 0430 April 10th

Narvik Harbour

The plan shows the harbour as it might well have been at 0430 on April 10th, 1940; yet it is only an incomplete jig-saw and not of the kind whose pieces interlock and prove their positions to be right. The fog of war, which had attended the British approach and frustrated the German patrols, continued to confound both the antagonists and their records. No single individual saw more than a small part of the whole picture and the evidence is often conflicting; nevertheless the plan is as faithful as much interrogation and study can make it.

The tide being high and the stream slack, most of the anchored ships lay with their bows into the nor'nor'easterly breeze. Deep inside the harbour however it is possible that a set came out of Beisfjord and swung the *Wilhelm Heidkamp* and *Anton Schmitt* the other way. Visibility had increased to nearly a mile and the snow had stopped, but it was still very hazy.

The German destroyers were at first invisible from the *Hardy* since they were berthed inside a screen of merchant ships. From north to south: the *Diether von Roeder* had anchored about 500 yards west of the Post Pier five minutes earlier; the *Jan Wellem*, east of the harbour centre, rode bows north with the *Hermann Künne* fuelling on her port side and the *Hans Lüdemann* to starboard. Astern, waiting her turn was the *Anton Schmitt*, and further south still lay the *Wilhelm Heidkamp*, with Kommodore Bonte asleep in his harbour cabin aft.

The *Blythmoor* and *Bockenheim* were the first ships to be individually distinguished from the *Hardy*, and as she neared them she slackened speed until she was just ghosting. The breeze fell away, not a ripple stirred the surface, and the only movement was an occasional whisp of smoke from a merchant ship's funnel; the snow-covered mountains appeared faintly in the growing light, the town slept, and Stanning thought, why have we got to do this?

At last there was life, a sentry on the deck of the *Blythmoor* now close to port; Stanning asked if he should hail him to ask where the enemy was, but was told, "No, we don't want to wake up the Germans in the town." Well, not yet. They knew that was ridiculous for the sound could not possibly have carried, but they were mentally on tiptoe and could not have shouted had they tried. All peered intently, and none more so than Heppel who knew that his torpedoes would be called upon the moment a target was sighted. He had

Right: Whose soldiers are standing where? An insupportable affront to the Royal Navy.
[Gerhard Stalling AG

Bottom: A general view of Narvik Harbour, looking approximately north-westwards.

Top: Kapitän zur See and Kommodore Friedrich Bonte. Senior Officer of the German Narvik destroyer force.
[Kapitän Böhme

Bottom: Kommodore Bonte's Flotilla Leader *Wilhelm Heidkamp*, flying his Broad Pendant.
[Bibliotek für Zeitgeschichte

Two destroyers of the 1936 *Leberecht Maass* class. The *Georg Thiele* (13) Korvettenkapitän Max-Eckart Wolff, and *Bernd von Arnim* (62) Korvettenkapitän Curt Rechel. This class carried five main armament guns (12.7cm, 5in) and eight torpedoes in two mountings. Note the low freeboard and tall funnels. Other ships of the class taking part were the *Wolfgang Zenker*, *Erich Giese*, and *Erich Koellner*. [Bibliotek für Zeitgeschichte

Two destroyers of the 1938 *Diether von Roeder* class. The name ship (51), Korvetten‍kapitän Erich Holtorf, and the *Anton Schmitt* Korvettenkapitän Friedrich Böhme. These ships carried the same main armament as the *Leberecht Maass* class, but their design was both more pleasing and seaworthy. The other ships of the class at Narvik were the *Wilhelm Heidkamp, Hans Lüdemann, Hermann Künne*. [MoD

Korvettenkapitän Max-Eckart Wolff (*Georg Thiele*). [Bibliotek für Zeitgeschichte

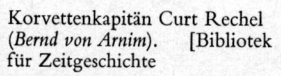

Korvettenkapitän Curt Rechel (*Bernd von Arnim*). [Bibliotek für Zeitgeschichte

Fregattenkapitän Erich Bey. Senior Officer 4th Destroyer Flotilla in the *Wolfgang Zenker*. Subsequently Kommodore Destroyers and finally lost with the *Scharnhorst*. [Bibliotek für Zeitgeschichte

Fregattenkapitän Hans-Joachim Gadow. Senior Officer 3rd Destroyer Flotilla in the *Hans Lüdemann*. [Bibliotek für Zeitgeschichte

Korvettenkapitän Karl Smidt (*Erich Giese*). [Admiral Smidt

Korvettenkapitän Fritz Böhme (*Anton Schmitt*). [Bibliotek für Zeitgeschichte

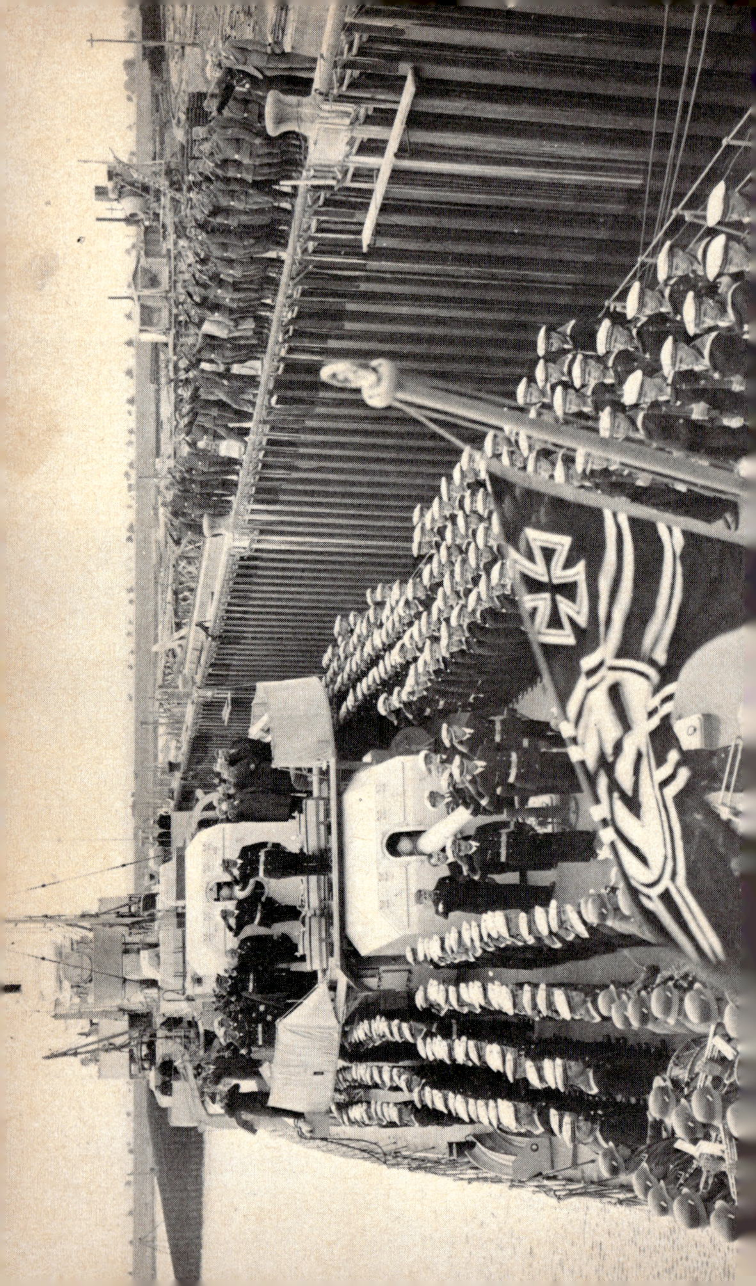

Opposite: Commissioning ceremony of the *Anton Schmitt*, September 24th, 1939. [Kapitän Böhme

Captain Bernard A. W. Warburton-Lee (known as 'Wash' or 'Wash-Lee') Captain (D) 2nd Destroyer Flotilla and Commanding Officer HMS *Hardy* [IWM

Vice Admiral W. Jock Whitworth, DSO. Vice Admiral Commanding Battlecruiser Squadron.   [IWM

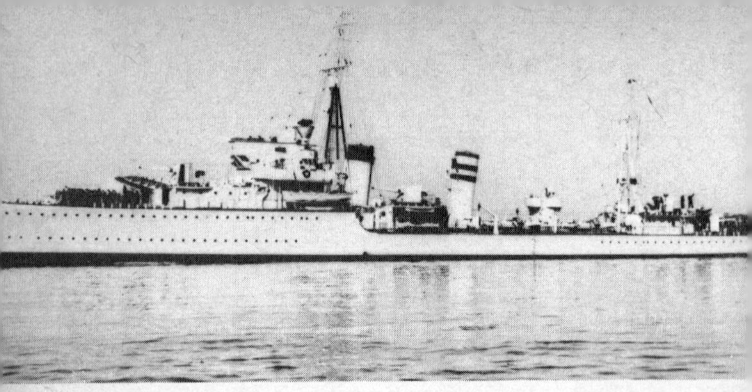

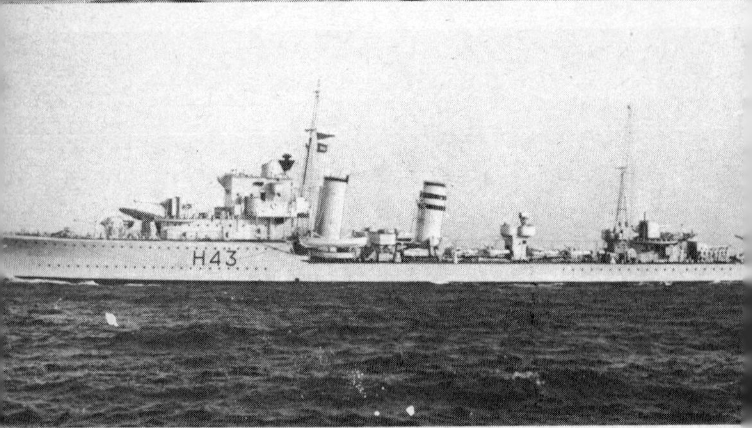
H43

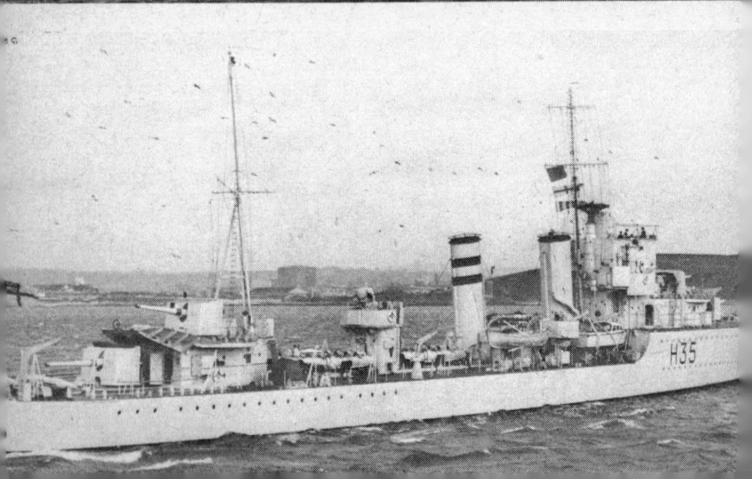
H35

HMS *Hero* and her Captain,
Commander Hilary W. Biggs.
[Admiral Sir Hilary Biggs

...posite, top: HMS *Hardy*
...aptain Warburton-Lee).
...tilla Leader, 2nd Destroyer
...otilla. Five 4.7in guns,
...orpedoes.   [Tom Molland

...posite, centre: HMS *Havock*
... Cdr Rafe E. Courage). Four
...in guns, 8 torpedoes.
... & J. Pavia

...posite, bottom: HMS *Hunter*
... Cdr Lindsay de Villiers).
...oD

The Germans arrive. [IWM and Bibliotek für Zeitgeschichte

Top: Norwegian Coast Defence Ship *Eidsvold* (Captain Willoch). Two 8.2in, six 5.9in guns.
[Real Photos

Bottom: HMS *Hostile*, Commander J. P. Wright.   [MoD

A 'K' Class destroyer, similar to HMS *Kimberley*.
Lt Cdr Richard G. K. Knowling. Six 4.7in guns, 10 torpedoes.
(Tom Molland)

Top: A British quadruple tube mounting (the shelter on top was not fitted in 1940). Note the expansion chamber into which the impulse cartridge was inserted to impel the torpedo out of the tube. The mounting had to be locked in the beam position for firing and was trained by the two handles, one each side. German torpedoes were set to 'angle' after firing, but the British ones ran straight in the direction they were heading when they were fired; control was achieved by swinging the ship. [MoD

Bottom: Launch. [MoD

Top: Launch. [MoD

Bottom: After an initial dive the depth-keeping mechanism would over-correct and the torpedo would often 'nose' or even, as here, 'porpoise' before achieving its set depth. [MoD

trained his forward tubes to starboard and the after mounting to port so that his reaction could be instantaneous; enemy speed zero, safety pins out of the whiskered pistols, impulse cartridges inserted, stop valves open.

Someone breathed, "There they are!" and the Chief Yeoman broke out the battle ensigns already furled at the two mastheads. They were the *Anton Schmitt* and *Wilhelm Heidkamp*, suddenly revealed indistinctly through a gap between the merchant ships and seemingly almost alongside each other. Heppel gasped, "There's a torpedo target such as I've never seen in my life!" "Well get on with it then," said Warburton-Lee, and ordered a touch on the engines to swing the ship to port inside the harbour from the *Blythmoor*; the *Hardy* was virtually stopped.

'Never fire torpedoes in penny numbers', was a principle well imbued in Heppel, and although it was theoretically impossible to miss a stopped ship at such a ridiculously short range he launched three in a narrow fan. On the foremost tubes Leading Torpedoman Cope's duty was to ensure that the drill went without a hitch, which he did; but being a man of acute awareness of his surroundings he also saw the targets. The torpedoes leapt from their tubes in small clouds of cordite smoke, in turn from aft to forward, their propellers already whirring; each splashed, dived, recovered, nosed the surface, achieved its set depth, and left a straight track to show that it ran true. Heppel heard the third one nose and thought it was a fourth being fired by the tube's crew, assuming a misfire from the bridge; he did not know therefore that he still had this torpedo pointing to starboard.

Warburton-Lee ordered revolutions for 20 knots and turned for the harbour entrance; why? Perhaps it was an instinctive reaction after firing torpedoes, or the end of a period of intolerable tension; or again there might have been some circumstance that was so obvious at the time that no one saw the need to record it. The effect was to end the phase when the harbour could be surveyed in detail and torpedoes fired with leisured accuracy. Enemy destroyers showed themselves between merchant ships and vanished again; Cope unquestionably saw the *Hermann Künne* alongside the *Jan Wellem* and even the oil hoses imprinted themselves on his photographic memory. The ship that Heppel saw was probably the *Diether von Roeder*, further to the left.

The *Hardy*'s torpedoes arrived as Stanning watched; the first missed to the right of the target as intended and hit the bow of a merchant ship. A torpedo explosion is usually impressive and this was no exception; but seconds later the centre one detonated not just its own warhead, but the *Wilhelm Heidkamp*'s after magazine. Her stern blew off; her three after guns hurtled through the air and one landed on the forecastle; the flash was brilliant and skyhigh, and ammunition continued to explode in the air for several minutes. Narvik stirred in its sleep, but not Kommodore Bonte and 80 of his men. Sensitive and conscientiously devoted to his duty, he may have been fortunate to die before he could realise the disastrous results of his misjudgement, for they would surely have been intolerable to him for years to come. Had, however, that exceptionally able soldier General Dietl died instead, the German operation could have been more seriously affected.

It is not surprising in the holocaust that no one saw what happened to the third torpedo. Silence was no longer a virtue, and the *Hardy* opened fire on either the *Diether von Roeder* or the *Hermann Künne* but does not seem to have hit them. Heppel frantically ordered his after tubes to train to starboard and the crew, with equal fervour, heaved and strained at the great handles on either side. Snow, slush, and cold lubricating oil made the task herculean, and Cope brought the forward tubes' crew to help. With shoulders to the breeches and striving for footholds on the icy deck, they succeeded in turning the ten-ton mass through 180 degrees, and just before it locked into the firing position Heppel pulled his first trigger. The mounting jerked in the reverse direction with the recoil, but the torpedo missed the ship's structure and no one was hurt. With a last heave the locking-bolt slipped home, and the second, third and fourth torpedoes fired normally.

The *Hardy* was already gathering way and it was too late; neither German destroyer was hit and the Norwegians later reported that the torpedoes detonated on the quays in the northeast corner of the harbour. If only Heppel had known he still had a torpedo pointing to starboard! If only the ship had not been moving so fast! Only a few rounds of light calibre followed her out of the harbour, and the Germans were bemused for several more valuable minutes.

As the *Hardy* left, the *Hunter* entered. Her records are sparse to the point of being almost non-existent for good reasons which will become apparent, but from what little is known of her circular tour of the harbour she seems to have laid about her with right good will.

Unlike Warburton-Lee, de Villiers felt no inhibition against sinking merchant ships; why should he? Paragraph 2 of the orders and the Admiralty's 0104 left no doubt that they had equal priority with warships. The *Hunter*'s guns blazed; she fired at least four, and possibly eight torpedoes into the crowded concourse, and the chaos she created was indescribable.

In one instance however, the *Hunter*'s achievement can be surmised with less imprecision. Many of the *Anton Schmitt*'s crew had been awakened by what they thought was gunfire, though it may be imagined that the *Wilhelm Heidkamp*'s devastating explosion close by was what did it in the first place. Indeed, when they arrived on deck they thought they were being attacked from the air; but then their ship was hit forward by a palpable shell and they realised the truth. Their Captain, Böhme, having been awake and intensively active for the previous 48 hours, had slept for only 90 minutes and reached the most profound state of unconsciousness. The *Wilhelm Heidkamp*'s end and the outside gunnery failed to stir him, but the hit on his own ship jarred him more insistently and he sprang up. As he did so a torpedo hit the first turbine-room, and his cabin door jammed; he struggled with it, trapped.

After ten minutes or so of crowded life, the *Hunter* followed the *Hardy* out of harbour, undamaged; but the enemy's fire was beginning to kindle and de Villiers thought it prudent to use smoke to cover his withdrawal. The *Havock*, ready and waiting, came in notwithstanding; she was just 16 minutes behind the *Hardy* and followed the same track round the *Blythmoor*; it took courage, but Courage was there. The natural visibility was no better than it had been, and now it was further reduced artificially by cordite, high-explosive, and funnel smoke; it hampered the *Havock* in her task but also protected her.

Courage saw first a series of gunflashes, and then made out that they came from a destroyer alongside a merchant ship; he opened fire, but for whatever reason, bad luck or bad management, no hits were scored on either the *Hermann Künne* or the *Jan Wellem*. At this moment Kothe was at last told that steam was on the main engines and rang down for astern power; never mind the wires or the oil hoses, all that mattered was to get under way. The *Havock*'s Torpedo Gunner, Mr Leslie Millns, saw this happen from his action station at the tubes, and as he then received the order, 'Ready starboard', from the bridge he naturally assumed that the *Hermann Künne* was the target. But Courage had sighted the *Anton Schmitt*, who seemed through the haze to be floating normally, and directed his Torpedo Control Officer, Lieutenant John Burfield, to sink her.

We should say today that Burfield's triple salvo was cost-effective. One torpedo hit a merchant ship; another, following the first's track, was displaced by the explosion so that it neatly dodged the stricken ship and hit another beyond her; and the third, though they were not necessarily in that order, took the *Anton Schmitt* in her second turbine-room. Böhme had wrenched his door open and run out on to the starboard side of the after deck. The ship had already taken an alarming list that way, but he just had time to run round the quarter-

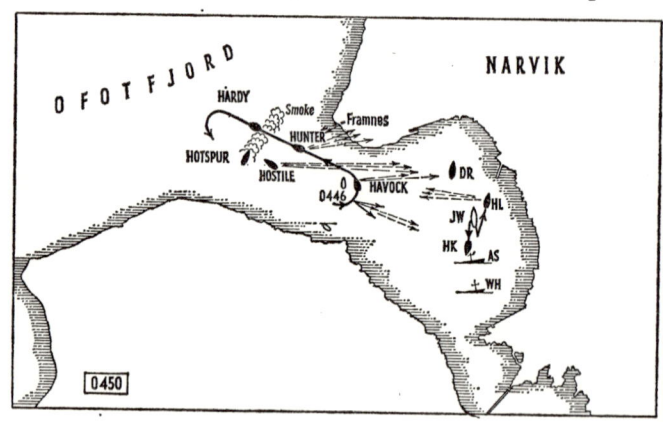

Narvik Harbour 0450

deck and up hill to the port side before the torpedo arrived. Böhme was blown over the side but his life-jacket saved him, and he was able to watch his ship break in two and sink in a minute; he took half an hour to swim to the Railway Quay with most of his men, but 63 were lost. His wife would need her bicycle again.

Three torpedoes, three hits; but that was not the end of the devastation wrought by the well-named *Havock*. The *Hermann Künne* dropped rapidly astern from the *Jan Wellem* and was within 40 yards of the *Anton Schmitt* when the latter was hit for the second time. The detonation jarred the *Hermann Künne* from stem to transom and her engines seized; the fore part of the *Anton Schmitt* rolled over, laying the mast quite gently on to the *Hermann Künne*'s deck, where a sailor thoughtfully unbent the Captain's pendant, returning it to Böhme in due course. The *Hermann Künne* was immobile for the next 40 minutes, and scraped over and through the wreck several times.

Courage withheld his remaining torpedoes because, as he put it, 'the *Hunter* seemed to have hit everything in sight'. But as he completed his turn he sighted another enemy just as his torpedo sights were past her, exactly as had happened to the *Hardy*. 'As the enemy gunfire was getting hot and they had the advantage of the light,' he wrote, 'I increased speed and cleared out.' The *Blythmoor*'s German guard, presumably the same man whom Stanning had wanted to hail and a brave one at that, emptied his revolver at the *Havock*'s bridge as she passed. A supernumerary Marine replied with a Lewis gun and notched up '1' in the snow on a bulkhead.

The *Havock* did not have an easy run out of harbour like her predecessors, being straddled several times while in the vulnerable attitude of having her stern to the enemy and only her after guns bearing. She was probably being engaged not only by the *Diether von Roeder* but also the *Hans Lüdemann*, who had slipped from the *Jan Wellem*'s starboard side and was lying off, using her as cover and shooting round her bow. The *Havock* was not hit, but it is possible that it was at this stage that the *Hans Lüdemann* was, twice and damagingly; her No 1 gun was wrecked, a fire was started aft necessitating flooding the after magazine, and her steering failed. She also worried her Captain, Friedrichs, by taking on a list and settling by the stern, but that was found not to be serious.

This was the chaotic scene which confronted Captain Evans of the *North Cornwall* when he had rushed on to the *Jan Wellem*'s deck, along with the other prisoners and crew. The big whaler bore a charmed life, but those below had been awakened and alarmed by such a violent explosion that they thought she must have been hit. This was probably the *Anton Schmitt*'s second torpedo, which also had such a drastic secondary effect on the *Hermann Künne*; if the detonation was completely tamped by water and the ship's hull, it would have had a greater underwater shock effect than the far larger one in the *Wilhelm Heidkamp* which was dissipated in the air.

Evans first saw a turmoil of water on the *Jan Wellem*'s starboard side with hoses and wires hanging down into it, and logically concluded that the destroyer he knew to have been there had sunk *in situ*;

but in fact he could see her, the *Hans Lüdemann*, lying off to starboard and in action. Astern were the two wrecks.

The *Havock*'s last trial in this first phase was a hail of rifle and machine-gun fire from the German troops on Framnes, which she returned in good measure with her foremost pair of 4.7s and got clear away. As the Royal Navy reports during exercises, 'Run one completed'.

The tranquil harbour at dawn twilight which the *Hardy* had entered less than 30 minutes earlier was now transformed into a scene of horrible destruction. Rudely awakened on the second morning in succession, Mayor Broch surveyed the collapse of much that had raised his beloved town from a minor fishing village into—what?—an important factor in world strategy. The mainspring of his life as he had lived it so far had also apparently snapped. As a progressive socialist with no interest in war, no comprehension of it, and certainly no premonition that it might ever engulf him however much outer barbarians might indulge in it to satisfy their brutish lusts, his life until yesterday had been devoted to the peaceful progress and fulfilment of ordinary people. But he did not despair; 24 hours of tyranny had shown him that great ideals must be defended, if necessary at great sacrifice, and the new revelation that his country and his cause had powerful friends became more important than the horror, and he watched with grim satisfaction.

Carry Out Run Two

There was in fact no pause, but since it was now impracticable to enter the harbour different tactics were adopted. The *Hotspur* and *Hostile* had made a short sweep to the northward outside the Framnes peninsula, and encountered no opposition or shore batteries. Their orders did not require them to search the outlying fjords but merely to engage any ships that might appear from those directions, and since there were none the *Hotspur* reported, 'Nothing to northward=0440', and returned to join the main battle. It seems that Wright, being of an independent turn of mind, had done so even earlier and was engaging the *Diether von Roeder* even before the *Hardy*, *Hunter* and *Havock* were clear of the entrance. To maintain a clear line of sight to his target he kept the *Hostile* stopped. The gun-direction telescopes were opaque with snow that could not be wiped clear fast enough, but over open sights it was hardly any easier to aim. Spotting fall of shot was almost impossible so 'blind ladders' were used, groups of three salvos fired rapidly, with an 'up' 400 yard correction between each; then the same with a 'down' correction, and so on. Steady nerves and good drill resulted in the *Diether von Roeder* being hit twice, seriously, while the *Hostile* remained unscathed.

The *Hotspur* had delayed in order to lay a smoke-screen* through which the three inner ships retired on leaving the harbour, and it can be supposed that they were glad of it, particularly the *Havock*. Then Warburton-Lee told Layman to clear his funnels and fire torpedoes into the harbour; he fired four and hit at least two merchant ships, of which one may have been the British *Blythmoor* who had hitherto borne a charmed life at the very focus of the battle.

On both sides gunnery was blind but intense, and the mountains echoed the thunder of discharge to join with the next salvo and amplify it to the level of the crack of doom. There was no formation, and each British ship positioned herself so as best to engage the stabbing, lurid gun-flashes when they appeared. The *Hardy* lay off behind the *Hotspur*, supporting her, and then edged closer again herself when the latter moved off northeastwards. The *Hunter* was in there too, and the *Hostile* circled to port and returned, determined to re-engage the *Diether von Roeder* and finish her off with a torpedo.

Somewhat enigmatically the *Hardy* signalled a group from the Fleet Signal Book that meant, 'Are you picking up torpedoes?' But before any wit among the Captains could be ready with a suitably pungent reply, assuming that any of them had the audacity so to address their austere leader, the question was changed to, 'Report number of torpedoes fired=0456'. The answers snapped back: *Hotspur* four, *Hunter* eight, *Havock* five (an error, she had fired three and five remained), *Hostile* nil. The *Hardy* herself had fired seven.

The British ships continued to jockey for firing positions outside the harbour, and gradually their movements combined to form a rough, anti-clockwise circle, with each engaging as she came abreast the entrance. The smoke however allowed less and less to be seen, there were noticeably fewer gunflashes, and the *Hostile* never got off her torpedoes at the *Diether von Roeder*. Warburton-Lee took the opportunity to assess the results so far:

'From (D)2. Report damage to enemy seen=0505'
'From *Hostile*. Left hand destroyer hit by 4.7 inch shell=0505'
'From *Hotspur*. Two merchant ships sinking=0505'

*See Operation orders, para 2, p. 48.

'From *Hunter*. Five torpedoes hit, damage to enemy destroyer not observed=0509'

'From *Havock*. Destroyer hit by shell=0507'

To these reports could be added the *Hardy*'s torpedoing of a destroyer and a merchant ship, but the combined reports do not begin to convey an impression of the havoc actually wrought. It is no wonder that the action was continued, and that Warburton-Lee told the *Hostile*:

'If you can find suitable warship target send four torpedoes in=0510'

It is fairly clear from this signal and his own actions that in spite of the Admiralty's order to sink German merchant ships, Warburton-Lee considered their warships to have first priority; but since he had never laid this down as a policy, the private ships had to make up their own minds and did so in different ways. The *Hostile* acted as did her leader; the *Havock*, compromised and spared the *North Cornwall* whom she recognised as British, but the *Hotspur* and *Hunter* treated all merchant ships as their legitimate prey whenever no warship was in sight. The latter may have been right, since time pressed, all German ships were firmly believed to be part of the operation and it was the luck of the draw that the only one which was, the vitally important *Jan Wellem*, escaped serious injury.

Wright continued to manoeuvre the *Hostile* for a torpedo shot at his old adversary, the *Diether von Roeder*, but now torpedoes coming out of the harbour became markedly more interesting than those going in. The three German destroyers inside engaged whenever they saw a target; although the *Hermann Künne* was immobile and entangled with the wreck of the *Anton Schmitt*, she had nothing wrong with her guns. The *Hans Lüdemann* had drawn clear of the *Jan Wellem* and, while groping her way between the wrecks, engaged with her four remaining main armament weapons, as well as with her 3.7cm AA automatics whose tracer shells misled the British into thinking that they were being fired by shore batteries.

It was the *Diether von Roeder* however who had initially shown up most clearly to the aggressive British and taken the most punishment. The *Hostile*'s two hits on the port side below the bridge had ruptured a fuel tank and turned No 2 boiler-room into an inferno. Having only just anchored no preparations had been made for slipping the cable, so she too was unable to move and Holtorf decided to get his torpedoes away while he still could; he fired all eight towards the entrance between the two merchant ships. Only the German control system whereby each torpedo was 'angled' at the last moment could manage such a shot.

Had the German torpedoes themselves however been as effective as the British ones, that would probably have been the masterstroke which ended the battle. Out of the harbour came the tracks until there seemed to be no parcel of water without at least several, and as there was a British ship on every one, each had her problems. Six, one or two surfaced, approached the *Hotspur*'s bow and Layman felt like shouting at those around him to stop reporting any more while he

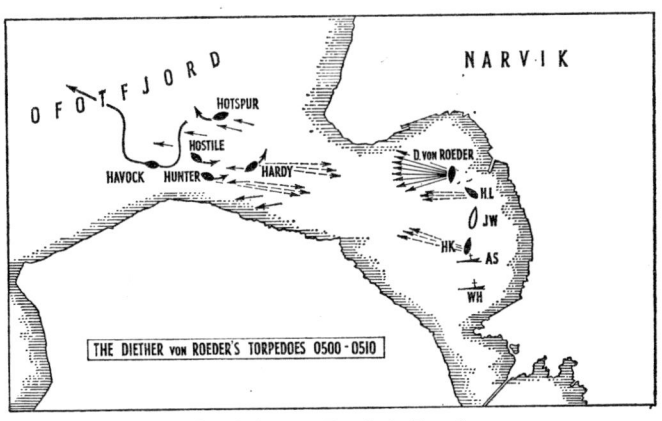

The Diether von Roeder's *Torpedoes*

concentrated on avoiding those he could see himself; he managed to do so, just. The *Hostile* too wriggled out of trouble, one passing ahead and one astern, both very close; but the *Hardy*'s beam was irrevocably presented to the oncoming missiles. Stanning watched one, fascinated, as it approached him directly, and remembered that one should bend one's knees to avoid jarring or fracture; he did so accordingly, preparing himself, body and soul, for lift-off. But the mood on the bridge was still extraordinarily carefree and euphoric; they could not lose, and sure enough that torpedo and another ran harmlessly underneath.

The *Hunter*'s scanty records also mention a torpedo under her, though not at what time. The *Havock* was furthest to seaward when those with her name on them approached, and Courage saw that he must turn away to the west in order to comb the tracks. He managed it and was starting to come back when three more threatened. "Full ahead, hard-a-port!" and still all was well, but he was not going to be caught again and continued west for the best part of two miles to make absolutely sure. Then he slowed down and turned to port, and at that very moment another torpedo was seen to be steering surely for the bridge. A habit of Courage's which endeared him to his people was to drape himself over the compass in a careless and most unmilitary attitude, becoming more languid the greater the excitement. Now he verily wrapped himself round the binnacle, hanging his head and thinking of the stokers in the boiler-rooms; "Sorry chaps!" he said. But that torpedo too sped on, deep and impotent; the Havocks immediately perked up and, like the Hardys, thought themselves invulnerable.

The two left-hand torpedoes of the zone ran scampering up the beach to the west of Ankenes and lay there whirring; even they did not explode.

The *Diether von Roeder* had shot her bolt and was fit for nothing more than to try and keep herself afloat. The boiler-room blazed fiercely, the main armament control system broke down and the guns were directed locally for as long as they could be manned. A hit in the forward stokers' messdeck set the fore part of the ship on fire, killing eight men and wounding two; a Leading Stoker rushed out in flames, was instantly pushed over the side by the First Lieutenant who then jumped in himself and pulled him out again. A hit on No 3 gun destroyed it and killed six of the crew; an ammunition locker ignited with a roar; and the last hit, near the after magazine, necessitated its flooding. To cap it all the anchor could not be weighed because the capstan was electrically operated and the power supply had failed.

However the main engines were all right and Holtorf used them to drag the ship and her anchor to a place of comparative safety. Slowly, stern first, she moved between the wrecks; at first towards the Ore Quay and then, doubtless because of the shorter distance, to the Post Pier, to the root of which a wire was secured; her bow was held pointing to seaward by her anchor, and there she stayed.

Captain Evans and his Chief Engineer had made their way to the *Jan Wellem*'s boat deck and watched the awesome events around them from that vantage point; seeing ship after ship hit, set on fire, listing, sinking, or disappearing under columns of water. They awaited their turn, for it was as incomprehensible to them as it must be to us today that the great *Jan Wellem*, conspicuously anchored in the centre of the harbour, should have escaped injury for so long. The whaler's Captain was equally apprehensive and asked Evans what he thought of the situation; Evans replied staunchly that knowing the Royal Navy as he did they would assuredly not rest until the *Jan Wellem* had been accounted for. That started a train of thought, and when the Captain asked Evans what he would do were he in command, he responded readily that he would give the prisoners a chance to get away while they still might. There the matter rested while the Captain digested the proposal.

Had the *Hardy*, *Havock* and possibly the *Hunter* been hit by torpedoes, it may be supposed that the British attack would have been blunted, if not defeated. As it was Warburton-Lee reorganised his ships:

'Stand by to follow round again. Keep a sharp lookout for enemy torpedoes=0512'

The British maintained their pressure, but Wright searched vainly for his old enemy who had probably already started her movement. A note of testiness crept into Warburton-Lee's signal to him: 'Have you fired any torpedoes yet?=0519', to which he replied: 'Intend to fire when going round this time.' But there was no warship to be seen, probe as he might, and that he did so is delightfully clear from this rap over the knuckles: 'Follow round, don't go the wrong way each time=0530.' Warburton-Lee had ordered the ships to circle at 20 knots, perhaps to offer more difficult torpedo targets and to allow instant response to emergency helm orders, and if the *Hostile* was not conforming to the others' movements she may well, at that speed, have been something of a menace.

Two minutes later, the enemy's guns silent, the harbour totally obscured and re-penetration being clearly out of the question, Warburton-Lee decided that Run Two had been completed. He led the Flotilla slowly westwards and again consulted with his staff, this time on the bridge.

The lull thus brought about, an hour after the action had begun, gave the Germans' their first opportunity to shake their heads and remember that a vital action should have been taken long since. All the evidence combines to suggest that only at this late time did the Flotilla Adjutant originate a message from the *Hans Lüdemann* to the outlying destroyers:

'Alarm, attack on Narvik.'

The Second Council of War

The young staff officers were still on top of the world; success, continued survival, and perhaps suppressed fatigue helped them to feel that there was nothing the Flotilla could not do. Their leader on the other hand had lived long enough to know that emotion is often an untrustworthy guide to decision and his maturity, together with the lonely burden of responsibility for life and death, led him to suggest that perhaps it was time to withdraw; but first he would be glad of the staff's views.

Stanning again reports how they advised. 'The answer was unanimously in favour of going in again, for the following reasons:

1 We didn't know what damage we had done, nor what forces of the enemy were left. As all guns had ceased fire early in the second attack it was possible that all opposition had been silenced. It would be ridiculous to withdraw in the face of no opposition at all, and if there were any enemy forces left we ought to try and estimate their weight and report it.

2 At the same time Captain (D) was anxious that no one should get torpedoed, but it was pointed out that so many torpedoes had been fired at us already that there could not be many more to fire.

3 The *Hostile* had fired no torpedoes at all so far and Captain (D) wanted to let her have a turn.'

Heppel confirms that the *Hostile*'s full outfit of torpedoes was a key point; not, naturally, because all the children at a school treat must be given an equal share of the fun, but so that the weapons should be used for the deadly purpose in hand. Then there was the arithmetic; six German destroyers were believed to be present, and four if not five had been located and some damaged in the harbour. If a further one or two were patrolling somewhere in the fjord they could be dealt with by five undamaged British ships, and the glowing possibility of achieving permanent control of the fjord became apparent; for all they knew it might have been won already. Leading Seaman Cope even received a message by his bridge telephone ordering the *Hardy*'s platoon to be ready to land at a moment's notice. That concerned him directly; not only was he in charge of the forward tubes, not only was he an electrician as were all torpedomen in those days, with his bag of tools handy, but he was also a makeshift soldier complete with Lewis gun, greatcoat, gaiters, and bars of pusser's nutty. He remembers hearing the words, "This time we're going to stay."

The arguments for turning back were sound enough, but Warburton-Lee would have found them hard to resist had he wished to do so; with his sense of military honour it would have been even harder to order a retirement with all his officers in favour of attack. But there is no evidence whatever that he did so wish; just a vague unease that has been transmitted through the years, a small red light flashing dimly in some far recess of his mind.

Run Three

The Flotilla had re-formed in line ahead, this time in the order *Hardy*, *Havock*, *Hunter*, *Hotspur* and *Hostile*, and steered east. Warburton-Lee ordered 20 knots at 0644, but following ships felt free to snake the line and vary their speeds so as to engage the more effectively. The mist and smoke were still thick and they could see very little, not much more than the poor *Blythmoor*'s near vertical stern, and gunflashes from the *Hans Lüdemann* and *Hermann Künne* which were taken as points of aim.

It was evidently easier to see out of the harbour than into it, and the *Hans Lüdemann* fired four torpedoes at the British line from a position near the western shore off Ankenes. Captain Evans also had an excellent view and watched his Navy with pride, though he knew it might be the death of him. He was distressed to see a vivid shell-hit on a British ship, and when she heeled violently to starboard and vanished behind Framnes he thought she was finished. It was the *Hostile* at the tail of the line who, under orders to fire torpedoes, had approached closer than the rest; still unable to make out any warships Wright launched four torpedoes into the brown, and was hit in doing so. That was the first British damage after over an hour's action and even then it was high up under the forecastle where there was nothing to hurt.

The harbour again erupting with noise, explosions, splashes and smoke, Evans and the *Jan Wellem*'s Captain thought very reasonably that the ship's last moment was at hand and the latter ordered her to be abandoned. He did not just leave it at that but chivalrously told Evans to take the port bridge boat with as many British prisoners as it would hold; he even delayed saving himself to supervise the operation, and only when 47 men and two armed guards had been crammed in and the boat floated down to her gunwales did he order, "Cast off."

'Numerous wrecks exist in all parts of Narvik Harbour'*

Evans saw no reason why he should land in German occupied Narvik and steered unobtrusively for the opposite shore through a graveyard of ships, an untidy one with the tombstones at all angles. There were ships with their bows in the air, their sterns in the air; ships with only lolling masts and funnels in the air; ships with little to show that they had ever been; marble slabs of ships; sacred to the memory of *Freilinghaus, Hein Hoyer, Neuenfels, Martha Hendrik Fisser, Aachen, Altona, Bockenheim, Blythmoor, Anton Schmitt, Norge*, and so on, late of this parish. Over them all hung a sepulchral, acrid mist.

The Battle in the Fjord

A New Enemy

As the *Hardy* led the line north past Framnes and continued her turn to the west, three fresh enemy ships were seen approaching down Herjangsfjord with smoke belching from their funnels as they strove for every available knot. Warburton-Lee sighted them himself; that was typical of the mature officer whose life at sea has conditioned his instincts to an awareness that things can happen at any point of the horizon, and not just the one at which present interest is concentrated. The opening range was 7,000 yards, effective for gunnery in theory but rarely in practice. The *Hardy* engaged on her starboard beam with her full broadside, and simultaneously the *Wolfgang Zenker, Erich Koellner*, and *Erich Giese* opened fire, but with only their six forward guns. Fregattenkapitän Bey had providently formed his Flotilla in port quarterline so that they could fire ahead without endangering neighbouring ships.

The *Havock* swung to port after the *Hardy* and was soon in action, though the *Hostile* in the rear was completing her attack on the harbour with singleness of purpose, unaware of the new development. The *Hunter* followed the *Havock*, then the *Hotspur* turned and all guns delivered their full output. Hits were claimed by both sides, who also condemned their respective enemy's fire as wild and ineffective; the latter was the more objective view since it coincides with the firm evidence that no hit, or even near-miss, was scored by either side. The British fall of shot was consistently short, which may be accounted for by their reasonable assumption that the Germans were steaming at full speed; but not knowing that the *Erich Giese*'s

* British Admiralty Chart No 3890, Caution No 2—1972.

desperate fuel shortage allowed only two boilers out of six to be steamed, they probably over-corrected.

On the *Hardy*'s bridge Warburton-Lee said, "This is our moment to get out," and initiated an enemy report:

'One cruiser, three destroyers off Narvik. Am withdrawing to westward=0551'

There was no cruiser and no one else thought he saw one, but all agree that the German ships, particularly their leader, looked extremely large as indeed they were, and that the error was under-

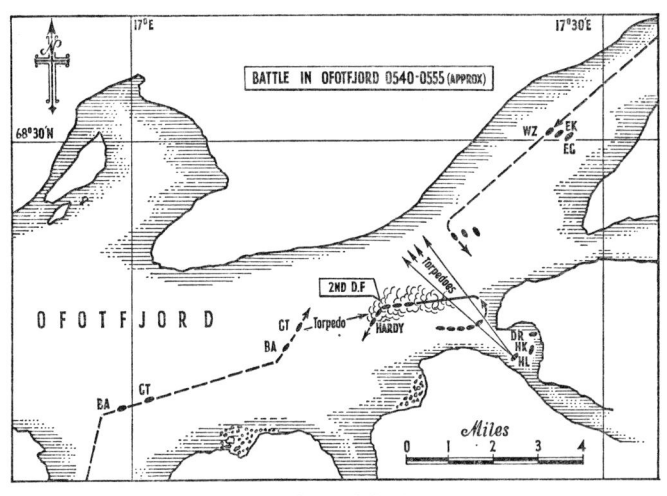

Battle in Ofotfjord

standable. They also agree that they were in no doubt whatever that escape had become a first priority; except for Clark who, like a good Staff Gunnery Officer, urged an intensification of the battle. Warburton-Lee however believed there to be a cruiser and over-ruled him, ordering a speed of 30 knots and the emergency withdrawal signal to be fired by Verey light. The *Hardy* made smoke, and most if not all her line followed suit so that the screen was soon dense. The British aim thus changed from aggression to evasion, and the Germans became free to seize the tactical initiative.

Command of the German force descended on to the shoulders of

Fregattenkapitän Bey with shocking and unwelcome suddenness, by means of the *Hans Lüdemann*'s amplifying report:

'*Wilhelm Heidkamp* sunk, Bonte killed. In the harbour three destroyers ready as protective batteries'.

Bey's reputation as a destroyer Captain and the respect in which he was held were considerable; yet the situation was one to daunt any but the most quick-thinking and decisive officer, and he failed to recognise his golden moment. He must have concluded that a disaster of such magnitude could only have been perpetrated by a massive enemy force, and that his first duty must be to save what ships he could. His three were trapped and must if need be fight to the end; but the *Georg Thiele* and *Bernd von Arnim* were clear of danger and fuelled, and had just a chance of breaking home to Germany as the Operation Orders required them all to do. He therefore signalled:

'Break out to the west'.

The Trap

A dense snow-squall enveloped Ballangen when Wolff of the *Georg Thiele* received the alarm signal, but still his reaction was the opposite of Bey's. Blind though he was he ordered his cable to be slipped, and sallied forth with but one object, to give battle. Rechel of the *Bernd von Arnim* weighed his anchor and followed, gradually overhauling his leader until he was about 1,000 yards astern; on his advice both ships flew huge recognition pendants (Wimpels), and this showed prudent foresight for the danger of mistaken identity was real.

A column of smoke-enshrouded ships was already in sight when Bey's 'break-out' signal was received. It caused momentary indecision lest the ships were fellow-Germans conforming, but very soon the distinctive British destroyer silhouette showed clearly and the signal, says Wolff, was "now uninteresting to me".

When the two big Germans were sighted from the *Hardy* they were end-on and fine on the port bow. Someone said, "Birminghams!" but although the thought was quite reasonable in the light of the agonised appraisals before the battle in the Admiralty, the *Renown*, and in the *Hardy* herself, it was also subjective. Only when Wolff turned 30 degrees to port to open gun arcs could Stanning, the unruffled Secretary with Jane's Fighting Ships open on the Asdic cabinet, point out that funnel-hoods must in the circumstances almost certainly be German. He wrote, "it looked as though we were in a tight corner". Right.

Two Against Five

Precious moments thus elapsed before the *Hardy* reached the same state of awareness as the *Georg Thiele*, and the forces were closing each other at the rate of a mile a minute. Wolff 'Viewed the situation with the eye of a seaman determined on attack' (Nelson), and used the time to collect himself and his men before their supreme effort; the British occupied it in taking false comfort, in doubt, and in making the recognition signal, so that when the *Georg Thiele* opened fire at the potentially decisive range of 4,000 yards she had achieved a classic crossing of the 'T' and all her five guns bore, as against only the *Hardy*'s foremost pair and they were in local control to start with as the director was still pointing astern. Warburton-Lee led round to port to expose the after weapons, but reacting rather than initiating as he had perforce to do, vital seconds were lost.

The *Hardy*'s smoke partially screened her from her following friends and exposed her to Wolff's and Rechel's mercy, which the latter were by no means disposed to exercise. The *Havock* saw fairly well and engaged the *Bernd von Arnim* to the left of both the *Hardy* and *Georg Thiele*; but the other three British ships could not see the enemy ahead and had to concentrate on keeping station in close order in appallingly difficult conditions, though the intensive training imposed by Warburton-Lee and men like him admirably qualified them to do so. But no one, and certainly not Warburton-Lee, could now see the enemies astern, and it was therefore assumed that they were following in hot pursuit to crush the British in a grim vice.

Mistaken Identity

In fact it was not so. The *Hans Lüdemann*'s torpedoes had emerged from the harbour, run round and *under* the *Hostile*, and then sped on across Ofotfjord on a northwesterly course to endanger Bey's 4th Flotilla; one of them was surfaced and clearly visible. A combing turn to the south was imperative and, worse, as the harbour was neared their friends inside opened a hot fire. Visual recognition signals were either not seen or believed, and tense minutes elapsed while identity was established by radio, though by great good fortune no hits resulted. But three German ships were out of the fight at the most critical time, and the *Georg Thiele* and *Bernd von Arnim* were left alone to deal with the five British. That might be called an example of what is meant by 'the best of British luck' had Warburton-Lee been able to see it, for he would then have realised that his problem lay with the two Germans ahead, against whose 10 guns he had 21. The two key factors at this crucial moment are seen to be Wolff's and Rechel's aggressive determination, and the British smoke; and they led to the worsting of five British destroyers by two Germans.

The smoke continues to blind us to this day, for no British ship except the *Havock* could report with any precision what she did or where she went during the next fateful 30 minutes, the narrative of which can only be an intelligent stringing together of disconnected incidents. But there is no doubt at all that the *Georg Thiele* straddled the *Hardy* with her fourth salvo and then started to hit. Her Gunnery Officer, Oberleutnant zur See Fuchs and his Director Layer, Bootsmann August Mandalka, were a formidable team; they and their ship were steady, the range was short, and the enemy's fire ineffective. Seeing the *Hardy* to be already engaged, the *Bernd von Arnim* replied to the *Havock*, but neither of these ships hit the other.

Warburton-Lee signalled:

'Keep on engaging enemy=0555'

Although in the context of what was to follow that message has assumed the aura of an heroic gesture, Stanning is sure that it was intended as a tactical instruction to the three rear ships to keep the enemy astern occupied while the *Hardy* and *Havock* dealt with the two ahead, and that it was not more explicitly addressed and phrased should be attributed to the stress of battle.

The *Hardy* Hit

A lucky hit on the *Georg Thiele* might yet have saved the *Hardy* but she scored none; then, at least two shells of a salvo struck her bridge and the wheelhouse below it. To describe the event is not permissible because nobody saw it happen, everyone in both positions without exception having been either killed or wounded into insensibility. The forward guns were destroyed too, but the engines and boilers were untouched and the telegraphs still showed revolutions for 30 knots. The Flotilla Leader raced blindly and uncontrolled towards the rocks of the south shore, and the other ships followed.

General Action

While still on a northeasterly course the *Georg Thiele* fired two single torpedoes at the British line. Heppel would certainly not have approved such 'penny numbers' and indeed they had no effect, other than to force the *Havock* to comb a track which she easily did by delaying her turn to follow the *Hardy*. Courage shifted his fire to the *Georg Thiele* when he saw she was no longer engaged, and ordered his five remaining torpedoes to be launched as she passed.

Burfield had been in an agony of indecision as to which side of the ship to train his tubes. During the head-on approach phase with the enemy on the port bow he had logically ordered, "ready port"; but when the *Hardy* turned to port and the *Havock* followed it had to be, "ready starboard" and quickly. The ponderous mountings were hove round only just in time, but since Burfield allowed the *Georg Thiele* only 20 knots deflection and she was doing 27, all five torpedoes ran between the two Germans. The range was point-blank at 3,000 yards and the gunnery intense, yet there were no hits except one of light calibre on the *Havock*. Perhaps both antagonists were finding the new gun data after shifting target; and one can imagine that however hot the blood, those who could see their enemy, look into his blazing muzzles and feel the brutal, deadly fact of war as it really is for the first time in their young lives, must have had steady hands indeed to have laid their telescopes and followed their pointers with the precision taught in their respective gunnery schools.

The *Hunter* came into action in her turn; and then the *Hotspur*, who only now became aware of the *Georg Thiele* when Layman sighted her on his starboard beam at very close range. It was a nasty shock but still there were no more hits. The *Bernd von Arnim* fired her last torpedo and that too missed. The *Hostile* had probably taken her time in her last run across the harbour mouth, for when Wright says he went in closer than the rest he unquestionably meant it. Having done the job thoroughly he turned to port to follow the Flotilla westwards, and must soon have become enveloped in smoke since for several minutes he saw no enemy. He was greatly exercised in finding and keeping station, and only just before the *Hardy*'s bridge was hit did he sight the German 4th Flotilla, on his *port* quarter in line with Narvik, and report:

'Three destroyers leaving harbour=0555'

The *Hardy* did not acknowledge because she no longer could.

No German ships left the harbour however. Of the five there only the *Hans Lüdemann* and *Hermann Künne* could possibly have done so, but the former's No 1 gun and steering were damaged, while the latter was only just coming back to life after her severe shaking. They took up positions, like the *Diether von Roeder*'s, where their weapons would bear on the harbour entrance in case of yet another attack, which they had naturally assumed the 4th Flotilla's passage to be.

Wright's first action on transferring his attention from the enemy astern to those ahead was, typically, to turn the *Hostile* to starboard through the smoke to see what was going on. He found himself on the *Georg Thiele*'s bow at some 5,000 yards range and fired his remaining four torpedoes, but no hit resulted.

The *Hardy* out of Control

The British followed a riderless horse, themselves blinkered by their own smoke which both prevented them from realising their temporary numerical advantage and hampered their gunnery. It did also protect them for no ship other than the *Hardy* was seriously hit during this phase.

Stanning slowly came to his senses and found himself to be sagging on his belly over the *Hardy*'s compass binnacle. Around him was death, bloody and revolting, with hideous destruction; all his friends of a moment before lay still, and one glance at Warburton-Lee told him that he, the Secretary, was the Captain now. On lowering himself to the deck his left foot, shattered, refused to support him and a racking pain shot through his back. Perhaps his physical agony hastened his restoration to what soon proved to be a particularly unpleasant consciousness, and he became aware of the overriding consideration: snow covered rocks lay ahead and the *Hardy* was rushing towards them at 30 knots. Supporting his weight by the compass, he shouted down the voice-pipe to the helmsman; but there was no helmsman.

If Stanning could not walk he could at least hop. "It took me a minute or two to get down the ladder, and another minute or two to get into the wheelhouse because of the wreckage. There was only a small part of the wheel still there and I was very surprised that something happened when I turned it." He put on starboard wheel to take the ship away from the shore, but that was only the first of his problems for there was no compass and he could not see out because the wheelhouse was darkened. He hopped round the wheel, found that the square port in front had been loosened by the blast so that he could lift it and look out. He had overcorrected alarmingly and the ship was swinging fast towards the enemy, so he let the flap fall and hurried back to the wheel.

Step by step, each time splitting the difference, Stanning achieved a roughly steady westerly course. The impression was growing on him that he was quite alone in the ship, but after what seemed to him a long time but could not have been more than another minute or two, his Man Friday turned up in the form of Able Seaman Smale and Stanning hobbled and hoisted himself up to the bridge.

His first view in the open was of the two German destroyers broad on the starboard bow at frighteningly close range and firing in rapid salvoes. He looked over the front of the bridge to see why the forward group was not replying and saw them to be completely wrecked, and although some of the after guns still seemed to be in action he realised that the ship was no longer much of a fighting unit. At that moment the relative positions of the *Hardy* and the nearest German made it practicable to ram, and Stanning resolved that this must be his next duty; he hopped to the starboard wing of the bridge to check the positions of the following ships, but was not allowed time to see anything. A boiler-room was hit, and escaping steam roared and billowed in a great cloud that blotted out the view; none reached the engines which whined to a halt. Ramming was forgotten and Stanning, lonelier than ever on that ghastly bridge, quickly decided to save what lives remained by putting the ship ashore, using what momentum remained.

"Port 20," he ordered Smale.

Heppel had also survived the fatal hit by having been at the back of the bridge structure where he could see his torpedo tubes, and a quick glance persuading him that the ship must be out of control he had run aft to organise emergency steering. Now, having found that the ship was being steered from forward, he raced back to the bridge to find the ship heading for the shore, barely 200 yards distant.

"Starboard 20", he panted, appalled. But then Stanning hurriedly explained his reasoning; the ship had no steam and could no longer fight; to stay there stopped would invite a massacre and surely the safety of life was now paramount? Heppel quickly agreed and re-ordered, "Port 20". The ship had already lost most of her way.

Wolff Turns West

While the *Georg Thiele* was still just to the west and north of the British line, Wolff turned hard round to port and steered west, the *Bernd von Arnim* following. He wanted to keep ahead of the enemy and expose him to two diverse fires, on the unverified assumption that the 4th Flotilla was hard on the British heels. He must have realised that had he and Rechel been on their own, as in fact they were, they would become the targets for every British gun without any longer possessing the advantage of surprise. It was an act of considerable courage and faith.

Wolff was not helped by his friends. Whereas his aim was to keep the British destroyers in Ofotfjord for ever—on the bottom, Bey evidently wanted nothing more than to see them out of it with as little hurt to his own ships as possible, a viewpoint that could be said to comply with the Operation Orders. No; Wolff was saved by his enemies. It was the wretched smoke again; but for that, they would have seen the German tactics and been able to react aggressively, for they certainly did not lack courage and offensive spirit. As it was, nothing illustrates the British confusion more graphically than the fact that no ship realised that the Germans had turned west, even afterwards.

The British line followed its new leader, the *Havock*. Those Captains could really handle their ships, and although confused they were no longer surprised and fought hard whenever they saw the enemy. They themselves may not have been consciously aware of the Germans' westerly heading, but some at least of their gun control officers must have noticed it or they would hardly have scored the hits that now started to arrive on their targets.

The *Georg Thiele* took a 4.7in semi armour piercing (SAP) shell in No 1 boiler-room and the boiler had to be shut down. Another started a fire which endangered the after magazine and the order to flood was given; but the pump had been damaged and an anxious wait ensued while the water level slowly rose by natural flow. The *Bernd von Arnim* may also have been hit during this phase, at any rate Rechel thought it best to present a more difficult target by weaving. A salvo of torpedoes passed harmlessly through the line, possibly those fired by the *Hostile*.

The Germans claimed damaging hits on the British and indeed both the *Hunter* and *Hotspur* appear to have been hit at about this time; but not the *Havock* in the van who did what seems to have been an extraordinary and gallant thing. Courage could see no enemy to the west, perhaps the *Georg Thiele* was obscured by her own gunsmoke, and turned 180 degrees to starboard to relieve what he thought was the pressure from astern. Although no other British ship reported the movement the Germans did so, and there can be little doubt that it was made.

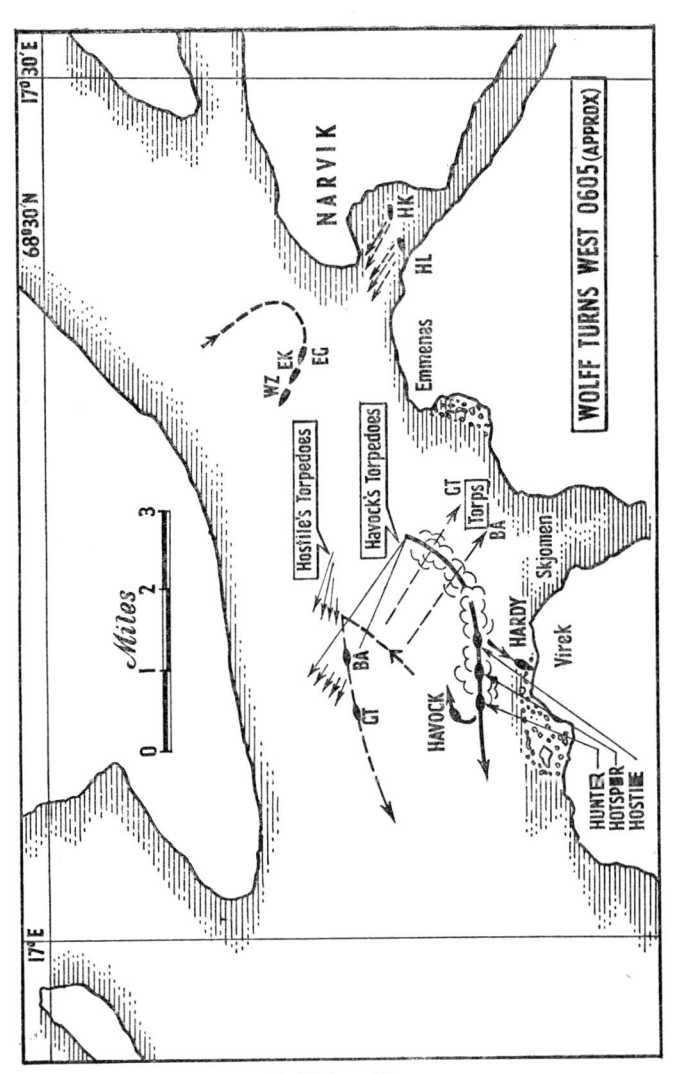

Wolff Turns West

As the *Havock* flashed down her own line at a relative speed of 60 knots, Courage saw, first the *Hunter* on fire and slowing down, then the *Hotspur* with something seemingly wrong with her steering, and lastly the *Hostile*. Of the enemy he thought he saw four, and ordered fire to be opened by his forward guns at 10,000 yards range, only to be told that those weapons were temporarily out of action. Realising that to close any further with only two guns and no torpedoes would be foolhardy, he turned to starboard under the *Hostile*'s stern and through her smoke, engaging with his after pair of guns. The Germans returned the fire with well-placed salvos, and the *Havock* was straddled and hit by splinters from near-misses; she then resumed her westerly course on the *Hostile*'s port quarter.

Whether it was wise of Courage to run down his own line in such a way that he might be mistaken for the enemy cannot be judged from the available evidence; that there was no trouble is probably the best answer. On the positive side he may well have deterred Bey from pressing his attack, and thus gained time at a moment when that commodity was to prove nothing short of vital.

The Kill

Wolff could not make out at all clearly what the British were doing, but thought they must be protecting their damaged ships for he found himself gaining distance to the west. If that was so, now was the moment to turn for the kill, and there followed several bloody minutes of intensive fighting with no tactical niceties, no quarter asked or given and no ship turning away from her enemy.

Even as the *Georg Thiele* turned to starboard she was hit. Her forward guns had necessarily been ordered to check fire and train to starboard in readiness for the new course, and as they did so No 1 was struck in the pivot from behind the shield; nine of the crew died, the weapon was wrecked, and ammunition in the hoist was set on fire causing much smoke and anxiety between decks. As the ship began to expose her starboard side, a shell triggered on passing through the foremost funnel and exploded behind the signal deck doing minor damage and wounding two men. Fortunately most of those on the bridge had moved over to starboard and escaped, but as soon as the ship had steadied on her easterly course she took a really nasty one in the stokers' messdeck. A fire started immediately, solid chunks of SAP shell penetrated to the fire control room, killing or wounding the entire crew and destroying the calculator and telephones. More fragments holed the airlock to No 3 boiler-room and allowed clouds of poisonous fire-extinguishing gas to be drawn in, so that this boiler too had to be shut down. The same shell destroyed a second fire and bilge pump at a moment when all the ship's fire-fighting capacity was desperately needed.

The far-reaching damage caused by just one shell was undoubtedly

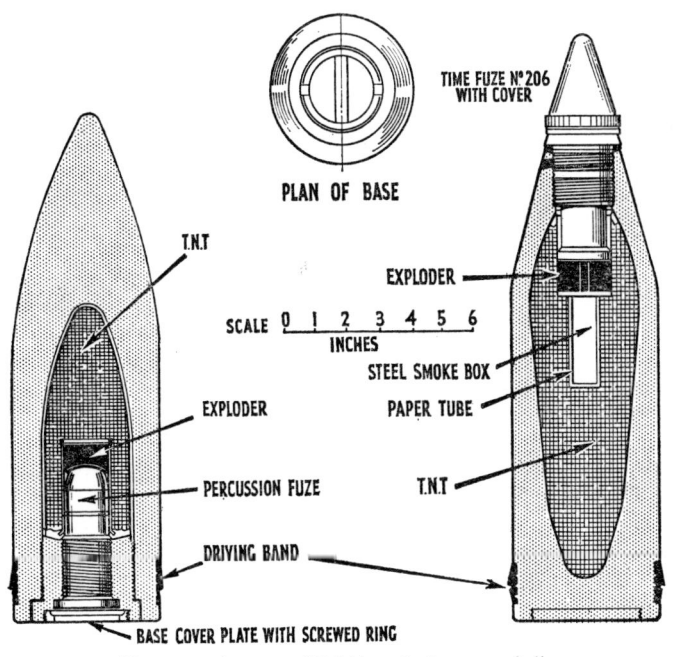

The two main types of British 4.7in destroyer shell.

Left: *Semi Armour Piercing (SAP) with small explosive charge and thick case which shattered into large fragments by the action of a percussion fuze in the base. It was British policy to use this type in the expectation of doing serious damage deep inside the target ship.*

Right: *High Explosive (HE) with thin walls, large charge and nose fuze, which could be either 'Time-Mechanical' against aircraft (as shown here) or instantaneous 'Direct Action'. This was the type favoured by the Germans because it would explode whatever it hit, even the thinnest plating.*

a tribute to its designers, since a thin-walled, instantaneously-fuzed high explosive projectile, such as the Germans were using, would have triggered on the ship's outer plating with only localised effect. On the other hand an SAP shell that did not encounter something solid could go right through a destroyer's light structure without exploding. On balance, observing that hitting was a comparatively rare phenomenon at medium to long ranges, a bang of any sort may be thought better than no bang.

In spite of this punishment the *Georg Thiele*'s four serviceable guns shifted to local control for laying and firing; it was still possible to order range and deflection from the bridge and a guess was as good as a computer, the range being so short. Wolff was not in any way diverted from his aggressive purpose and thrust home resolutely.

The British line, if line is the right word which it probably is not, continued to press westward at 30 knots in the order *Hunter*, *Hotspur*, *Hostile* and *Havock*; but not for long. As Courage saw when he darted back the *Hunter* had been hit; now she was overwhelmed. Wolff reported that the range reduced to as little as 1,700 yards and that he was able to use his 3.7cm as well as his 12.7cm guns. Transformed in a few moments into a flaming wreck, her forward funnel incandescent, the *Hunter* lost all power and control, turned involuntarily towards the enemy and stopped instantly, like a speed-boat coming off the plane. Few of those on board can have had any clear idea of what had hit her, and fewer still survived their wounds and the icy water to tell their story. The only contemporary report, an unofficial one, states that she was badly holed forward; that and the extreme suddenness of total disaster makes a torpedo hit at least possible, and the *Georg Thiele* had fired a salvo of three as she passed, claiming a visible hit abreast the bridge.

The *Hotspur* followed about 1,000 yards astern of the *Hunter* but Layman could see nothing of her but smoke. He fired two torpedoes at the *Georg Thiele* approaching and then his ship was hit twice though not, it seemed at first, very seriously. The *Hostile* and *Havock* in the rear were often blind but still fighting fit; the former was making smoke like the rest, but hers served the useful purpose of isolating the German 4th Flotilla that was following somewhere astern. Wright estimated the *Georg Thiele*'s closest range as 1,000 yards; "You had only to squint along the barrel and let fly." Even so Wolff's ship was only hit twice more, once by a near-miss fragment; her last excitement was to dodge the *Hotspur*'s torpedoes which were very accurately aimed and missed astern by just a few feet.

Collision

Far from being slight, the damage caused by the *Hotspur*'s two hits was calamitous. All telephones failed, the engine-room telegraphs jammed, the hydraulic leads from wheel to steering engine were severed, the ship took a slow swing to starboard and Layman was appalled to see the *Hunter* lying nearly stopped across his bows. Collision at sea is seen to be inevitable so long before the event that its accompanying agony of apprehension has time to mount steadily to a nerve-rending climax; but at last the *Hotspur*'s stem sliced inexorably into the *Hunter*'s engine-room with a clash of steel on steel that was clearly heard in the *Havock* and *Hostile* through the din of the guns. Wright managed to put his wheel hard-a-port just

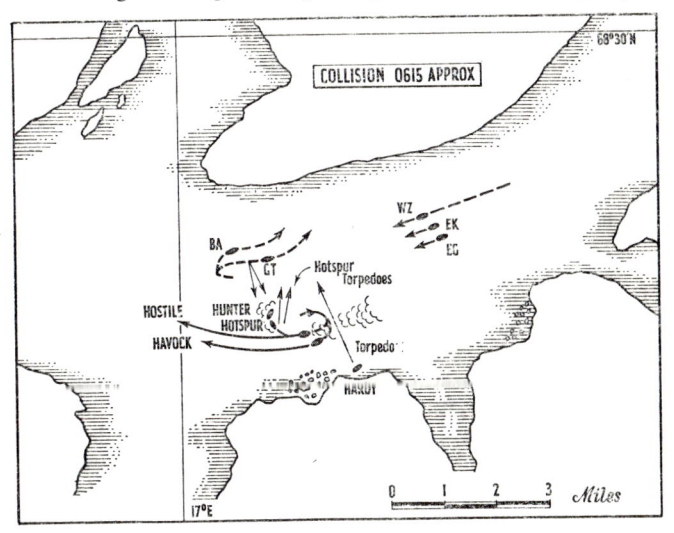

Collision

in time to avoid making a third in the pile-up.

The *Hunter* reeled to port under the tremendous kinetic energy of 1,400 tons being stopped dead from 30 knots. Her Engineer Officer, Alick Reed, was just emerging from his engine-room hatch to investigate the loss of steam, and was confronted by the *Hotspur*'s bow cutting through the metal towards him. Stuart-Menteth the First Lieutenant was also there starting to plug the hole made by the shell that had ignited No 3 boiler-room. They will neither of them ever forget that moment.

Hit after hit slammed into the two ships; the *Hotspur*'s engines continued to push the *Hunter* over with a thrust of 34,000 horsepower and Layman was powerless to stop them. He left the bridge and as he did so a shell hit the rangefinder and killed nearly everyone there; he half slid, half jumped down the ladders to the iron deck, sprinted aft, and shouted down the engine-room hatch to the nearest Stoker who in turn took a message to the Engineer Officer, Johnny Osborne. At long last the engines were put to full astern and the *Hotspur* drew clear.

The *Hunter* sluggishly righted herself and then lolled to starboard, sinking. There was a look about her that said that must be so; yet one gun continued to fire and to good purpose, for the enemy was very close and must not be allowed to come any closer. Chaos and carnage were everywhere; typically, the starboard torpedo davit collapsed over Stuart-Menteth trapping him, as water lapped the deck-edge. Then with her last gasp of steam her siren blew involuntarily with a high-pitched shriek that was like the cry of a wounded hare. It was the most terrible sound Burfield in the *Havock* had ever heard; the *Hunter* was being killed and screamed as she died.

The *Hotspur* in Peril

The *Hostile* and *Havock* having swept on to the westwards and vanished behind their smoke, the *Hotspur* was quite alone and the target for all five German ships. True, the *Georg Thiele* had shot her bolt; seven times hit, flaming forward and aft necessitating the flooding of two magazines, her fire-fighting capacity largely destroyed, and with no means of controlling her four remaining main armament guns, even Wolff could not reasonably be expected to bring her back into action again. Indeed there was no need to do so, for he had sighted the 4th Flotilla at last and the *Georg Thiele* had been recognised by her big red 'Wimpel'; although she continued to fire astern until out of range, she then passed out of the battle to lick her wounds, leaving Bey to finish the job so well set up for him.

Bey closed the range indeed, cautiously because he could not see what lay in and beyond the smoke pall that surrounded the *Hotspur* and *Hunter*; but the latters' main tormentor was the *Bernd von Arnim* passing close to the northward. During the long minutes while the two British ships were locked together and swinging slowly to starboard so that the *Hotspur*'s bows pointed to the east of north, and continuing while she came astern and then with painful slowness checked, turned west and gathered headway, they suffered dreadfully. The *Hunter*'s distress will never be known in detail, even the cause and time of her Captain's death was not recorded, but the *Hotspur* was hit seven times in all; that she was not destroyed is remarkable, and the factors that saved her were human ones.

Layman had started the process by inspiring a happy and efficient ship in the best Royal Naval tradition; everyone could therefore be guaranteed to do his duty without orders, and not merely the duty for which he had been trained but anything that his initiative told him was his duty. Layman jumped up to the after gundeck whence he could see, and established two chains of messengers, to the engine-room and to the tiller-flat which housed the steering engine and rudder-head. He was greatly helped by Marine Donald Thomas, specially embarked for the minelaying operation in case a prize crew should be needed, who saw the point instantly and rushed to and fro with great zeal, while not forgetting to hand a shell up to the gun every time he passed it. Thus the ship came under her Captain's control again, albeit with little precision.

That there was any movement to control was a tribute to Osborne's prescience and efficiency. To use sea water in the boilers was normally anathema, even a tiny percentage of salt being enough to cause serious damage, yet Osborne not only did it but had evolved a method in advance and trained his people in its use. Now, all distilled feed water was quickly lost through a shattered pipe in No 2 boiler-room, but the ship continued to steam.

Layman wrote formally: 'I personally noticed that the two after guns were keeping up a rapid fire in group control at the enemy in the rear.' Himself preoccupied with saving his ship, he stood too near the muzzle of No 3 gun and suffered a burst ear-drum, so that the process of 'noticing' must have been peculiarly painful. Twenty-year-old Sub Lieutenant Leo Tillie was directing these guns so calmly and effectively that they must have deterred Bey from closing to killing range. Leading Seaman Watling found that his gun, No 1, was still operable after the collision and engaged the *Bernd von Arnim* with rapid fire over open sights. Equally calm, and thus able to size up the unexpected problems of the moment, he had found that snow and slush prevented the breech closing readily and had sent for a can of boiling tea-water from the galley to pour over each round as it was loaded. He guessed the range as 2,000 yards and the first splash was short; an 'up 400' correction hit and then he went on hitting. How many times he did so cannot be analysed, but it is certain that the *Bernd von Arnim* was struck by five shells in all and that, having passed the *Hotspur*, she followed the *Georg Thiele* out of the battle.

Thus did resolution triumph. Bey brought the 4th Flotilla to within 5,000 yards of the *Hotspur*, and although that range might have been decisive had he been more concerned with hitting than being hit, he zig-zagged across the fjord and the accuracy of his gunnery suffered accordingly. The *Erich Giese* fired a torpedo but no one saw what became of it. As though by a miracle the *Hotspur* survived.

This Time We're Going to Stay

The *Hardy* touched ground almost imperceptibly with the last knot of her way, Stanning having skilfully steered her to the gently shelving beach at Virek, above which dwellings promised shelter and succour for the wounded. His ship-handling had been faultless, and highlighted the fatuity of the regulation debarring him from executive command because of a minor physical disability; Nelson would have been similarly excluded. From having thought himself almost alone, Stanning was both delighted and appalled to see the large number of men who poured up from below. Lieutenant Commander Victor Mansell the First Lieutenant, who had known nothing of the bridge catastrophe, took charge and organised the abandonment of the ship.

Heppel went down to the tubes and personally fired his last torpedo by training the mounting, probably at either the *Georg Thiele*, who reported a torpedo close to her, or the *Bernd von Arnim* when they were steering east for the last time. Either the *Hostile* or the *Havock* crossed Heppel's line of sight at the time and he took care to avoid them.

To the Rescue

When the *Hotspur* emerged from the smoke and followed about two miles astern of the *Hostile* and *Havock*, she presented an astonishing appearance with two enormous sprays of water either side like ornamental fountains, caused by her jagged bow and a shell hole. The sight was also immensely gladdening and just what was needed to inspire Wright and Courage to save her at any cost. Wright the realist had decided that if she had been stopped there would be no justification for such a last ditch throw; but now the two ships turned back boldly, at first apparently independently and simultaneously, though soon Courage, the junior, conformed with Wright's movements without signal. It was a cold-blooded move for they had thought the battle was over and no further demands would be made on their scant stocks of nervous and physical energy. Burfield records that this was his worst moment yet; however as Nelson said, 'The measure may be thought bold, but I am of opinion that the boldest

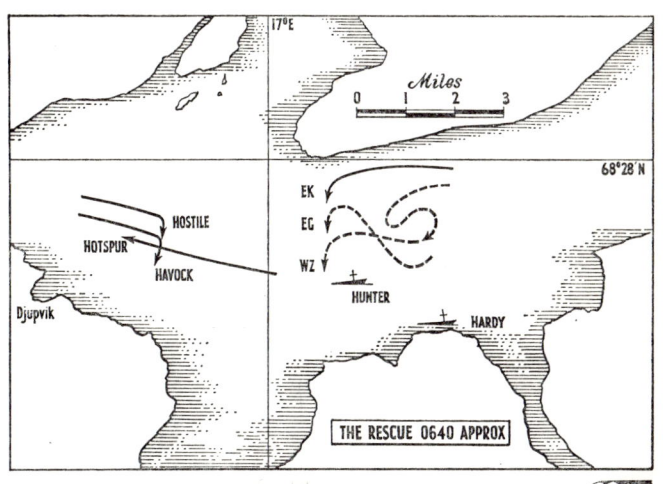

The Rescue

measures are the safest.' The Germans were clearly dismayed by the two ships, so steady and purposeful, closing at high speed and shooting as they came (the *Havock*'s forward guns were again in action thanks to the skill of Ordnance Artificer Abnett) and continued to hold back. Like two sheep-dogs, the *Hostile* and *Havock* closed in behind their stray ewe lamb and hustled her away from the snarling wolves; it was beautifully done.

The *Hunter* Sinks
She settled further and the order was given to abandon ship. That

meant nothing to Stuart-Menteth pinned under the davit, until he was noticed by Able Seaman Norman Stewart who postponed saving himself to extricate him and propel him to a raft. Reviving, Stuart-Menteth gave as good as he got, and finding life on the raft 'a bit crowded' he pushed off, with his broken leg and dislocated shoulder, to make space for others in even worse case; he clung to a piece of wreckage and then passed out. Such stories could probably be repeated many times but there are few to tell them.

The German 4th Flotilla continued its dodging progress down the fjord. The *Hardy* was still firing with No 4 gun as it passed and she was therefore engaged, to the discomfiture of her crew abandoning ship; the *Erich Giese* fired a torpedo at her but it malfunctioned. That ship was so low in fuel that her Engineer Officer anxiously awaited signs of the fuel pumps losing suction, as they had already done in the rough weather at sea. She at least was in no state to pursue the British. Bey's Flotilla Leader, the *Wolfgang Zenker*, returned eastward to engage the beached *Hardy*, the reason for doing so not being easily comprehensible from the available evidence. The *Erich Koellner* however did follow as far as Djupvik; had she gone further she might have seen something greatly to her country's disadvantage.

Bey being satisfied that the retreating British were not going to return again, all three ships closed on the *Hunter*'s last position. She had sunk, and the greatest pains were taken to search for and rescue every possible survivor. The normal life expectancy of an unwounded man in water at zero degrees Centigrade is about 20 to 30 minutes, and these had had to endure considerably longer than that; only 48 finally lived, but all bore witness to the generous humanity meted out to them by the German destroyers' officers and men. Stuart-Menteth came to, gazing at a framed portrait of Hitler, but that was all right by him.

The tension with which the Admiralty, the Commander-in-Chief, and Admiral Whitworth awaited news of the battle can be imagined. They had all known in their hearts that Warburton-Lee should have been reinforced, and his last report of an enemy cruiser would have turned their nagging anxiety into dread conviction. Now, after an hour's silence, they were told the bare facts of what Wright knew, and he of the British Captains had seen as little of the German losses in the harbour as any; neither was it in his nature to sugar the pill. He made:

'From *Hostile*. Returning with *Hotspur* and *Havock*. *Hunter* sunk

Running true; the track was caused by the exhaust of the internal combustion engine, this torpedo is shallow. When watching an approaching track it had to be remembered that the torpedo itself was considerably ahead; the deeper, the farther. [MoD

British contact pistols after test. The fan revolved initially, arming the fuze when the required safety range was reached. Then the least movement of any whisker would fire the 750lb warhead; a very fine strike angle was sufficient. [MoD

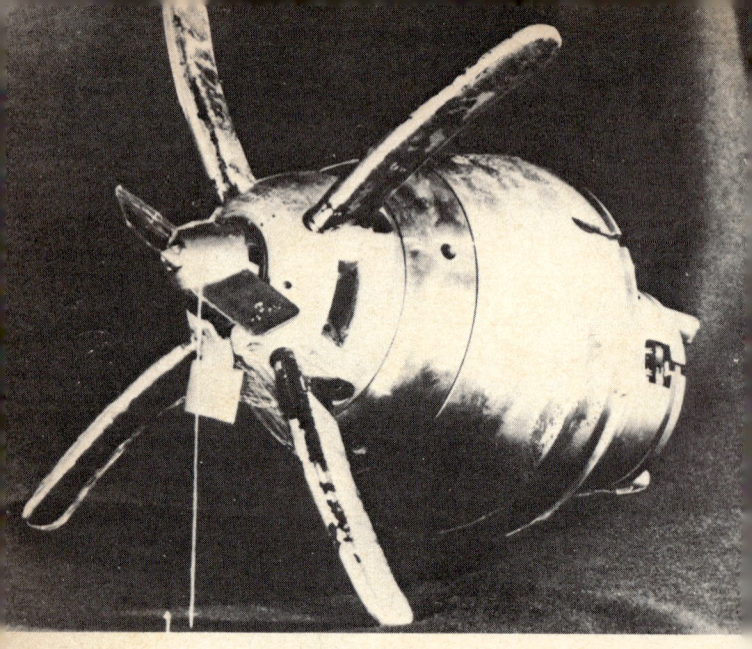

A German pistol. Similar in principle except that the arming vane was separate from the whiskers. As might be guessed from its appearance, this pistol proved to need a broader strike angle than the British one. [MoD

The very simple British bridge sight. Mental or rule of thumb calculation determined the deflection which was set on the sight, and a zone of torpedoes was fired by triggers underneath when the target passed between the prongs of the foresight. A torpedo being only marginally faster than its target, much could change while it was running and great precision was unnecessary. The German system was more advanced, with the great advantage that torpedo 'angling' obviated the need to swing the ship.   [IWM

Narvik Harbour after 0500, April 10th. [Bibliotek für Zeitgeschichte

Action in Ofotfjord looking west of north. Taken by Lt John Burfield, HMS *Havock*. *Left:* The *Georg Thiele* or *Bernd von Arnim* steering west. *Centre:* A German torpedo running surfaced and a shell burst. *Right:* Funnel smoke.
[Cdr Burfield

Rescue of the *Hotspur*. Looking north. *Left: Hotspur. Centre: Hostile.* Foreground: *Havock*.
[Cdr Burfield

Top: Before. [Cdr Burfield

Bottom: During. The Germans watch from Narvik, delighted because they think it means the end of a British destroyer. [Bibliotek für Zeitgeschichte.

Top: After. [Cdr Burfield

Bottom: April 10th. The *Wilhelm Heidkamp* slowly sinking, stern awash. [Bibliotek für Zeitgeschichte

A hit in the *Diether von Roeder*'s boiler-room, probably scored by the *Hostile*. [Bibliotek für Zeitgeschichte

April 10th. At the Post Pier. *Left: Hans Lüdemann* berthed so that her after guns bear on the harbour entrance. *Centre:* Destroyer manoeuvring. *Right: Hermann Künne.* The ships alongside are landing wounded and starting to repair damage. Out of the picture to the right the *Diether von Roeder* is anchored with bows to the entrance and stern secured to the shore near the Pier. [Bibliotek für Zeitgeschichte

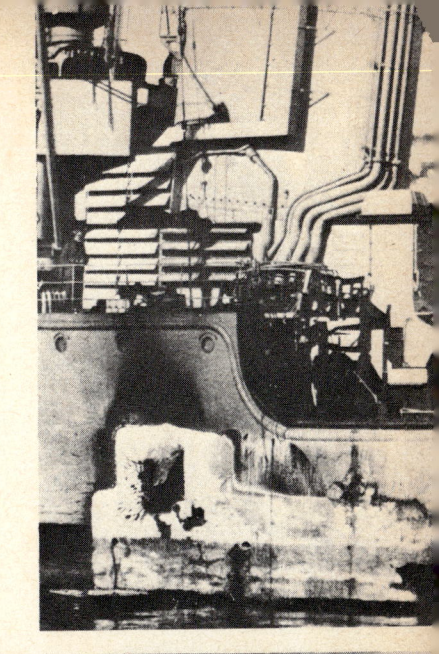

Top: The *Erich Koellner* (*above*) and *Hermann Künne* refuelling from the *Jan Wellem* after the first battle.
[Bibliotek für Zeitgeschichte

Bottom: A Torpedo, Spotter, Reconnaissance Swordfish lands on a carrier. [IWM

Top: HMS *Hotspur* in Skjelford, repairing damage after the First Battle. [Capt Layman

Bottom, left: The *Hotspur*'s crumpled bow after ramming the *Hunter*. [Capt Layman

Bottom, right: Typical large hole made by German high-explosive shell. [Capt Layman

HMS *Warspite*, Captain Victor Crutchley VC. Eight 15in, eight 6in, eight 4in AA guns; two or three aircraft, with hangar and catapult abaft funnel. Note blast bags on 15in guns. [MoD

Top: HMS *Punjabi* (*Tribal* class),
Commander J. Trevor Lean.
Eight 4.7in guns, four torpedoes.
Sister ships at Narvik were the
Bedouin, *Eskimo* and *Cossack*.
[Rear Admiral Micklethwait

Bottom: HMS *Forester*, Lt Cdr
E. B. Tancock. Four 4.7in guns,
eight torpedoes. Sister ship,
HMS *Foxhound*. [P. A. Vicary

Commander 'Bes' McCoy.
Bedouin and Senior Officer
Destroyers.   [Lt Cdr Henley

Commander Trevor Lean,
Punjabi.   [Mrs Lean

Commander St J. A. Micklethwait, *Eskimo*. [Rear Admiral Micklethwait

Commander R. St V. Sherbrooke, *Cossack* [Mrs Sherbrooke

Top: Lt Cdr E. B. Tancock, *Forester*. [Commander Tancock

Bottom: Commander G. H. Peters, *Foxhound*. (Lt Cdr in 1940) [Capt Peters

Opposite, top: U-boat. [IWM

Opposite, bottom: A battleship's Swordfish on floats. [IWM

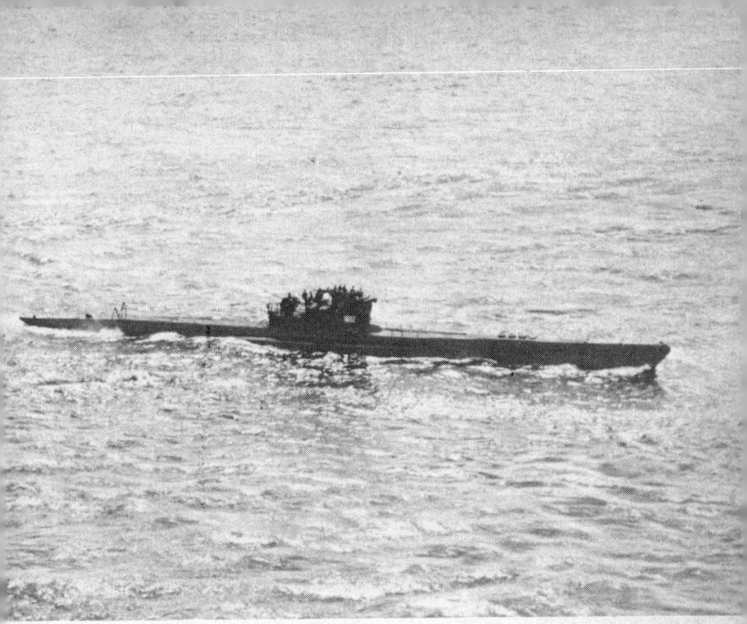

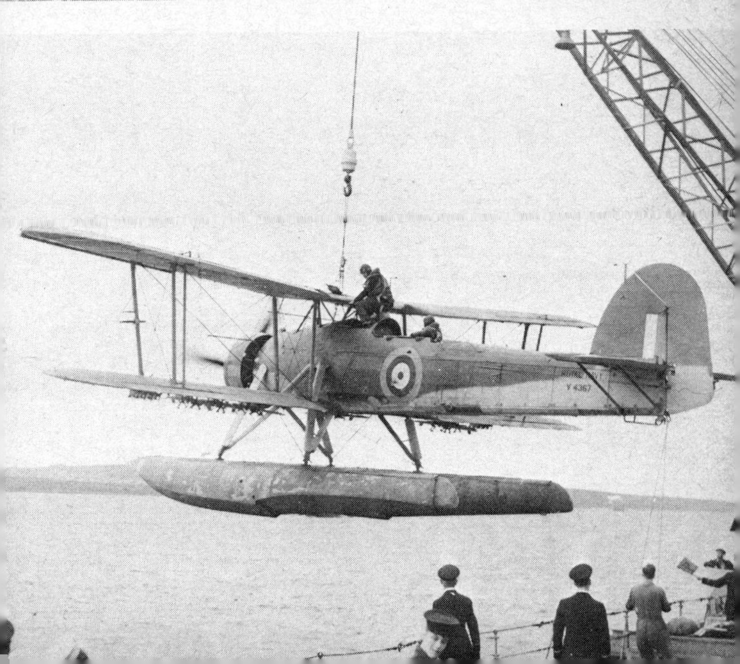
Y 4367

Petty Officer Airman 'Ben' Rice, Pilot. [Cdr Rice

Approaching Djupvik. In the foreground are two of the minesweeping destroyers, probably the *Hero* and *Foxhound*. Beyond them the starboard division of Tribals, *Bedouin*, *Punjabi* and *Eskimo* move ahead. [IWM in Vestfjord, *Hardy ashore*. 5 or 6 large German destroyers in Narvik = 0645'

The Rauenfels

No one at Narvik had any idea when the supply ships might be expected, for secrecy was naturally essential to every part of their voyages; but it is a common error in such cases to overdo the concealment of information from the enemy to the extent of withholding it from friends. General Dietl was acutely conscious of their importance, but in spite of his close relations with Bonte it does not seem that the latter had grasped the point, or he would surely have deemed it his prime duty, after landing the soldiers, to do everything in his power to assist the ships' safe arrival. In practical terms that must have meant establishing a patrol of the first ships to fuel as far to seaward as he dared, as much to meet the supply ships and escort them in as to obtain early warning of an enemy attack.

If not Bonte, far less Bey who certainly had had little leisure to consider such matters; but if the *Rauenfels* and *Alster* had been graven on his heart as they should have been, he had no option but to follow the British with such ships as had any fighting capability and fuel left, and in such a manner that he could have re-engaged and at least prevented the enemy from interfering. For on the supply ships might well depend the outcome of the Narvik operation, and their safe arrival demanded the utmost effort and justified any sacrifice. So are merchant ships often the focal points of maritime situations, which naval sailors do well to remember.

If Bonte and Bey made errors of judgement, so unquestionably did Schütze of *U25* as he watched the *Rauenfels* round Baroy through his periscope. U-Boat Command had clearly failed to emphasise her importance to the submarines, or to give them her detailed description. Schütze gave the matter 'much thought'; he had heard gunfire in the distance and perhaps assumed that this was a British military transport, though the very improbable circumstance of her being unescorted should have cast doubt on that argument. He was however an enterprising officer who probably took as his motto, 'If in doubt, attack'; he fired one torpedo but it missed, either because the track angle was too fine or because it failed to function properly.

Sohler of the *U46* near Ramnes had also heard gunfire from the direction of Narvik, but was certainly not expecting three British destroyers to come charging at him from that quarter. He had time to crash dive without being sighted but not enough to close to a good attacking position, and the British ships swept by in blissful ignorance of their danger.

Layman was the senior British officer, but since his ship had no communications and was only barely under command, needing his constant personal attention to keep her moving in even approximately the right direction, he had wisely turned over tactical command to Wright who had therefore to face the next problem. On rounding the bend in Ofotfjord at Hamnesholm he saw the *Rauenfels* ahead.

Wright did not know who this large merchant ship might be, any more than had Schütze, but he was in a better position to find out. He ordered her to stop; she did not which was suspicious, and then he recognised her. He fired two high-explosive rounds into her and she ceased prevaricating, whereupon he ordered the *Havock* to deal with her by the signal:

'Let crew escape then sink him=0703'

He then continued to escort the *Hotspur* towards some temporary refuge outside Ofotfjord.

A fire started in the *Rauenfels* and she not only stopped instantly but her crew abandoned ship with remarkable and possibly significant alacrity. Courage however sent an uneasy Burfield to investigate in the whaler, which crossed the *Rauenfels*' boat half way between the ships. There were cups of coffee in the Master's cabin and everything was thrown about, presumably as part of the process of destroying vital papers; the ship was quickly searched and her identity firmly established, though nothing more of any interest was found. Burfield heard a 'sizzling' noise from below, escaping steam 'or something', and forebore opening the main hatches; the ship was on fire; her cargo might very well prove to be exactly what it was; the enemy destroyers might appear in pursuit from behind Hamnesholm; and finally he could not see that he was doing any good by staying a moment longer. His guardian angel said, 'Leave!' and he left.

The *Rauenfels*' fires were spreading and Courage too became uneasy; but the whaler returned safely and as soon as it was at the davit-head he ordered two more rounds to be fired to hit. The result must have been one of the most shattering explosions of those good old days before nuclear weapons; Mr Leslie Millns, Torpedo Gunner, saw a bright flash in the centre of the ship which expanded until she shone from end to end; it seemed that it was not just the cargo which detonated but the whole ship.

Millns shouted to those around him to take cover, for what went up must come down and a great deal of ironmongery had gone up. Wright in the *Hostile*, now well round Baroy and separated from the *Rauenfels* by the 500 foot contour or higher, saw what he swore was her funnel gyrating in the sky; certainly no funnel remained in the wreck. His heart sank and he asked the *Havock*:

'Are you all right?'

Her welcome reply was:

'Only just. Merchant ship contained all reserve ammunition for Narvik and I blew her up.'

'*Havock* from *Hostile*. Well done=0850'

A similar distance to the east and also over the hills, the Germans saw the huge white cloud and hoped, as Wright had feared, that it came from a British destroyer, perhaps torpedoed by a U-Boat. Bey never even guessed at the disastrous truth; and neither did Sohler of the *U46* who saw both the *Havock* and the burning hulk, but without curiosity. Another observer of the British departure was the *U25*; but she was on the north side of the channel opposite Baroy, too far off track to fire. The First Battle of Narvik was over.

'*And we saw the giants, the sons of Anak; and we were in our own sight as grasshoppers, and so we were in their sight.*' (Numbers 13, 33)

Although the surviving British were encouraged at the moral ascendancy they seemed to have achieved over their superior enemy at the end, they greatly doubted whether results had justified their severe losses. Whether in fact they had won or lost is best discussed at the end of the story when the battle's effect on subsequent events will become clear; but one aspect of the encounter may be remarked while it is still fresh in the memory: the often decisive importance of the tactical initiative which it graphically illustrates. An Alladin's Lamp, as it were, was tossed from side to side and conferred on its possessor extra strength and courage, which were translated into tactical advantage and fed on themselves; while those without it sought only to defend themselves against an enemy who seemed to be nine feet tall.

Kommodore Bonte possessed the initiative when he first arrived at Narvik. Certainly his success depended on surprise, which often accompanies the exploitation of the initiative but is not the same thing. The Captains of the *Norge* and *Eidsvold* were not in fact entirely surprised for they had been warned to expect a German attack and ordered to resist it; nevertheless they felt lost and indecisive in the face of an enemy who knew where he was going and was not prepared to be stopped.

In Warburton-Lee's attack, surprise was again predominant to the extent that the operation would have been impossible without it. Yet it was his initiative that gave him the tactical advantage; first through the medium of surprise, and then by imposing on the enemy a sense of inferiority when the odds were, in fact, over two to one in the latter's favour. Had the three surviving German destroyers in the harbour striven to regain the initiative they would have alarmed their five outlying consorts half an hour earlier and then been prepared to sally forth, however damaged, to join in what should logically have resulted in the annihilation of the British. But when one does not have the initiative such reversals of fortune are hard to envisage, and few are they who can do so.

In Ofotfjord the initiative transferred to the outlying German ships. Bey made no use of it but Wolff seized it, putting it to dramatic use and proving the proposition: two, plus initiative are greater than five. Finally, the *Hostile*'s and *Havock*'s rescue of the *Hotspur* turned the tables yet again, shocking Bey into surrendering both the initiative and his prey, when he had no need to do either.

To seize the initiative postulates a decisive commander imbued not only with courage, but with faith in the probability of success; for if victory depends on surprise there will often be the temptation to wait a little longer so that the enemy's circumstances will become clearer. That may be fatal as the situation will also then become clearer to the enemy, and the attack must take place to some extent against the unknown, in the belief that the momentum of initiative will override whatever shocks may be in store.

As in all academic arguments concerning war, the danger of accepting any one aspect as an immutable principle must be avoided. To seize what one believes to be the initiative and attack an enemy who then, like Wellington at Torres Vedras, proves to be a master of war and has carefully lured one into doing that very thing so that the initiative is truly his, is the very proper fear that must always confront a commander before taking the plunge. He has a very lonely job.

CHAPTER FIVE

The Vortex of the Storm

The battle was over but little else was clear; and men's minds, in trying to assess the situation and decide their proper courses of action, revolved turbulently like a tropical storm around an inert centre, which withstood the assaults of those who pressed for decisive action without a tremble.

The first to try was Wright of the *Hostile* who, with the *Havock*, was escorting the crippled *Hotspur* through Vestfjord. It can be supposed that even he had had his fill of battle for the time being, but on sighting the *Penelope* coming up to help he had no thought but that she would at once lead them, and any other fit ships there might be, back up to Narvik to finish off the job. He and Courage were in no doubt that it could be done and that this was the moment to do it, while the Germans licked their wounds. He closed the cruiser and started to tell her Captain what to expect, but the latter had only been ordered by Whitworth:

'Your object is to support retirement of 2nd Destroyer Flotilla, counter-attacking enemy forces as necessary. Then establish a patrol off minefield with object of preventing enemy force reaching Narvik=0823/10th'

and so that is what he did. He may perhaps have been disappointed, knowing that the three Tribals and the *Kimberley* were hurrying to the scene; indeed he signalled to the *Bedouin* when they arrived:

'I hope there will be a chance for us very soon.'

But Wright having done his duty, saw there was to be no immediate re-engagement and concentrated on getting the *Hotspur* to a place of safety, for she was in a very poor way indeed. As a haven he selected Skjeldfjord in the Outer Lofotens where they arrived at 1640, utterly exhausted but safe.

In the meantime Wright had amplified his report of the action in a slightly less sombre vein. He judged the enemy force at Narvik to comprise five or six *Leberecht Maass* class destroyers of which one had possibly been sunk and three damaged and on fire; he thought he had been engaged by shore batteries of up to 6in calibre; he reported the end of the *Rauenfels* and the British losses and damage. The Admiralty, to their credit for they could not yet know whether the affair had been handled competently or otherwise, replied:

'Their Lordships congratulate all concerned on your determined action against superior forces, and on the successful results you achieved despite severe losses=1639/10th'

Wright made no mention of an enemy cruiser; nevertheless Warburton-Lee had done so in his last report and it continued to influence future plans as well it might. Indeed the Admiralty made it official, and for some reason doubled it, in a signal timed 1107/10th.

Since there was to be no immediate attack the first thing to be done was to organise patrols; both so as to prevent any more enemy forces breaking in—a wise precaution by Admiral Whitworth for the *Alster* and *Kattegat* were still at large, though he did not know that —and also to intercept those inside should they try to break out as the Commander-in-Chief, equally wisely, ordered at 0808. The forward patrol was to go as far inside Ofotfjord as it dared to mark any movement through the channels to the north, Tjelsund and Ramsund, as well as through Vestfjord.

What, in retrospect, was not so wise was the evident lack of awareness of the possible, indeed likely, presence of U-Boats, which could be particularly dangerous against a patrol that must cross and recross a very confined stretch of water. It was not that the British were unappreciative of danger for they were extremely sensitive about mines and shore batteries; but of these there were none, in contrast to a veritable hornet's nest of U-Boats. After sighting the 2nd British Flotilla the evening before, the *U51* had moved further up Vestfjord and taken station just southwest of Tranoy; the *U25* was still to the north of Baroy, while the *U46* patrolled further up Ofotfjord in the Ramnes area. In addition, Admiral Dönitz now ordered two more U-Boats, *U64* and *U48*, into Vestfjord. As early as 1000/10th *U51* was contacted and attacked by British destroyers but the latter did not report the incident, doubtless because the poor quality of the Asdic echo did not confirm a submarine's presence.

Thus was the first evidence of U-Boats understandably missed, but the second was astonishing. In the evening the advanced British patrol, the *Bedouin* and *Eskimo*, penetrated north of Baroy where they were sighted by the *U25* at 2050. Schütze took his time and 17 minutes later fired four torpedoes at 1,200 metres; it was a perfect shot and when he heard detonations after the right time intervals he assumed he had sunk his targets. The latter were certainly surprised, but not sunk, by two explosions within 100 yards and a third on the rocky shore, and prudently retired round Baroy. Although it was appreciated in both ships that a U-Boat must have been present, McCoy later reported:

'Explosions appeared to indicate controlled minefield and shore-fired magnetic torpedoes. Acitivity was also observed on Baroy. The indications were that shore defences were fully prepared.'
And so the British myth of mines and shore defences built upon itself.

The Germans on the other hand began to be aware of a dreadful reality; that their new magnetic pistol was ineffective in these latitudes. Worse still, later experience was to show that this defect in combination with the faulty depth-keeping mechanism, which was common to both submarine and destroyer torpedoes and caused them to run either too deep or surfaced, rendered the weapons nearly useless. As the story progresses it will be seen that this handicap to the Germans had fateful consequences, while the bonus to the British was one they by no means merited. Nevertheless a Navy gets the weapons it deserves; such faults as skimping in research, development and testing, and lack of interest by user departments, invite operational failures like this one, or the British heavy shell at the Battle of Jutland.

The German Dilemma

Fregattenkapitän Bey assumed the unwelcome burden of command and set about solving the problems of which he had inherited a super-abundance. The toll of battle made depressing reading:

The *Anton Schmitt* had sunk, with 50 dead.

The *Wilhelm Heidkamp* was sinking slowly and 81 of her crew were dead. Strenuous efforts were in train to salve her torpedoes, light AA weapons, ammunition and stores before she went.

The *Diether von Roeder* was immobile after five shell hits. She had lost 13 dead, but her two forward guns could still engage to seaward. Her surplus ammunition and stores were also being landed.

The *Hans Lüdemann*'s No 1 gun was destroyed and her after magazine was flooded. Two men had been killed.

The *Hermann Künne* had sustained no damage and her engines were now serviceable.

The *Georg Thiele* was severely damaged by seven hits. No 1 gun and the fire control system were irreparable; there had been two major fires, the appropriate magazines being flooded, and she had widespread damage to hull and machinery. 13 of her crew were dead.

The *Bernd von Arnim* had been hit five times, with a boiler out of action and holes in the side and stern which rendered her unseaworthy. Two men had been killed.

The *Wolfgang Zenker*, *Erich Giese* and *Erich Koellner* were undamaged, but had expended half their ammunition and were empty of fuel.

As the outcome of a contest between ten large and five small destroyers the score was hardly favourable; in the light of the vital need for the German ships to return home at once it was appalling, and when Bey told Group West they were duly appalled.

At Wilhelmshaven, the degree of gamble inherent in the Narvik operation became depressingly clear. At all the other landing places it had been possible to establish air bases which had immediately proved to be the dominant factor in disputing local command at sea. On the afternoon of the 9th the British Fleet had been attacked off Bergen, the battleship *Rodney* being hit and the destroyer *Gurkha* sunk. As a result, and highly significantly for both the Norwegian campaign and the general conduct of war at sea in the future, the Commander-in-Chief decided to move north and leave the Royal Air Force to attack Bergen. At Narvik the boot was on the other foot; the only air power available derived from British aircraft carriers, and the Royal Navy could therefore use the sea and its arms for whatever purposes it chose. There was little doubt in the German mind that it would choose to recapture Narvik at the earliest possible moment, and this was entirely correct as the following Admiralty message shows:

'Recapture of Narvik is to take precedence over operations at Bergen and Trondheim. Expedition being prepared. Primary importance in meantime to prevent reinforcement by sea = 1904/10th'

That the importance of the air took even the Germans by surprise is shown by an instruction to General Dietl:

'Urgently necessary to make temporary runway at Narvik. Use the local population if you can, payment is to be assured = 1408/10th'

This was clutching at straws indeed, for it should have been well known in Germany that there was no flat ground near Narvik closer than Bardu Foss, 50 miles to the northeast across forbidding mountains in Norwegian held territory. Dietl and Bey together recognised the order for an admission of a major planning failure, and composed the only reply that made any sense:

'Absolutely necessary to prepare a landing area for seaplanes as reconnaissance units and possible use as bombers = 1850/10th'

Nothing could however be done on these lines in a hurry, or indeed on any lines other than to make a desperate attempt to save those destroyers which could still keep the sea, even in the face of ever-growing British naval forces. The situation became even more depressing during the day when Bey revealed that not only would none of the damaged ships be ready to sail that evening, but of the three operational ones only the *Wolfgang Zenker* and *Erich Giese* could be fuelled in time. In contrast to Warburton-Lee who had been more apprehensive before his proposed attack than had his Admiralty, Group West did not seem able to convince Bey of the perilous nature of the trap he was in. Press as they might, they only just persuaded him to sail with the two ships; this was to be done at twilight so that Vestfjord would be traversed entirely in darkness.

The *Hardy* Ashore

The *Hermann Künne* was sent to examine the *Hardy* on Virek beach during the afternoon. Boarding her was no problem, but the fore part was still on fire and could not be approached; her No 1 boiler-room and stern were burnt out and she seemed to be hard aground forward. She was certainly no use to the Germans; though in her Captain's coat pocket were some interesting documents. the orders for the operation, several signals with both coded and clear versions, a short gunnery manual, and orders for formation steaming. Other trophies included some Long Service and Good Conduct Medals awaiting presentation when a pause in operations should allow.

The *Hardy*'s abandonment had of course been achieved in the most trying conditions imaginable. As she glided ashore a blazing wreck, her No 4 gun nevertheless gallantly continued firing and naturally attracted return fire from the enemy; simultaneously men struggled in the icy water, half swimming, half clinging to damaged boats, rafts and planks, amid the shell-bursts. Stanning destroyed confidential documents; the strong helped the weak, the brave encouraged the fainthearted. Warburton-Lee rallied momentarily to his knees and pointed towards the shore to indicate, it was thought, that he wished the ship to be abandoned. But even as he was carried down and lowered gently on to a raft it was terribly clear from his head-wounds that he could not live long. Heppel looked at the unconscious Gordon-Smith and judged that to move him then might prove fatal; he made him comfortable, murmuring, "I'll come back for you".

Stanning's watch had stopped when he jumped into the water at 0712. An hour later, from the near-by house of a Mrs Christiansen, to whom the Royal Navy will always be profoundly grateful for her and her daughter's devoted tending of its wounded and shipwrecked mariners, he was startled to see the brave Navigator alive and wandering dazed and aimless around the *Hardy*'s forecastle amid desultorily exploding ammunition. But Heppel and a small team were already on their way to the rescue, and also to ensure that the confidential safes in the Captain's harbour cabin were destroyed. Having retrieved Gordon-Smith, Heppel placed a small explosive charge against the safes and blew them up; he did so with sadness for it had been Warburton-Lee's conceit that he would live and if necessary die like a gentleman, and the cabin was beautifully furnished, complete with family silver and sporting trophies*. To have lowered a 300lb depth charge into the engine-room and touched that off would not have been a great deal more difficult; but it was firmly in his mind to return at nightfall for an attempt at salvage, which he thought might just be possible.

With the unstinting help of the Norwegians the *Hardy*'s 140 survivors found their way to the small town of Ballangen where they later met some unexpected friends.

The Pied Piper

As the battle in Narvik Harbour drew to its close, 47 British merchant seamen stamped and hugged themselves in the snow on the southwest shore among a crowd of Norwegians, watched by their two guards. There they might have stayed had it not been for Captain Evans, an officer of infinite resource and powers of persuasion, who manoeuvred his men unobtrusively into a tight and perhaps somewhat grim circle round the guards. He then suggested that since they were all on

---

* 30 years later the Norwegians salvaged a silver tankard from the wreck and returned it to Mrs Warburton-Lee; it had been a wedding present.

neutral ground he and his men no longer considered themselves prisoners and that it would be wise of the Germans to drop their weapons. His logic achieving its purpose, the circle then slowly expanded and the sailors mingled with the crowd; when he judged the moment to be right, Evans told them to start walking.

The coast road to the west led first through Ankenes where Evans paused for a last look at the desolation. Of the 25 merchant ships in the harbour the conspicuous ones were now the handful still afloat, and he identified the *Jan Wellem*, *North Cornwall*, *Mersington Court*, and a big German, the *Lippe*. Then they trudged through Emmenes to Skjomnes, whence they could see the *Hardy* beached, on fire and with ammunition exploding. As they continued Norwegians encouraged them with gifts of warm socks, food, and a free ride over the Skjomenfjord ferry. At 1500 they came abreast the *Hardy* at the same time as the *Hermann Künne* was searching her; they stopped and hid, watching and fearful that the Germans would land a force and cut the road, but at 1600 the destroyer moved away and the marchers rested at a friendly house. They saw the *Hardy* lift with the flood tide and drift eastwards, still burning, to ground again on the east side of Skjomenfjord. Then they plodded on, weary and unsure of their future but the kindly Norwegians sent trucks to meet them and by 2230 they were snugly in Ballangen School, sharing experiences and their hosts' generosity with the men from the *Hardy*.

The Break-out

Whether Bey really intended to leave Narvik may be doubted, for at 1914/10th he sent a signal to Group West complaining that the British 2nd Flotilla had not been reported or attacked by any of the U-Boats, and requesting 'instructions to the Senior Officer U-Boats to appear for a discussion with me'. This was acted upon at 2235 when the nearest submarine, the *U46*, was ordered to Narvik, even though Bey was not expected to be there, for at 1930 the latter was told somewhat brusquely:

'Leave with *Wolfgang Zenker* and *Erich Giese* as soon as it gets dark=1812/10th'

He may or may not have been further encouraged by:

'There is a possibility that besides the two *Renowns* a southerly group with three battleships is making for the Lofoten area=2004'

This information was uncannily accurate, for the *Repulse* had joined the *Renown* and the Commander-in-Chief was coming north with the battleships *Rodney*, *Valiant* and *Warspite*. Also with him was the aircraft carrier *Furious*.

Bey embarked in the *Wolfgang Zenker* at 2040 and the two ships sailed down the fjord at high speed; it was not yet dark and the visibility was very good, too good. The first surprise was the *Hardy* in her new position, and two other ships were sent to check that the British were not up to any tricks; all they found was a hulk starting to settle by the stern. Had the *U46* been keeping a good lookout she should have seen the two friendly ships off Ramnes; but she did not, and such was the lack of co-operation between the two arms that she had not been told to expect them. Next, the smoking wreck of the *Rauenfels* was sighted and the alarm sounded for fear she might be a lurking British destroyer; her true identity remained a mystery. Off Baroy the *U25* had unwittingly cleared a path by driving away the *Bedouin* and *Eskimo* only 50 minutes earlier, and now at 2200 Schütze saw the two German ships and identified them correctly; he was beginning to reveal himself as an experienced officer who missed few tricks.

Five minutes later Vestfjord opened ahead of the *Wolfgang Zenker* and Bey saw what he both expected and feared, a shadow. Then there was another, much larger, and finally a third; they were the *Penelope* and two destroyers, probably the *Bedouin* and *Eskimo*. Bey allowed the range to close to 7,000 yards but saw no opening, neither could his reason persuade him that he had the least hope of breaking through. At 2220 he turned about under smoke, and the British saw nothing in spite of his beams being exposed, not even the smoke.

The British Dilemma

As far as the Captain of the *Penelope* knew he might be confronted at any moment by two German cruisers and three or four destroyers which he had specific instructions to prevent escaping. They would have been formidable adversaries to his little 5,000 ton, six inch cruiser and two destroyers, yet his ships were in no sort of fighting formation, nor were they looking out as though they meant it. Perhaps he had more than half an eye for the latest Admiralty message which had been addressed to him personally:

'If in light of experience this morning you consider it a justifiable operation, take available destroyers in Narvik area and attack enemy in Narvik tonight or tomorrow morning=2012/10th'

Three hours later he replied:

'I consider attack justifiable although element of surprise has been lost. Navigational dangers from ships sunk today eliminate chances of a successful night attack. Propose attacking at dawn on 12th since operation orders cannot be got out and issued for tomorrow in view of escorting ships' dispositions and destroyers on patrol=2310/10th'

The contrast between this signal and Warburton-Lee's of the previous afternoon is remarkable. The key consideration was the two cruisers and they are not mentioned; had they been judged too powerful well and good, but if the attack was considered to be justified the weak 'propose' was inappropriate since no new circumstances had arisen unknown to the Admiralty who had already given the go-ahead. Comment on the proposed delay of 30 hours is scarcely necessary.

Admiral Whitworth, doubtless piqued at being again overridden by the Admiralty, complained bitterly that his forces had been given three conflicting aims: to prevent the enemy going into Narvik, to stop them coming out, and to attack those ships that were there. Which of these were meant? In his view an attack would risk further casualties and jeopardise what he considered the main aim of preventing reinforcements reaching Narvik. To this the Admiralty paid no attention and the Commander-in-Chief kept well out of the controversy.

Vestfjord, April 11th

The fjord now teemed with British destroyer patrols and it was inevitable that the brave but luckless *Alster*, in the final stretch of her run to Narvik, should meet one. Unluckier still she had for her assailant the *Icarus* whose Captain, Lieutenant Commander Colin Maud, possessed the daunting outward appearance of a latter-day buccaneer and was endowed with exceptional boldness and tenacity to go with it. Before the *Alster* could fire her scuttling charges and abandon ship, the *Icarus* ran alongside and her sailors swarmed on board. The position of the capture was conveniently close to Skjelfjord, and she joined the crippled *Hotspur* there in the morning.

The *U51* attacked a destroyer southwest of Tranoy at 0219; the torpedoes missed or failed to function, and although one exploded, the target was not alerted and Knorr took another shot 20 minutes later, again without result. At 0300 the *U25* was in contact with two ships who had ventured into her area north of Baroy, probably the *Bedouin* and *Eskimo* again, but thought she had been detected before attacking and retired. Life was hard for the U-Boats; the waters were narrow and offered few opportunities for charging batteries unobserved, and they were deep so that a boat could not bottom to rest and conserve electricity but must continue under way amid navigational hazards; the nights were short and British destroyers were everywhere. Even so the number of attacks the submarines achieved over a period of three days would have amply justified their deployment in such unusual surroundings had it not been for their useless weapons. For the British part, their ships continued to share patrol areas with the U-Boats whom they often detected and attacked but never sank or damaged seriously.

In the morning of the 11th the *Penelope*'s Captain heard the *Bedouin*'s imaginative assessment of the German defences at Baroy which, to modern ears, recalls those of a James Bond villain. He signalled the Admiralty relating this and concluded:

'*Bedouin* is of opinion that the operations on the lines of yesterday's attack could not be carried out successfully. In the light of this report I concur and regret that I must reverse my decision given in my 2310/10th=0930/11th'

There was thus to be no attack, and since word had arrived through roundabout Norwegian channels that a German transport, a tanker, and possibly a warship were in the Bodo area, the *Penelope* was sent to investigate. She ran on a rock and damaged herself so badly that she had to be towed by the *Eskimo* to Skjelfjord, which then became known as Cripples' Creek. Her golden moment had flitted by and now there could be no second chance. The information that had led her astray was founded on fact but tardy; both the *Kattegat* and the *Alster* had been there, but the Norwegians had sunk the former and the latter was now safely in the British bag.

Narvik, April 11th

The *U46* berthed alongside the *Wolfgang Zenker* in the early hours so that Bey and Sohler could discuss their mutual problems. They ended in a more understanding mood than they began, the destroyer side having been not a little irked at the U-Boat's failure to report the British entering on the 10th, and instituted a method of direct communication; the U-Boats were also to be kept in constant touch with the developing situation. Bey was reassured that he could rely on better warning in future; but it was not to be.

Tremendous exertions by the destroyer crews were in progress.

There was no saving the *Wilhelm Heidkamp* who capsized and sank at 0600; but not before four torpedoes, much 12.7cm ammunition, some of the close range weapons and a great deal of equipment had been landed. The *Diether von Roeder* was similarly de-equipped, except for her forward pair of 12.7cm guns which were pointing to seaward, for it seemed that she was unlikely to be able to steam again in less than a week. Of the other ships the *Georg Thiele* was in the worst case; her structure was distorted, large areas were burnt out and smelt horribly, fire-fighting water slopped over the decks and could not be pumped out because there was no power of any sort, neither was there any warmth. She could however be made partially ready for action in three or four days, given the full resources of the *Jan Wellem* and the untiring efforts of her own crew.

No one had any rest however, and the need of it was keenly felt. Worse, the night's abortive break-out had shown them all, not just the Captains, that Narvik was a trap from which escape was only possible by the aid of a miracle; and if the British had come for them once they could do so again. Backs to the wall they nevertheless turned to with spirit.

Bey, it is clear, decided that another break-out would invite a worse fate than staying put, even though four ships became operational. He did so in spite of further pressure from Group West, and the fact that visibility in the evening was again very bad and consequently favourable. Was he wrong? He does not seem to have carried the argument much further than the very reasonable assumption that he would probably be intercepted at sea; but naval actions, especially at night, were rarely completely overwhelming in their results when one side was bent on evasion, whereas at Narvik there could be no sanctuary at all until strong air power could be established for defence and to keep the Royal Navy at arm's length, and there was no hope of that for many days. On the other hand, he may have thought that the crews of sunken ships would be safer in the landlocked fjords; and the General may have foreseen what was to become very clear later, that his toe-hold on Narvik would be in jeopardy without the 2,500 sailors.

As with the *Penelope*, so with Bey; having decided that he should take no action, fate stepped in to ensure that there could be none, for two of his good ships grounded while moving to their night dispersal anchorages. The *Wolfgang Zenker* merely bent her port propeller and the ensuing severe vibration reduced her speed to 20 knots, but the

Erich Koellner suffered considerable structural damage with much flooding; she could not steam safely at over seven knots, her fire control system was useless, and like the *Diether von Roeder* she became an immobile gun platform.

British Initiative

Also during the 11th the Commander-in-Chief steamed northwards to the Narvik area, and on the way he ordered the *Furious* to launch a strike of Swordfish torpedo bombers against the German ships at Trondheim. This had no success, and it was resolved to arm the aircraft with bombs for an attack on Narvik planned for the next day.

In the morning of the 12th news was received that the German battlecruisers were as good as home in Germany, having encircled the British forces without being sighted by any, or from the air. This was humiliating, but at least there was now nothing to distract the Commander-in-Chief from concentrating his forces against the Germans at Narvik, the recapture of which had become his first priority. It may be presumed that he did not intend to mount any direct assault, other than an air strike, until the promised military expedition should arrive; it was to sail that day. The Admiralty however was not prepared to wait, and spelled out its wishes with insistence and precision:

'An operation to clean up enemy naval forces and destroy shore batteries in Narvik is to be carried out using synchronised dive-bombing attacks from *Furious* in combination with attack by surface forces. It is considered that the latter should consist of a battleship heavily escorted by destroyers.

'On completion of the operation *Furious* is to remain in the Narvik area and assist coming land operations. Fuel for *Furious* is being sent. Risk of U-Boat attack should be slight if suitable anchorage is selected with destroyer patrol outside= 1033/12th'

The importance given to the air arm in this signal is interesting, though the effectiveness expected from the old Swordfish smacks of wishful thinking. Also important is the reference to the 'coming land operation', which was clearly intended to be later than and quite separate from the assault now ordered. Although the massive naval force to be sent up to Narvik could reasonably be expected to achieve its expurgatory aim, the Admiralty did not envisage that a naval victory would surely throw the enemy into such confusion and dismay that the landing would be best carried out at that moment.

A day or two would have sufficed for the main troop convoy to arrive, and half a battalion of the Scots Guards with the Military Commander in the cruiser *Southampton* would be there even earlier. If however further delay was not to be tolerated, there were the Royal Marine detachments from three battleships, two battlecruisers and the *Furious* available on the spot, a sizeable force of trained soldiers which could have been backed up by soldiers. It might of course have proved impracticable to transfer these men at sea, but the fact is that the Admiralty did not mention landing and had therefore no right to expect later that the commander on the spot would make good their omission.

Air Attack

In the afternoon the Commander-in-Chief detached part of his force to cover the troop convoy from Scapa, and went on with the rest to a position close to seaward off Moskenes Island in the Lofotens where the *Furious* flew off nine Swordfish of 818 Squadron under Lieutenant Commander P. G. Sydney-Turner at 1615. The Commander-in-Chief told them:

'Attack on ships in Narvik to be pressed home and I hope to hear that all ships, including merchant vessels which are either transports or store ships, have been sunk. No shore AA batteries so far as known and most of the enemy destroyers are badly mauled. One aircraft is to take photographs.'

The Squadron was spotted over Vestfjord, presumably by a U-Boat, and the German destroyers were alerted. The weather started to play up again, but Sydney-Turner found his way up Ofotfjord and attacked the ships in the harbour. It was a gallant effort but quite hopeless; the Swordfish had never been designed for divebombing, their crews were inexperienced, and they had to fly through fire from the very effective 3.7cm and 2cm automatic weapons, which were far in advance of anything carried in British ships, as well as through a 12.7cm barrage. And they were almost unbelievably slow; "Look at those tired ducks," exclaimed a German observer. "Biplanes gentlemen! They look as though they're standing still in the sky. They have spirit though." It was about all they did have; none of the destroyers was hit and the only results were a few splinter casualties in the *Erich Giese*, a small Norwegian patrol craft sunk, and a party of German sailors who were unluckily caught in the open on the Ore Quay lost eight killed and 20 wounded when a bomb hit the land. Two aircraft were shot down, the remaining seven landing on safely at their limit of endurance at 2010.

'When the visibility is less than a mile, cloud base below 200 feet, and it is raining, deck-landing can be hazardous, at night.' (Guidance to naval aviators)

After 818 Squadron left Narvik, the visibility closed in and the Germans felt safe from further air attack; they were fully justified. 616 Squadron under Lieutenant Commander H. Gardner flew off at 1708, and one of his Telegraphist Air Gunners, Frank Smith, tells the story:

'In those days it was not considered necessary for TAGs to attend pre-flight briefing so we had to rely on our pilots to give us the "gen". Each Sub-Flight carried an observer, but we lost ours as soon as we hit the coast.

'I plotted the inward course on a piece of paper and drew a rough map for the first hour or so; I noted a lighthouse on the port side as we entered Vestfjord. After that, a turn north and then by guess and by God up and down fjords in blinding snow. After about two hours we turned south and were very lucky to arrive back at the entrance. I saw this same lighthouse to starboard through the snow and murk (it was practically dark by now) and put the pilot on to a reciprocal course for the ship. There appeared to be three or four aircraft in a very long line abreast. I have a feeling that our own ships opened fire on us, we dropped our bombs in the sea and forced on.

'My pilot had never done a night deck-landing—nor did he now—touched the deck and cartwheeled over the port side—no dinghy—45 minutes in the water in a howling gale, temperature 28° F—picked up by *Hero*'s boat—lucky.'

Lucky indeed, and brave. The flyers did all they could to fulfil the Commander-in-Chief's grandiose exhortation; but that would only have been realistic had the Royal Navy devoted the previous ten years to developing its aviation to that pitch of efficiency which technical advance had made possible. Other nations had done so, but in Britain the Trenchard doctrine of concentrating virtually all air forces on strategic bombing, together with the Navy's almost obsessive cult of the gun, had ensured that the air could not yet take its rightful place as the main strike weapon.

The *Furious* reported:

'In Narvik 5 Maass class destroyers and 11 merchant ships. One destroyer at Ore Quay, three at Post Pier and one at anchor. All attacked, two hit, one seriously. AA battery on point and neck of Narvik peninsula. Aircraft fired on by ships and batteries. Two mines seen in Vestfjord. No batteries on Baroy and none seen in Ofotfjord. Batteries seen half way up hill behind Narvik. Entrance to harbour partly blocked by sunken ships. Photos taken but visibility bad. 12 aircraft now available for service, two lost, all officers and men now accounted for=2215/12th'

The AA batteries were by no means imaginary, consisting of automatic weapons salved from the *Wilhelm Heidkamp* and *Diether von Roeder* mounted on shore. There was of course no mention of German cruisers.

CHAPTER SIX

The Second Battle

The Commander-in-Chief's Staff Officer (Operations), Commander Cecil Hughes-Hallett, spent the day of the 12th drafting orders for an operation to comply with the Admiralty's instructions:

'1 Operation DW will take place Saturday, April 13th.

2 Object: Destruction of German warships, merchant ships and defences in Narvik area.

3 Ships of Force 'B' are to consist of *Bedouin*, *Punjabi*, *Eskimo*, *Cossack* (Commander R. St V. Sherbrooke), *Kimberley*, *Foxhound* (Lt Commander G. H. Peters), *Forester* (Lt Commander E. B. Tancock), *Hero*, *Icarus*, are to rendezvous with *Warspite*, flying the flag of Vice Admiral Whitworth (Short Title: BC1) in position 67° 44' N, 13° 22' E (In Vestfjord) at 0730/13th.

4 & 5 Not applicable.

6 After arrival of other destroyers *Hero*, *Foxhound*, *Forester* will be detached to stream minesweeps. *Icarus* is to stream bow sweeps and form ahead of leading sweeping destroyer when latter is on station on *Warspite*, the four destroyers working their Asdics as far as possible. Other destroyers form anti-submarine screen as ordered by BC1.

The force will proceed up Vestfjord in this formation, and it is suggested that a destroyer should be detailed on either side to throw a depth charge into any likely inlet that could harbour a submarine.

7 On reaching Baroy, which is the suspected minefield area, the anti-submarine screen should as far as practicable move into the swept water until past the island.

8 The force will proceed into Ofotfjord, engaging shore defences in passing and making full use of short-range weapons as well as heavier guns. Non-sweeping destroyers and *Warspite* cover advance of sweeping destroyers with gunfire. It is especially important that

destroyers sighted should be engaged before they can fire torpedoes at *Warspite*.

9 Minesweeping is to be continued to longitude 16° 55′ E (Ballangen Bay). Sweeping destroyers are then to haul clear of *Warspite*, recover or cut their sweeps, and assist the non-sweeping destroyers. Failing other targets they may drop back and destroy shore defence guns on Baroy or elsewhere.

10 *Warspite* will proceed to about five miles from Narvik depending on circumstances, and from there cover the advance of the destroyers into the harbour where enemy ships may be located.

11 Destroyers are only to make smoke if ordered by BC1.

12 Force will withdraw as ordered by BC1.

13 *Furious* is to arrange air attacks on following enemy positions:
(a) Baroy about 1215.
(b) Ramnes and opposite shore about 1300.
(c) Warships in Ballangen, Narvik and Herjangs, and batteries at Narvik about 1345.

BC1 will signal exact times at which these attacks are to commence.

14 *Furious* is to provide anti-submarine air patrol for *Warspite* from 0730.

$$= 1909/12\text{th}'$$

Information concerning the enemy was also signalled:

'1 Minefield reported in entrance to Tjeldsund.

2 U-Boat reported in Vestfjord.

3 Five or six *Leberecht Maass* class destroyers, some damaged, and six merchant vessels sunk inside harbour.

4 *Hardy* beached one mile west of Virek.

5 Baroy Island fortified, including possibly magnetic torpedoes

6 Three 12 or 18pdr guns on Framnes facing northwest. 4in guns on both sides of fjord at Hamnes.

7 One or two unidentified aircraft sighted in Vestfjord on 12th.'

Admiral Whitworth welcomed these excellent orders, and if it should seem strange that he did not resent being told how to fight his battle in such minute detail, the answer may be that he considered himself lucky to be allowed to take part at all as this signal to the Commander-in-Chief shows:

'As I was unable to prevent the Germans entering Narvik, may I hoist my flag in *Warspite*?'

The precautions to be taken against mines and shore batteries were realistic in the light of available intelligence, and the aim was crystal clear, with nothing about landing. Admiral Whitworth and a small staff set out from the *Renown* for a rough ride in an oared cutter, and in the *Warspite* the word spread rapidly, for an Admiral appearing unannounced from the waves at dead of night must surely portend something unusual. The truth must have been hard to guess for the project was both unconventional and bold; better indeed to risk an old battleship than one of the only three battlecruisers, but capital ships took years to replace and the risks were very real. The air threat was not mentioned in the orders, but the Fleet had already been bombed twice and knew it to be serious. Although it was not thought that Narvik was in range of enemy strikes, eyes were kept skinned.

The risk from U-Boats had been recognised but seriously underplayed, for to reach Narvik the *Warspite* would have to pass not one but five. On the morning of the 13th the *U48* was off Tranoy, the *U46* was in the Ofotfjord narrows between Baroy and Ramnes, the *U25* was near Lilandsgrund, the *U51* was in Narvik Harbour fuelling from the *Jan Wellem*, and the *U64* was anchored at the head of Herjangsfjord conserving her batteries but at instant readiness to sail. Had these dispositions been known or even guessed at it is to be wondered whether the *Warspite* would have been allowed into the fjord, especially as the two mythical cruisers were no longer taken seriously. Yet if minefields and shore batteries were guessed at, why not submarines which are self-contained and easy to pre-position for a planned operation? The frequent submarine contacts by the British destroyer patrols in Vestfjord seem to have struck no warning note.

The German Order of Battle
Although the British thought that Bey's force consisted of five or six ships, and the true figure was eight, only one, the *Hermann Künne*, was fighting fit. The rest, despite the prolonged and devoted efforts of their weary crews, were still in various degrees of unserviceability:

Hans Lüdemann. Her No 1 gun was permanently out of action but otherwise she was in good shape. Her after magazine had been pumped dry and the ammunition proved usable; four torpedoes remained.

Wolfgang Zenker. Until the action started her speed was though to be limited to 20 knots by her propeller damage, but when circumstances demanded her being driven at full speed come what may, the vibration ceased entirely. Whether this merely seemed to be so amid the distraction of even more pressing emergencies, or was brought about by a providential dispensation in the field of harmonics, cannot be said with assurance. She had all her eight torpedoes.

Erich Giese. She had neither been hit nor run aground, but from the moment of her return from the break-out attempt a defect had developed which defied all efforts to correct. The only fault positively identified was a massive loss of feed water through leaking boiler-tubes, but the ship's ability to steam was further inhibited by parts of the main machinery being in pieces when the alarm was raised on the 13th. She had eight torpedoes, having received two replacements from the *Wilhelm Heidkamp*.

Bernd von Arnim. Her five shell holes had been welded over, and strenuous efforts below had brought five (out of six) boilers into use, albeit with heavy loss of feed water. She could thus steam at 33 knots, her gunnery system and weapons were unimpaired, and she had embarked six torpedoes from the *Wilhelm Heidkamp* and *Erich Koellner*.

Georg Thiele. Determination to get back into the fight had achieved four boilers and an emergency speed of 27 knots; without the port main circulator and feed pump this could only be maintained briefly, but the time when it was to be needed would be only too brief. Four main armament guns were serviceable in local control; the torpedo control system was also inoperable but six torpedoes were ready in the tubes, four having been borrowed from the *Erich Koellner*.

The *Diether von Roeder* was still anchored by the bow on a westerly heading and had her stern secured to the root of the Post Pier. Although it had been assessed that her boiler damage might have been partially repaired in a week or so, she was most unlikely to be allowed so long and had been stripped of everything that could be useful to other ships or ashore; for instance stores, AA guns, ammunition, and a radio transmitter that became General Dietl's only means of communication with the outside world. The Captain and bulk of the ship's company had taken up residence in a tunnel in the hillside just over their ship, and all that remained on board were the crews of Nos 1 and 2 guns. Two depth charges were rigged for demolition.

The *Erich Koellner*'s plight after grounding posed Bey a problem as to what to do with her, and he decided to put her at the village of Taarstad on the north shore three miles east of Ramnes, where there was a wooden jetty behind which she could lie unobtrusively with a clear field of fire, but protected from torpedoes and to some extent from gunfire. Since she could not have used her torpedoes from this position they were to have been removed, together with all other useful equipment, but it so happened that the one positive effect of the *Furious*'s air raid had been to delay her movement, then just about to begin, and to bring about that some torpedoes remained on board.

April 13th

The day dawned for the Germans with no more foreboding than those preceding it, but offering like them a bleak prospect of wearing mental stress and physical toil. But the *Warspite* was already steaming majestically up Vestfjord and collecting her destroyers as she came. The weather was overcast with heavy, melting snow clouds that precipitated intermittent rain; the wind was light in the southwest, the visibility was as much as ten miles, and snow lay thick on the mountains and down to the water's edge. The omens were propitious and no second thoughts obtruded.

Admiral Whitworth had plenty of time to get his team together and tell it his wishes; firstly he ordered the *Furious* to carry out the air attacks at the times proposed by the Commander-in-Chief, and then he signalled his force:

'We are proceeding to attack the defences of Narvik and any German warships or merchant ships met. I am sure that any resistance on the part of the enemy will be dealt with in most resolute and determined manner. I wish you all success=0915/13th'

Finally, the Admiral added three of his own points to the Commander-in-Chief's orders:

'1 Any sign of enemy activity on Baroy is to be destroyed by gun fire.

2 If a guide to fire distribution is necessary odd numbered destroyers (those on the starboard side) take south and even numbers north side. Enemy warships take precedence over shore targets.

3 When east of 17° E (Ballangen Bay) destroyers may use high speed but should not lose support of *Warspite*'s fire. Any enemy warship in fjord to north of Narvik is to be provided for before harbour is entered=1009/13th'

Fateful Resolve at Narvik

One minute later Fregattenkapitän Bey received this awful intelligence from Group West:

'Special enemy action this afternoon in the Narvik area. Ships taking part: *Repulse*, *Warspite*, five Tribal destroyers, four destroyers, and possibly an aircraft carrier=0838'

If in that terrible moment any German Captain considered acting like Langsdorff of the *Graf Spee* and scuttling his ship rather than meet the enemy in battle—and there is reason to believe that some did, very properly for it was a reasonable alternative course of action in the circumstances—he put the thought behind him and prepared to fight to the last round. There was real, if slight hope of staving off defeat; while there is life there usually is, and the British might be thwarted by a number of known and unknown factors, not least the U-Boats; but honour, and the upholding and indeed creation of tradition, were also taken into serious account. The destroyers being probably doomed, to have landed the sailors unharmed and fully equipped would have added greatly to the Army's strength and been entirely logical; but to have given in without a fight would have invited the scorn of the Norwegians, the British, and the world. If the numerically inferior German Navy could not be guaranteed to fight when outnumbered, it would have little value. Besides, such a decision properly belonged to the higher command where the advantages or otherwise of resistance could be viewed against the background of the campaign as a whole, and where it was known whether last-minute help in the form of air power could be given. It may be thought that Group West, like the Admiralty with Warburton-Lee, should have grasped this nettle; but they said nothing, not even goodbye.

Steam was ordered to be raised in all ships, and at 1030 the *Erich Koellner* sailed for her ambush at Taarstad escorted by the *Hermann Künne*; but she could only make seven knots and had 17 miles to go. She carried just her weapons, crews and a steaming party, the rest having been landed. Bey intended to disperse his other mobile ships in the side fjords as had been done on the 10th, so as to seize the enemy light forces as in a vice and also, doubtlessly, to enable them to fire torpedoes from the beams. However, the time taken by the damaged ships to get under way prevented this plan from maturing.

The British Approach

A newcomer to Skjelfjord, and no cripple, was the tanker *British Lady* who was enabling the destroyers to maintain their constant patrols. The *Eskimo* had replenished during the night and then relieved the *Bedouin* and *Punjabi* who proceeded to do the same. Back on patrol between Baroy and Tranoy the former sighted a Junkers flying boat who assumed her to be German and carried out recognition procedure. Even more strangely, a U-Boat suddenly surfaced two hours later, at 1040, four miles to the southwest and did exactly the same thing. This was the *U48* (Kapitänleutnant Schultze), newly arrived from seaward and to whom sympathy is due, for clearly no one had told her what to expect by way of British patrols, which would have indicated the folly of surfacing in the middle of Vestfjord in daylight.

Micklethwait of the *Eskimo* had an immediate problem, for beyond the U-Boat the *Warspite*'s force could already be seen approaching; he hurled his ship at full speed at the submarine who dived, and then plastered the area liberally with depth charges. No Asdic contact was made nor damage inflicted, but the main aim was achieved since Schultze remained unaware of the British force, merely logging that life in Vestfjord that morning was particularly trying. Not only did other screening ships harass her as they passed, but three patrolling destroyers were later ordered by the Commander-in-Chief to hunt her remorselessly. Admiral Whitworth's comment however was, 'He may have been a Norwegian'.

The *Eskimo* then joined the starboard wing of the *Warspite*'s screen, and Force 'B' was complete. Proudly the *Icarus* led the way; as an erstwhile minelayer she had only two guns and no torpedoes, but previous operations had required her to be fitted with bow protection paravanes, designed to pioneer a path through a minefield without herself being endangered except by a mine struck directly by her forefoot. Astern of her came the *Foxhound* and *Hero* with their stern-towed sweeps widening the swept channel, sufficiently to safeguard the *Warspite* but not the remaining destroyers, who were disposed in a conventional anti-submarine screen. To starboard were the *Bedouin*, *Punjabi* and *Eskimo*, and to port the *Cossack*, *Kimberley* and *Forester*; the latter having managed to weave her minesweeping gear into something of a tangled web, she finally cut it adrift and gratefully took her place as a fully mobile fighting ship.

The Senior Officer Destroyers was Commander 'Bes' McCoy of

the *Bedouin*, an affable and well-liked officer who, as might be expected, made a signal:

'On passing Baroy, *Bedouin*, *Punjabi*, *Eskimo* proceed to the van. *Cossack*, *Kimberley* and *Forester* will form astern of *Eskimo*. If enemy warships are in Herjangsfjord leading ships will go for them. Rear ships use their discretion when to attack ships in the harbour=1101'

An advocate of the pragmatical approach, McCoy thus made clear to his Captains that he expected them to go for the enemy with as few restrictions as possible, and the signal is remarkable as being the only tactical order he gave during the entire battle; other than Flag 5—engage the enemy—which remained at his yard-arm throughout. He was perhaps wise, for the battlefield was so unlike anything envisaged by standard doctrine; the most effective tactics would be those which best countered the enemy's defensive moves, which in turn were best assessed by the very experienced destroyer Captains and translated by them into action on the instant. McCoy may also have surmised that these same Captains whom he knew intimately, might be tempted to do just that in any case and therefore the less he said the better. His signal could have been even briefer, for the first part seemed to imply that six ships were to steam up Ofotfjord in line ahead, with the probable result that should the enemy be massed at the far end, his own ship leading the line would be exposed to their concentrated fire without his consorts being able to join in. A more marked contrast between McCoy's and Warburton-Lee's methods can hardly be imagined.

The *Warspite's* Aircraft

On the battleship's bridge two members of the Ship's Flight, Lieutenant Commander W. J. M. 'Bruno' Brown (Observer) and Petty Officer Airman F. C. 'Ben' Rice (Pilot), were being briefed by the Admiral, the Captain (Victor Crutchley VC) and Commander Currie. They were to take one of the two Swordfish floatpanes and:

1 Carry out a general reconnaissance for the fleet advancing up Ofotfjord, with particular reference to the presence of German warships in side fjords, the movements of German forces, and the positions of shore batteries.
2 Bomb any suitable targets.
3 Return to Skjelfjord.

Brown did not fancy the last instruction because it would mean leaving the battlefield before the battle was over, and he tried to persuade his seniors to delete it. With the aircrew's safety in mind they would not do so, but Brown was not unduly discouraged; once in the air he would be more his own master, and naval tradition tended towards leniency for young rebels who erred on the side of closing the enemy.

A Swordfish on floats was allowed a bomb load of 1,000lbs, but Rice had crammed on two 250lb high explosive, two 100lb anti-submarine, and eight 40lb anti-personnel bombs. There was something for every eventuality, and although they totalled 1,020lbs Rice was confident that his aircraft was up to it; at the ritual of weighing out the cordite which would accelerate the catapult, he persuaded his colleagues, the Catapult Officer and Chief Stoker, to put in an extra soupçon. When the ship was five miles west of Baroy at 1152, the aircraft was launched over the starboard side without faltering and plunged at a headlong 85 knots into the great tunnel, comprising the sea, the mountains, and the cloud base at 1,000 feet, that was Ofotfjord. The third crew member was Leading Airman Maurice Pacey, Telegraphist Air Gunner, who shared the after cockpit with Brown, transmitted the signals on his morse key that were ordered by the latter, and took a series of outstanding photographs. Rice in the front seat could be contacted through a speaking tube, or by tapping him on the shoulder.

First Contact

There was no sign of any activity or batteries when the aircraft passed Baroy at 1157; but that was the only anticlimax of this memorable flight and very soon at 1203, Rice saw the *Hermann Künne* off Tjellebotn, on her own and still steering west. She opened fire but he scraped the aircraft along the southern mountains and pressed on eastwards as Brown reported the enemy to the *Warspite*.

It may be thought strange that the flagship did not pass this first sighting to the destroyers, and even stranger that all ships were not listening on Air Reconnaissance Wave which they were technically fitted to do; but this is comment from an age when everybody is air minded and it is hard to recall a time when they were not. Only the *Hero* was fully in the picture, because Frank Smith, the rescued TAG, appropriated a wireless set and listened to every dot and dash. The result was that the *Hermann Künne*, alerted by what was obviously a ship-based aircraft, sighted and was able to count the nine British destroyers ten minutes before she was herself seen. She raised the alarm at once, and continued westwards to get a clearer view.

Bey ordered all destroyers to sail immediately, but the U-Boats were not alerted in spite of the mutual promises of closer co-operation two days before. The *U64* had been ordered to sail from her anchorage in Herjangsfjord at 1200, but not urgently and since she had minor trouble with her periscope she delayed for it to be put right. Schütze of the *U25*, alert as ever, spotted the aircraft and dived to periscope depth, but the *U46* nearest to the enemy did not and knew nothing.

Rice pressed on and at 1210 sighted the *Erich Koellner* plodding westwards off Lilandsgrund. Her fire was easily avoided and then Brown looked keenly into the side fjords as the Swordfish flew eastwards; there was nothing in Bogen, Ballangen or Skjomen, but the *Hans Lüdemann* was clearly seen anchored in the harbour entrance and she was reported. Then over to Herjangsfjord and there, at the very head not 50 yards from the shore, was the *U64*. Sighting was mutual and the submarine just had time to man her guns.

Brown the Observer was an officer and consequently Captain of the aircraft, but he could only exercise that function by telling the pilot his general policy and leaving him free to take instant decisions. Whether or not to attack the U-Boat was one such and Rice, young, enthusiastic and uninhibited, said, "Let's have a go at the so and so!" Brown understood his man perfectly, and instinctively agreed so he said nothing; then he considered the arguments. If we attack and are shot down the fleet will have no more air reconnaissance because Rice is temporarily the only pilot; but we have already looked into the side fjords, and if we have to return to Skjelfjord we shall not have much longer anyway. On the other hand if the U-Boat is allowed to escape she will menace the fleet later; let's attack! It was fortunate that the decision fell out in this way because by the time it was taken all was over.

Rice selected the two anti-submarine bombs and put the Swordfish, floats and all, into a 50 degree dive starting at 1,000 feet, the height at which conventional dive-bombers usually pulled out. At 200 feet he released his bombs and pulled up hastily, thus blotting out his own view, but Pacey saw the starboard bomb fall close alongside and the port one hit just abaft the conning tower; the U-Boat was already sinking when Rice could see her again. 36 of the 48 man crew were saved however, including one hopes the brave

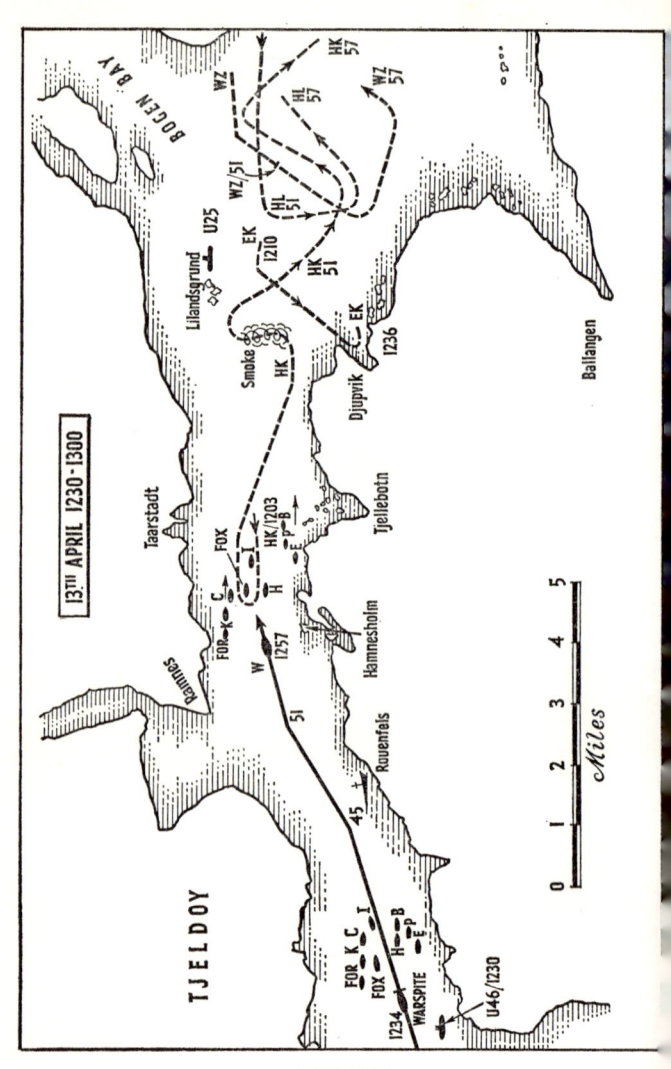

1230–1300

gunner who continued to aim truly even as the bombs fell and hit the aircraft in the tail plane; only the fabric was damaged, but response to the controls became somewhat sluggish and Rice told Pacey to watch it in case it became necessary to put down on the water. For Brown it was just the excuse he needed for staying at Narvik until the limit of endurance; he reported the sinking, but it so happened that this was the only signal that was not received out of 30 or more sent.

The time was 1230 when the Swordfish flew back past Narvik, and although the German destroyers inside were striving to clear the harbour none had yet succeeded. Brown ordered Rice to regain visual touch with the fleet and then to scout ahead of it.

Five miles up the fjord from Baroy, Sohler watched the armada approach through the *U46*'s periscope. His responsibility was heavy, and he must have been acutely reminded of a conversation two days before when General Dietl had asked him if the U-Boats could prevent enemy heavy ships coming up to Narvik. He had replied, 'Yes', and must now back his judgement with deeds; but there was no apparent reason why he should not succeed if he could only slip through the mass of destroyers, for the battleship was restricted in her movement and would pass within 650 yards. All British eyes were concentrated ahead and that gave him a further advantage; the *Warspite* sailed grandly on at an untroubled 15 knots, looking as though she owned the place while in fact being utterly vulnerable. But in the very second before firing time, the *U46*'s bow struck an uncharted pinnacle of rock and jumped skywards, breaking the surface uncontrollably. 'Enemy in sight!' The report flashed through the British force in an instant, and penetrated to the remotest part of every ship; but it was for the *Hermann Künne* at last, not for the *U46* who, with engines racing astern slid back into the depths and obscurity.

Had the *Warspite* been hit, what might McCoy have done? He could have pressed on and won the battle without the great ship's help, but he was not to know that and the question is, would he have done so? He could hardly have left her entirely alone, damaged and possibly sinking, in the presence of a known U-Boat, and to have had to reduce his force by perhaps two ships might have induced him to surrender the initiative. The argument is not entirely academic, since deep-draught ships were by no means immune to the German torpedoes, as witness the *Royal Oak* and *Courageous* which had already been sunk by the self-same mark of weapon. Thus if a judgement is sought on whether it was wise to employ the battleship in narrow waters, it may be observed that not only was she herself in peril, but that the aim of the operation might have been prejudiced as well.

Kothe of the *Hermann Künne* had closed the range to something under ten miles, and while doing so his ship's head-on silhouette was not seen by the British through the misty drizzle; but as soon as her beam was exposed it was a different story, and their leading ships, *Cossack*, *Icarus*, *Punjabi* and *Bedouin* were quick to engage. That was the opening of the surface battle, but it was only a token one for the range was far too great for effective shooting, and fire was checked after a few salvos when the *Hermann Künne* disappeared from view; she had not seen the *Warspite*.

Schulze-Hinrichs of the *Erich Koellner* had realised that he could never reach Taarstad in time, and had turned for Djupvik as a bad second best. He was unlucky enough to arrive just as the ubiquitous aircraft passed to rejoin the fleet, and Brown saw the destroyer point her bows east and expose her armament to the north across the fjord. He was in no doubt that this was an ambush and informed the fleet, amplifying his reports at five minute intervals to ensure that there was no doubt in any British mind. Just to the west of Djupvik the *Hermann Künne* appeared again, while astern, too far to see, the *Hans Lüdemann* and *Wolfgang Zenker*, the latter with Bey embarked, had left harbour and were hurrying to the scene. The *Bernd von Arnim* did not take much longer to pick her way through the wrecks and out into the fjord, but the *Georg Thiele*'s and *Erich Giese*'s engineers still struggled frantically to close up their main machinery and get their ships to move, however temporarily; they had been ordered to be ready by 1300, an unfortunate guess by Bey.

Knorr of the *U51*, who thought the alarm was for an air attack, cast off from the *Jan Wellem* at the Ore Quay and dived his boat to the bottom of the harbour, whence no amount of signalling, by light at the periscope or radio, could shift him.

The *Hermann Künne* turned in her tracks at about 1245 and laid a smoke-screen, with the double intention of hiding her consorts' approach and of using it as cover for firing torpedoes. It did not lie well, and the range being reduced to 13,000 yards a further short exchange of fire took place with the *Cossack* and *Bedouin*. The British force was approaching Hamnes and Ramnes at the time, with their weather eyes cocked for the reported batteries, and were relieved

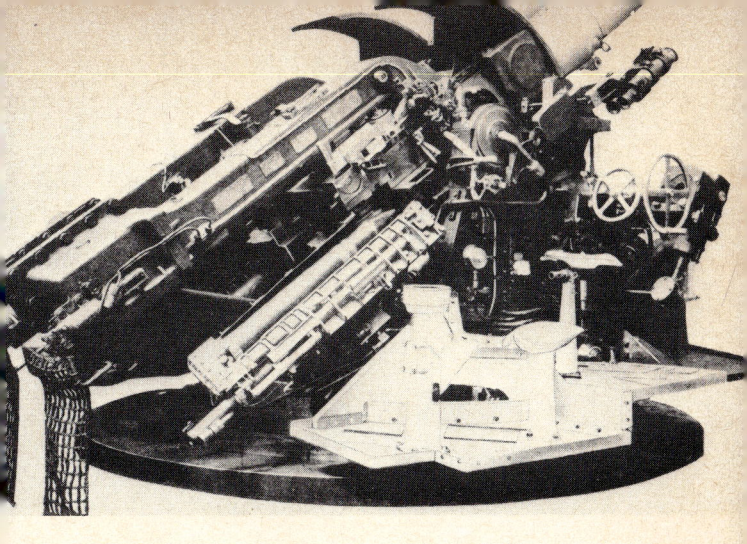

A *Tribal* class destroyer's gun-mounting and its crew.
10 rounds per minute could be achieved, and the design was excellent for surface action; but since its maximum elevation was only 40° it was useless against the main air threat, dive bombing.

The piratical appearance of the crew does not indicate an advanced stage of ill-discipline but the fact that the Royal Navy had given no thought to arctic clothing. 'Comforts' were greatly in demand and the *Tribals* were lucky in being bountifully supplied.
[MoD and Capt Dickens

Top: The *Erich Koellner* after being hit for first time. [Lt Cdr Henley

Bottom: The *Warspite* completing the *Erich Koellner*'s destruction. [IWM

Top: The *Punjabi* and *Eskimo* engaging ahead with their forward guns. The photo is taken from the *Bedouin* who is doing the same.
[Capt. Garnett

Bottom: The *Hermann Künne* was very thoroughly demolished.
[Bibliotek für Zeitgeschiehte

Top: The *Erich Giese* silent, burning and sinking. [IWM

Left: The *Hermann Künne*'s funeral pyre. [IWM

Opposite, top: Narvik Harbour as the British approach. Note the small number of ships left afloat out of the original 25. [IWM

Opposite, bottom: Narvik Harbour as it was when the *Cossack* entered. In the foreground is the stranded *Bochenheim*; directly beyond her is the *Diether von Roeder* at the Post Pier; to the left is the Ore Quay where the *Jan Wellem* is lying; and in the entrance is the wreck of the British *Blythmoor*. Note the shell damage to the Swordfish's tail plane. [IWM

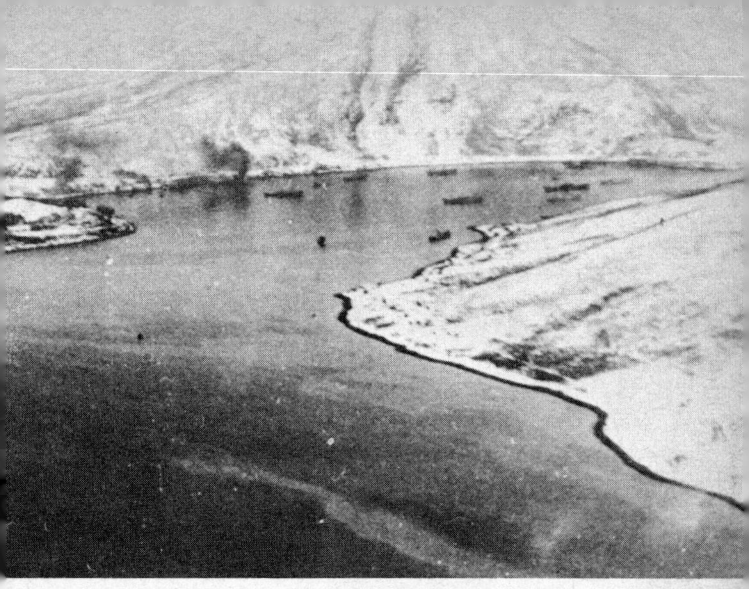

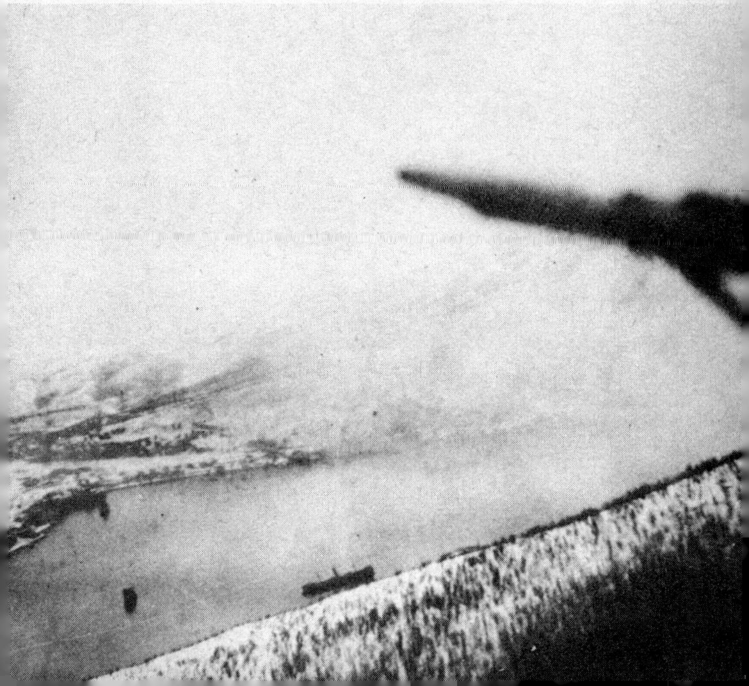

Top: The *Kimberley* hurries to join the *Cossack* in the harbour. [IWM

Bottom: The *Cossack* aground on Ankenes, still engaging. [IWM

Top: Inner and Outer Rombaksfjord, showing the Straumen Narrows and the Ore Railway. [*Via Rear Admiral Micklethwait, believed to be originally Illustrated London News*

Bottom: The *Bedouin* and *Icarus* passing the *Warspite*, probably in the Outer Rombaksfjord to join the *Eskimo* through the narrows. [*The Times*

Top: This photo, taken from the *Forester*, of the *Eskimo* in Rombaken has so far been thought to show her being torpedoed; but angles do not coincide with Pacey's aerial photo and it is now thought more likely that it shows her turning through the narrows and engaging with full broadside.
[Admiral Micklethwait

Bottom: Artist's impression of the last stand of the *Georg Thiele*.
[Admiral Wolff

Top: The *Eskimo* has just been struck by the *Georg Thiele*'s last torpedo; her bow has drooped and the shock wave from the explosion expands around her. Her wash indicates that she has been moving astern. The German destroyer is visible up the fjord, and in the foreground the *Forester* manoeuvres frantically to avoid one of the *Hans Ludemann*'s torpedoes. This unique action photograph was taken by Leading Airman Maurice Pacey from the *Warspite*'s damaged Swordfish. [IWM

Right: The track of the *Georg Thiele*'s torpedo which ran on the surface is still clearly visible after it has hit the *Eskimo* (just left of picture). [Public Records Office

Top: The *Georg Thiele* ashore. She must have struck with great force for the bow to be raised to such an angle. [IWM

Bottom: Later, the *Georg Thiele*'s back broke and her stern sank in deep water. [IWM

Top: The *Eskimo* lies alongside the captured German Supply Ship *Alster* in Skjeldfjord, having lost her bow to the *Georg Thiele's* torpedo. [Rear Admiral Micklethwait

Bottom: The *Hans Lüdemann* aground, on fire and abandoned. She is being boarded by men from the *Hero* and *Icarus*, and the two whalers are lying off.
[Lt Cdr Henley

Top: The *Bernd von Arnim*. [Bibliotek für Zeitgeschichte

Bottom: The *Hans Lüdemann* after being torpedoed by the *Hero*. [Bibliotek für Zeitgeschichte

Right, top to bottom: Wolfgang Zenker, Bernd von Arnim, Hans Lüdemann. [Bibliotek für Zeitgeschichte

The *Foxhound* offers aid to the *Cossack* after the *Diether von Roeder* has blown up. [IWM

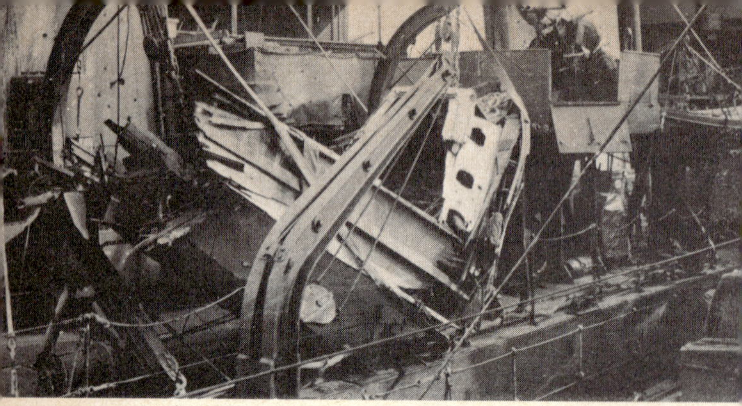

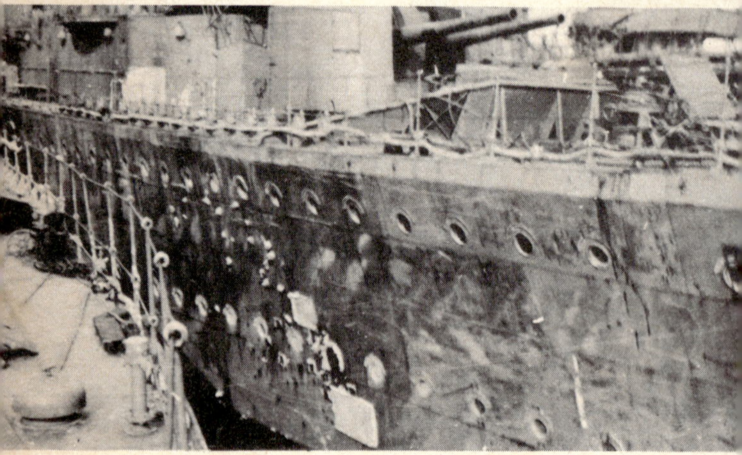

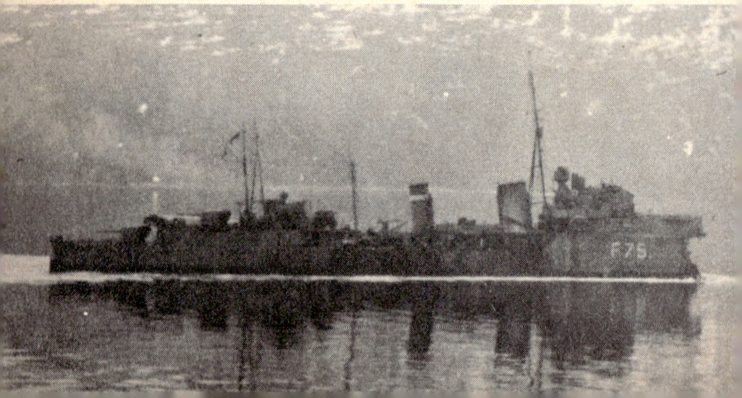
F75

posite, top and centre: Some of
 Punjabi's damage.

posite, bottom: The *Eskimo*
ed up and ready to sail for
me. [Rear Admiral
cklethwait

and right: Graves are
sual resting places for sailors
o die in battle. These were
otedly tended by the
rwegians throughout the
man occupation, and are
w in the care of the British
r Graves Commission.
M

CAPTAIN
B. A. WARBURTON-LEE
VC RN
H. M. S. "HARDY"
10TH APRIL 1940 AGE 44

CONTINUETH
R KNOWING

Top: Survivors from the *Hardy* return to London still dressed in borrowed Norwegian clothes, and are reviewed by the First Lord on Horseguards Parade.
[London News Agency

Bottom: Commander Herbert Layman (*Hotspur*) receives his DSO, accompanied by his wife.

when nothing happened; the aircraft from the *Furious* sent to pinpoint and bomb the batteries had met a patch of thick weather and been unable to reach its objective.

> '*So all day long the noise of battle roll'd*
> *Among the mountains by the winter sea.*' (Tennyson)

It began in earnest when the *Hans Lüdemann* came into range at 1251, followed by the *Wolfgang Zenker* at 1257. The Germans used the same tactics as on the 10th, zig-zagging over nearly the whole width of the fjord which enabled them to bring all their guns to bear while giving the enemy difficult targets; on the debit side was the difficulty imposed on the gun-control teams by the frequent and drastic alterations of course, but it is hard to see what else could have been done. The British destroyers maintained steady courses for the time being, their large numbers and the narrowness of the fjord dictating it, so that they could only shoot with their forward guns. That was however a small handicap to the Tribals and *Kimberley*, with their twin mountings, who might have been designed for this particular battle—which of course they had not for no planner in his senses could possibly have envisaged such a confrontation—but the little *Hero*, *Foxhound* and *Icarus* with single guns and firmly tied to the *Warspite* by the apron-strings of their paravanes, were not so happily placed. The *Icarus* was straddled by the third salvo fired at her and was considerably impressed by the German technique.

The fjord was full of noise, direct and echoing, while the air thickened with smoke from guns and funnels, and the sea boiled and erupted with shell splashes. But now came noise, smoke and splash that awed even the British, when at 1259 the *Warspite* engaged her first target. The word thunder had been used to describe it, but what thunder can of itself dislodge snow from mountains as the 15in salvos did? The *Hermann Künne* was alerted by the huge splashes that rose like stalagmites around her, and then saw their mighty source through the haze-curtain that hung over the British destroyers; inexorable and inevitable finality was spelled out clearly for all to read in that dreadful moment, yet the Germans fought on.

Effective shooting from the *Warspite* at $10\frac{1}{2}$ miles range was far from easy; the ponderous equipment had been designed to engage an equally ponderous battleship that must maintain an approximately steady course between salvos, a straight-flying pheasant rather than a jinking snipe of a destroyer. The revolving mass of one twin turret weighed 750 tons, each gun 100 tons, and a shell nearly one ton, so that powerful hydraulic machinery was needed for every movement and operation. To load, a three-tiered cage rushed upwards from the depths behind the gaping maw of each breech, a huge chain uncurled itself to ram the shell firmly into the rifling and then withdrew; the cage shifted up a notch and the first half-charge was rammed, then the second; down went the cage, the breech closed, and the gun was free to return to its firing elevation. The maximum rate of fire of two rounds a minute may be thought remarkably fast under these conditions, but to a destroyer it gave time to dodge. Then there was the difficulty of shooting over the bow which resulted in the view from the director control tower being totally obscured by cordite smoke for 20 seconds after each shot. From that position above the bridge the guns were controlled, layed, trained and fired, enemy data was assessed and splashes spotted; the problems were thus formidable and the rate of fire was further reduced.

No ship on either side was hit during this opening phase, though records seem to indicate that the German gunnery was if anything the more accurate. But that was not the point; the British advance was unfaltering and relentless, whereas each leg of the Germans' zig-zags took them a pace backwards towards the wall through which there was no escape.

By 1300 the *Warspite* had passed Hamnesholm and was into the final straight. Ahead and to port the British formation remained as it had been, but McCoy had taken the starboard division ahead according to his signalled intentions. An additional motive for doing so may have been to deal with the *Erich Koellner* before she could be a danger to the *Warspite*, but he did not say so being a man of few words, at least on paper.

The *Erich Koellner*'s Last Fight

As the *Bedouin*, *Punjabi* and *Eskimo* neared Djupvik they ceased firing ahead and trained their guns and tubes to starboard; the aircraft circled, watching both sides. The point opened to reveal the *Bedouin* and *Erich Koellner* to each other at 1305, the *Punjabi* and *Eskimo* following at two minute intervals. There followed a horrible little massacre that was carried out efficiently by the British but gave them no satisfaction. Fregattenkapitän Schulze-Hinrichs and his skeleton crew might well have escaped to shore when they saw the hopelessness of the odds against them, but they fought back stubbornly,

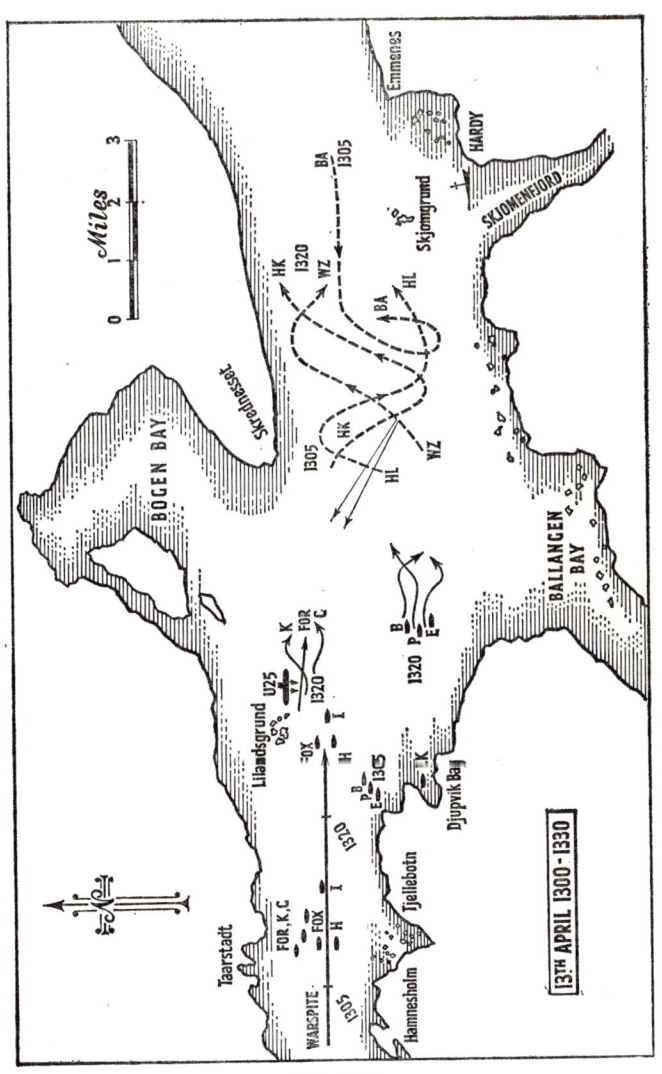

1300–1330

firing their two torpedoes, for a full ten minutes during which their ship was hit time and time again from a range of under a mile. The *Bedouin* fired a torpedo and the *Punjabi* and *Eskimo* two each, two if not three of which hit; but still one or two of the *Erich Koellner*'s after guns continued in action. Nevertheless McCoy was satisfied that he could safely leave her and did not slacken speed, continuing after the main enemy ahead; the *Icarus* and *Cossack* continued the engagement for a short time as they passed.

The *Erich Koellner* was wrecked and burning, and Schulze-Hinrichs sent most of the men ashore; but one gun could still fire and honour demanded that it should. Then the *Warspite* steamed across the bay and gave her two salvos of 15in, the force of which on striking made her heel visibly; they are thought not to have exploded, their base fuzes having been designed to trigger on a battleship's armour rather than a flimsy destroyer, but that should hardly have mattered. Nevertheless five minutes later a few men left on board were seen busy around the torpedo tubes and the *Warspite*'s Gunnery Officer was told to destroy her once and for all; he did so with four salvos and she slowly sank.

Was it worth it? The *Erich Koellner*'s sacrifice was 31 men killed and 39 wounded, and no British ship was scratched; but her honour was bright as was vouched for by the best of judges, her enemies. Bey's error lay in positioning her so far down the fjord, whether at Taarstad or Djupvik is immaterial, that she must inevitably engage on her own and not in concert with the mobile ships. He would have been wise to have given more weight to the principle of mutual support.

The Norwegians arrested the surviving Germans, but were kind to them. The *Hardy*'s survivors, still just over the hill from Djupvik, were not displeased at an enemy's misfortune in similar circumstances to their own; they sallied forth to appropriate an undamaged motor boat in which they were later able to make contact with their friends afloat.

Mounting Pressure

Meanwhile there was no let-up in the main fjord; the *Bernd von Arnim* had joined the fight and the *Wolfgang Zenker* had fired four torpedoes at the northern group of destroyers. These were sighted and reported by Brown in the aircraft and seen to pass clear on the *Warspite*'s port side to detonate on the shore, though not before the

Cossack had had to swerve to avoid one running on the surface. The latter now led her division forward on the port wing, and although she was still not so advanced as the *Bedouin*'s group, she was it seems the more heavily engaged of the two. The fjord had widened, and to confuse the German gunners both wings started to weave, though not sufficiently to bring their after guns to bear. The minesweepers still steamed slowly on a steady course and were more vulnerable; they were several times near-missed and the *Foxhound* even suffered a splinter casualty.

The *Warspite* engaged target after target, always ahead of her so that only the two forward turrets could fire, 'B' directly over 'A'. The latter's blast bags, loosely fitting canvas seals between gun and turret, were not man enough for the overpressure and blew off, so that the gunhouse filled with cordite fumes and earsplitting noise. Nevertheless Petty Officer Reardon and his crew carried out the drill impeccably, and with such self confidence that one member boiled a kettle on the electric radiator, lifting it with each fire-gong to prevent it being spilt.

The *U25*, waiting off Lilandsgrund, had ample time to prepare for her attack. Schütze had seen all the British destroyers, appreciated what they were doing and told his crew to be ready to join the battle. At 1319 he fired two torpedoes at the *Cossack*'s column from 800 yards, but of course nothing happened. Ten minutes later he came to periscope depth again and saw the *Warspite*, but too far south to reach; he realised that the German surface forces would be overwhelmed and that he could do nothing but sit there and watch. Rather than that he decided to make his way down the fjord, charge his batteries unobserved, and be ready for the British when they came out; at least the latter had no idea that he was there.

A Heinkel seaplane approached near enough to the *Warspite*'s stern to be engaged by her 4in AA guns. The shooting was ineffective, but the point was noted that if a reconnaissance aircraft could reach Narvik, so might a strike.

The German destroyers had zig-zagged their way back to Narvik by 1330, when the *Georg Thiele* at last joined them after herculean efforts in the engine-room, and frustrating manoeuvres with warps and springs between the wrecks because the port engine could not be used astern. The *Wolfgang Zenker* fired her last four torpedoes at the northern British group and one was seen to explode on the shore near Skrednesset. On the British side at this time the *Warspite* looked ahead from the *Erich Koellner* for a new target, and must have detected the *Bernd von Arnim* whom she straddled. The *Icarus* had reached the limit of her minesweeping task and dropped back to recover her sweeps. The *Cossack*, *Kimberley* and *Forester* weaved along the northern half of the fjord at moderate speed and without trying to overtake the southern group, in compliance with McCoy's signal. What the reasons for these orders were when they were given, or for conforming to them in the circumstances of 1330, cannot easily be fathomed. For the southern Tribals were racing ahead and attracting much of the German fire; the *Hermann Künne* fired all her torpedoes at them in two salvos, and the *Georg Thiele* also engaged them hotly with both types of weapon, as other German ships may also have done though their records are understandably imprecise.

McCoy's group was distinctly discomfited. As it approached the Skjomgrund shoal in rough line abreast, in order from north to south *Eskimo*, *Punjabi*, *Bedouin*, the latter received a damaging near-miss under her bow which splintered the hull and threw her No 1 gun up to its full elevation, whereupon the left barrel had a neat, 4.7in diameter gouge taken out of it by a shell from No 2 gun and was put out of action. That was not the *Bedouin*'s only near-miss, a bold alteration of course seemed to be indicated and McCoy took her south of the shoal. The *Punjabi* was also peppered and took the same avoiding action, though she did it even more drastically and found herself on the starboard wing. Pride of place thus passed to the *Eskimo* who now led the British force up the centre of the fjord, quite unscathed.

From 1340 to 1350 was a busy time for everyone except the *Hero* and *Foxhound* who were hauling their sweeps and had leisure to survey the extraordinary scene of seven destroyers weaving about in no sort of order, but pressing ever eastwards and firing continuously, while the *Warspite* steadily followed at ten knots and contributed the bass register to the cacophony. Biggs likened them once to a platoon of skirmishing infantry supported by a tank, and again to a huntsman with a pack of hounds in full cry, united relentless in a common purpose yet each achieving it in his own way. As Peters put it less poetically, 'The whole thing was a mess from start to finish but it didn't matter, they were all rugged individualists.' The Admiral never once gave an order or needed to; perhaps he felt as Nelson did: 'I had the happiness to command a band of brothers, each knew his duty and I was sure each would feel for an enemy ship.'

That ten minute period was climacteric for the five Germans in the fight who were already being pressed into Herjangsfjord; suddenly there was the wall, their backs were to it, and their ammunition was running low. There was no hope yet they fought well, as the British spontaneously acknowledged; and that was perhaps generous for it must be recalled that to them all Germans were barbaric huns, who with brutal savagery had gratuitously shattered the peace of the world and the integrity of defenceless small nations, and whose behaviour was not to be judged by civilised standards. Furthermore the British possessed the magic of the initiative, they were winning, their momentum rolled, and a personal, revengeful motive was evoked by the *Hardy*'s wreck which they were even then passing. That they were fighting fine professional naval officers and ratings like themselves was not a reflection to be expected at the height of battle; yet it is a tragedy of war that to be fit for the front line a man must be of high integrity, whatever he is fighting for. Where there is rottenness it is to be found in the rear.

The *Bernd von Arnim* made a bold dash to the southwest, then turned northeast and fired two triple salvos of torpedoes at the *Warspite* and the northern group of destroyers. Her aim was true for both the flagship and *Icarus* were endangered and the *Cossack* became the next on the now long list of ships to record one running underneath. By doing so Rechel had taken his ship nearest of all to the enemy and received the greatest volume of fire, but she emerged, miraculously, unharmed.

Air Strike

Then came the *Furious*'s ten Swordfish, led by Captain A. R. Burch Royal Marines, and punctual to the minute. They had had to struggle against snow squalls and a cloud base sometimes as low as 500 feet, but now they were able to climb to 2,000 feet and make what they could of the weaving, smoking ships below. Being sailors as well as airmen they identified their enemy correctly, selected their targets and dived their clumsy machines at them through streams of tracer, releasing their 250lb bombs at about 900 feet. It was a gallant effort, and although no hits were scored bombs fell very close to the *Hermann Künne* and *Bernd von Arnim*; so close to the latter that she bucked like a wild horse and threw Rechel off his balance, but no damage resulted. It seems that she, the *Georg Thiele*, and the *Erich Giese* in the harbour, all had a hand in shooting down the two aircraft

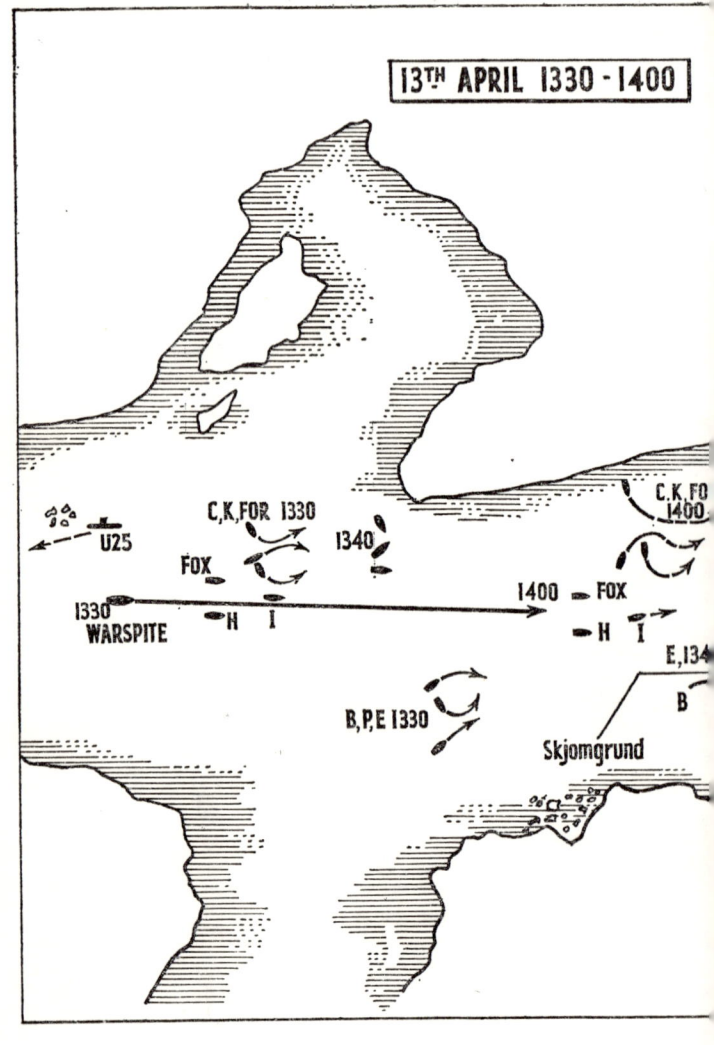

1330–1400

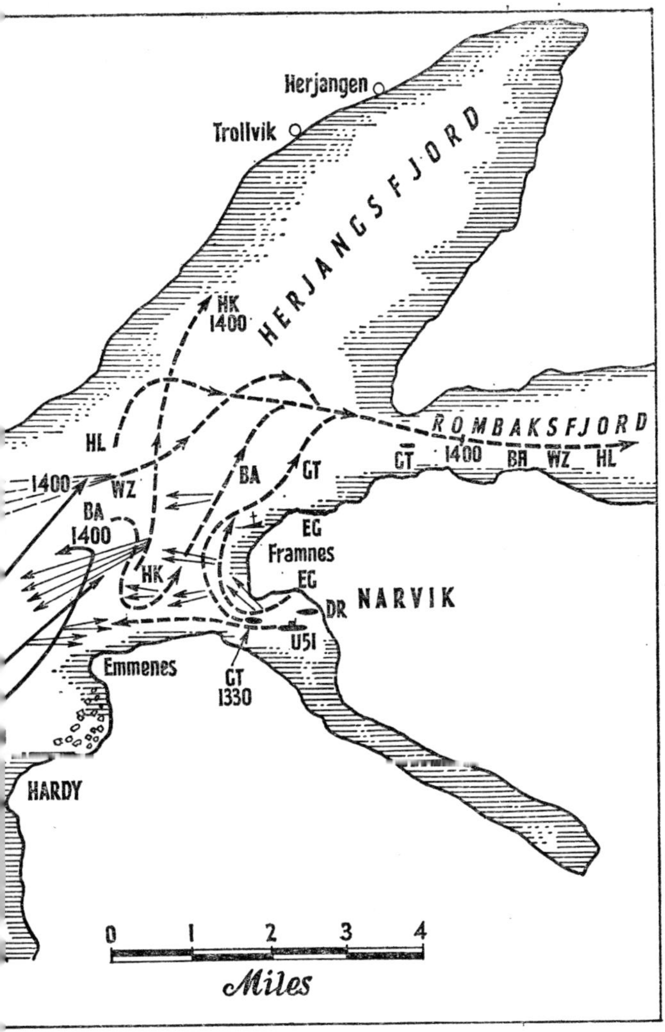
Herjangen
Trollvik
HERJANGSFJORD
HK
1400
ROMBAKSFJORD
HL
GT
1400
BA
WZ
HL
1400
WZ
BA
GT
BA
1400
EG
Framnes
HK
EG
NARVIK
DR
U51
Emmenes
GT
1330
HARDY
0 1 2 3 4
Miles

which were lost; one forced landed on the beach at Emmenes, watched by the *Punjabi*, and the crew was rescued later.

Technical Knock-out

The *Bernd von Arnim* made one more pass to the southward, and during it fired her last 12.7cm round. The *Wolfgang Zenker* too had no ammunition left; high explosive, starshell, practice, all had gone, and at 1350 Bey ordered his ships by voice radio to retire to Rombaksfjord where there might be some chance of destroying them and saving their crews.

So had the battle been effectively lost and won. For one hour and 20 minutes enemy ships had fired many hundreds of rounds at one another and, disregarding the *Erich Koellner* episode when the range was point-blank, not one single hit had been scored by either side. That was not the fault of anyone on the spot, for the weapon-systems were just not up to their designed task despite the research, development and money that had been lavished on them; and those ships were the élite of the two navies, built in peace and manned by highly trained regulars. Had those senior Gunnery Officers who controlled the Royal Navy and its policies fallen on their knees, before St Barbara* to seek forgiveness and guidance, who can doubt that that incendiary saint would have reminded them that her martyrdom was not in any way connected with a gun, but that any large explosion would please her equally well just so long as it landed on the target. Had the British Home Fleet contained more carriers than battleships, and had they been equipped with strike aircraft and weapons expressly designed to replace the gun as the Fleet's main offensive power, the two naval battles would hardly have been needed. And had the German establishment admitted to itself that destroyers' guns were virtually useless at ranges over 5,000 yards it would probably never have mounted the Narvik operation unless it could have found some means of providing local air power. The German torpedo failure was of course even more disastrous because it was one-sided.

Martyrdom of the *Erich Giese*

The tactical battle being over, the real fighting now began. At 1350 the *Erich Giese* was at last able to move astern from the *Jan Wellem* under her own power, but on approaching the harbour entrance the

* Patron Saint of Artillerists.

port engine failed and prevented her turning. The fjord seemed entirely filled with British ships, but of friends there was only the *Hermann Künne* and she was retreating rapidly up Herjangsfjord.

Was it really Smidt's duty to go out there, into the jaws of death? He thought so, without fanaticism but with cool, analytical courage:

'I could either destroy the ship in the harbour, in which case the crew would have been saved, or go out and fight. I was alone, I was the last, all the others had disappeared. It was a difficult question for me, but I considered that the proper duty of an officer and soldier is always to inflict as much damage on the enemy as possible for as long as he is able, and we had about ten minutes worth of ammunition and all torpedoes, so we could fight. But I had no hope that we should ever reach any port again.'

For 13 long minutes the *Erich Giese* lay stopped in the harbour mouth, but that did not prevent her from opening fire which she did the moment she saw a target, at 1352. The *Bedouin* and *Punjabi* approaching along the south shore, sighted the *Erich Giese* and *Diether von Roeder* at the same time and engaged; the opening range was 6,000 yards closing, and would soon reach that at which guns could, if well handled, begin to become effective. First however three of the ships fired torpedoes. The *Erich Giese* did so with the practical object of giving herself a respite, for no ship can afford to be hit by one and might well have to retire to avoid it. Unfortunately the Torpedo Officer selected as his target a ship on a northeasterly course which was probably the *Eskimo*, hot-foot after the *Hermann Künne* and no immediate menace. Worse, her high speed and crossing inclination produced on the calculator a large aim-off angle to the right, so that three torpedoes got no further than Framnes. The one that ran out of the harbour eventually overtook the *Eskimo*, who however had no difficulty in avoiding it.

The *Bedouin* fired three torpedoes and the *Punjabi* two, all they had left, and three of these almost certainly passed the *Erich Giese* without being seen and nearly hit the *Diether von Roeder* who was perturbed to see the Post Pier erupt about her. The ship heaved and most of her wires parted; but her gunnery was unimpaired and it seems probable that both German ships chose the *Punjabi*, who was nearest to them, as their target for the latter soon began to be hard hit. Firstly her fire control room was wrecked and the crew killed or wounded; the guns had to be switched to local control which must have reduced their accuracy and been a relief to the Germans. Then two shells hit forward almost simultaneously causing serious fires and more casualties; the fourth set an after storeroom fiercely alight so that No 4 magazine had to be flooded instantly, and the fifth detonated on the starboard motor boat abreast the after funnel, causing yet another fire and perforating a high-pressure steam-pipe in the engine-room; there were near-misses too, whose vicious splinters tore the side. It was a bloody few minutes, but Trevor Lean was not the man to give up while his guns could still fire, and indeed, the range having shortened to 3,000 yards, the 2pdr pom-pom joined in until its crew was killed or wounded by the fifth hit. The *Diether von Roeder* was hit too, twice, but aft where it did not matter.

Meanwhile the *Bedouin* had been engaging the *Erich Giese* without herself being fired at, and it seems that she hit her though not seriously. The *Warspite* also, after encouraging the German retreat into Rombaksfjord with her main armament, now had her attention drawn to the activity in the harbour and saw, not the *Erich Giese* but the *Diether von Roeder*'s gunflashes. These she took for a shore battery which in a sense they were, and engaged; the huge splashes drenched the ship and the ton-weight shells caused havoc around her and on the shore so that her Captain, peeping out of his tunnel, thought she must have gone down; but she suffered no damage and her two forward guns continued in action.

The *Erich Giese*'s port engine was made serviceable again at 1405, and Smidt's agony of decision was renewed for there was a strong argument in favour of remaining where he was. With the *Diether von Roeder*'s support he would stand the best chance of inflicting even more punishment on the enemy and then, when his ammunition ran out, he could slide his ship into the lee of Framnes to destroy her and save the crew unmolested. But he had made up his mind, and in such crises it is usually best not to change it; out of the harbour at her maximum speed of 12 knots came the *Erich Giese* to the slaughter—but she was no lamb.

Nearest of the British ships was the *Punjabi*, but now the *Bedouin* increased speed and closed determinedly; she hit the *Erich Giese* almost at once and then again and again. Nearly every British destroyer joined in whenever the range was clear; the *Warspite*'s 15in Control Officer had his binoculars fixed on the *Diether von Roeder*, but then saw the *Erich Giese* move into his field of view and shifted his point of aim to her. He hit her three times, but the Germans do not believe the shells exploded or the end would have come there and then. Telephone communication had ceased, so Smidt sent the Torpedo Officer aft to fire the four remaining torpedoes at any suitable target; the *Punjabi* was chosen, and in spite of many violent distractions his aim was true.

Lean, in spite of his many troubles, the latest of which was a message from the Engineer Officer that loss of steam would stop the ship very soon, saw the torpedoes just in time to hurl her to port with full helm and the port propeller at full astern. The torpedoes ran surfaced and were consequently dangerous, but the avoiding action had been timely and they passed clear up the starboard side. Belching smoke from three fires and listing with the turn, the *Punjabi* looked as though a torpedo had hit her and the German crew raised a cheer, even in their own extremity. Then they went on to hit her with a sixth shell which killed and wounded more men, including the Engineer Officer who was climbing the bridge ladders to report to the Captain. He struggled on, confirmed that the engines could not be kept going much longer, and collapsed. Lean, now perforce heading westwards, accepted with chagrin that he was temporarily beaten and continued in that direction away from the action. As he passed the *Warspite* he made to Whitworth:

'Am damned sorry, I have to come out of it= 1400'

The *Erich Giese*'s torpedoes pursued their northwesterly course and forced the *Cossack* to swerve to avoid them.

The *Bedouin* closed the range to as little as 1,000 yards, and as she closed her rate of hitting increased. Her Gunnery Officer, Ian Garnett, had trained his team well, and that probably contributed to her not being hit at all despite many splinter holes from near-misses. In the *Erich Giese*, stopped, without power, making water, with distorted structure and growing carnage, the guns miraculously survived and continued to fire until every round had gone; that is except three, for even after Smidt had at last decided that his duty was honourably done and ordered the ship to be abandoned, Gunnery Artificer Piening found them hidden and, with Ob Btsmt Gangelhoff, discharged them with stubborn defiance. German naval tradition could not have been better upheld and perpetuated, but the cost was 83 lives and many wounded.

The *U51* Opts Out

It was during this period that Knorr at last became seized with the imperative need to get away from the harbour. Nerve-racking as it was to find a way between the wrecks while submerged, his troubles increased outside for countless ships dashed in all directions at high speed, and torpedoes, with strident and bloodcurdling underwater racket, raced, it seemed, above, below and all around. Knorr was a very unhappy officer until he had made his way clear of the fighting, in which he found it impracticable to join, and found refuge in Ballangen Bay.

The *Hermann Künne*'s Turn

Four of the German destroyers were inside the Rombanksfjord by 1400 and the *Georg Thiele*, last to enter, covered their withdrawal effectively by leaving a line of smoke-floats on the water. Perhaps for that reason the *Hermann Künne*, who had missed Bey's signal, suddenly realised herself to be completely alone; on enquiring the ammunition state, Kothe was told that she was even then firing her last few rounds of practice shell. The British phalanx rolled on indomitably, spear-headed by the *Eskimo* whose Captain, Micklethwait, appreciated the German position perfectly and saw that the *Hermann Künne* must be his immediate objective; in doing so he precisely obeyed McCoy's order for the leading ships to go for any enemy in Herjangsfjord, wittingly or not as the case may be. Kothe's aim became to destroy his ship and save his crew; he fled, hotly pursued by the *Eskimo*, but there were no hits and when he drove the destroyer aground at Trollvik she was as immaculate as on the day she first commissioned the previous autumn, and none of her crew was scratched.

Seacocks were opened, demolition depth charges set and the ship was abandoned in a very short time, but before any explosion took place the *Eskimo* approached within 5,000 yards and fired a torpedo at 1413. There followed a great blast and smoke column, but from which source cannot be known; perhaps both achieved their purpose and symbolised an extraordinary unanimity between enemies who were equally determined to destroy the *Hermann Künne*.

The *Forester*, originally in the *Cossack*'s group, had zig-zagged to the north of Ofotfjord, and after engaging the *Erich Giese* in passing, Tancock considered he would be most useful with the *Eskimo* whom he followed in her chase after the *Hermann Künne*, firing a further two torpedoes. Then Micklethwait led the two ships towards Rombaksfjord where he had seen the enemy's main body disappear.

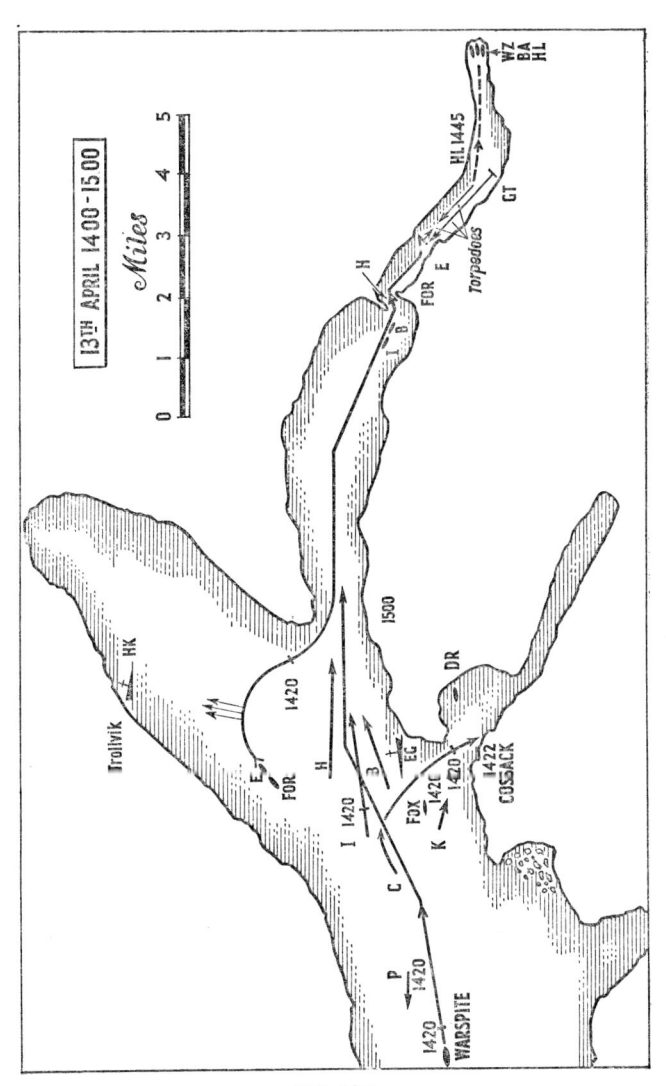

1400–1500

'Leave off Action? Now damn me if I do!' (Nelson)

The *Warspite*'s aircraft continued to circle and report the enemy's movements faithfully, a particularly valuable function being to give warning of approaching torpedoes which could be seen clearly from the air. At 1345 came the dreaded moment of leaving for Skjelfjord, but the damaged tailplane gave Brown a perfect excuse for turning the blind eye and there was no rebuke from below. At 1405 and 1410 he reported the *Diether von Roeder* alongside the Post Pier, so there should have been no reason for the *Warspite*'s Gunnery Officer continuing to think she was a shore battery when he engaged her again at 1412. This time the destroyer returned the battleship's fire directly with commendable cheek, watched by her Captain from the mouth of his tunnel until a near-by shell-burst indicated the prudence of retiring inside. The great bulk of a 15in shell often rendered it visible from its target and the sight, together with a roar like an express train, could be truly terrifying.

Duel in the Harbour

Admiral Whitworth had given his first tactical order:

'*Warspite* engage shore batteries at Narvik. Destroyers engage enemy destroyers = 1401'

This signal posed Sherbrooke of the *Cossack* a momentary problem. He had received the aircraft's report and knew there to be an enemy ship in the harbour which was the discretionary objective McCoy had given him as a rear ship. He could see the *Eskimo* and *Forester* racing ahead, and they were followed by the *Bedouin* who swept on past the *Erich Giese* when it became clear that the latter had been reduced to scrap. He decided, in spite of the Admiral's signal, that his duty lay in the harbour which he turned towards at 1415, ordering the *Kimberley* to follow.

As the *Cossack* passed close to the *Erich Giese*, Sherbrooke refrained from engaging for she was clearly finished and the crew were leaving her; two of her men were nearly run down accidentally, but such was their spirit that instead of crying for help they rounded on the *Cossack* with full-blooded Teutonic abuse. There followed several minutes of unaccustomed and pregnant silence as the *Cossack* fouled the *Warspite*'s range, compelling her to cease firing, and checked her own weapons which were then loaded and trained just clear of Framnes so that they would point at the *Diether von Roeder* the instant she came clear of the land. Sherbrooke now saw that the wrecks were formidable obstacles which would not allow an approach speed greater than 12 knots, and the tension on board mounted correspondingly as second after agonising second ticked slowly by. For once initiative conferred no advantage, nor was surprise a factor; this was to be a stand-up fight at 2,000 yards between an undamaged ship with eight guns and an immobile hulk with two, but resolution and determination were well matched.

The huntsman, having seen his hounds clear the main field of the quarry, now watched them transform themselves into terriers and gather round the several earths; he was pleased, and sounded his horn spontaneously:

'You are doing grand=1420'

Sighting was mutual and so were the first salvos, but the *Cossack*'s, despite the theoretically point-blank range, was a clean and disastrous miss short. There was no time to correct whatever mistake had been made before the *Diether von Roeder* hit her in the fire control room, necessitating the guns being switched to local control in highly distracting circumstances. More hits slammed home, the nose-fuzed German shells opening huge, four foot diameter holes in the *Cossack*'s side and sending jagged fragments tearing inwards to kill and wound men, wreck compartments, and perforate steam-pipes and hydraulic leads to guns and steering engine. It became terribly clear that the tactical factor which really mattered was the *Cossack*'s exposed beam as opposed to the *Diether von Roeder*'s narrow, end-on silhouette. The British guns fired rapidly and evidently scored some hits, though not near the two guns which was the only place that mattered.

The *Cossack* was hit seven times in two minutes at the end of which, without steam for the engines or control of the steering, but with nine men killed and 21 wounded, she had drifted past the *Blythmoor*'s wreck and joined the *Bockenheim* ashore on the strand of Ankenes. The battle then continued on more equal terms, for Sherbrooke, a subsequent VC, his First Lieutenant Peter Gretton who later led one of the most aggressive and successful Escort Groups in the Battle of the Atlantic, and his crew, were not the yielding sort. The end however was anticlimax, for the Germans soon fired their last available shell and then there was nothing for the 25 brave men who had caused all the trouble to do but leap for the jetty and race to the tunnel. Three remained on board to set two depth charges for demolition; but they did not touch them off, yet.

The *Cossack*'s fight had been over in such a very short time that the *Kimberley*, awkwardly placed initially, had been unable to join in the decisive phase; but she appeared in the entrance at 1422, the moment the *Cossack* grounded, and engaged the *Diether von Roeder* briefly until the latter ceased fire. The *Foxhound* too had lent a hand from outside until accumulating smoke obscured her vision. The *Kimberley* offered to tow the *Cossack* off the beach and out of harm's way, for although the Germans possessed no shore-mounted guns of any consequence, the British were not to know that and were extremely worried by her helpless and vulnerable situation. Sherbrooke however thought it best to have his ship's hull thoroughly examined before attempting to refloat her, to make quite sure that she would in fact float.

Valley of the Shadow

When Bey ordered his ships to retire into Rombaksfjord at 1350 they entered in the order in which their various zig-zags placed them at the time: *Hans Lüdemann*, *Wolfgang Zenker*, *Bernd von Arnim* and lastly, scattering smoke-floats to give a temporary respite, the *Georg Thiele*. They were all inside the outer Rombaksfjord by 1400 and steamed straight on up through the Straumen narrows into a veritable, crooked little finger of the sea.

Rombaken; 800 yards wide of deep, dark water, steep-sided to 1,000 feet of rock and scrub on which the snow could only lodge in patches; a place for trolls rather than humans, for it led to nowhere on earth and deterred intruders by its grimness; a place set aside by the god of war for arms to clash unsoftened by any kindly influence; a place where the only amenity was a narrow beach at the ultimate extremity, a mortuary slab where ships went to die.

There crept the *Wolfgang Zenker* and *Bernd von Arnim* straightaway; empty of ammunition, their crews' lives became their Captains' first priority, and soon the only men on board were those charged with destroying the ships before the enemy's arrival. To give them time the other two ships stood guard at the knuckle of the fjord whence they could see both ways and waited, utterly weary after a week's unremitting toil and trial, yet summoning their last reserves of strength and resolution for a final great endeavour which promised only to end many lives and offered no hope of victory.

The *Hans Lüdemann* retained four torpedoes and four guns, together with a limited supply of ammunition. She lay with her bows to the east, so that the three after guns and the torpedoes could fire down the fjord over the port quarter; and she was also well positioned to retreat to her final resting place when the time should come.

'And how can man die better than by facing fearful odds.'
(Macaulay)

Wolff placed the *Georg Thiele* athwart the fjord, facing the rocks of the south shore, in such a way that quick escape in action would be impossible but so that her four good guns and two torpedoes bore on the narrows. This was not the act of a fanatic but resulted from a coldly sober assessment of the classical advantage in defending a narrow pass against an enemy however superior in numbers, together with the very real likelihood it offered of allowing at least three crews to land unharmed. The alternative of allowing the British to pass the knuckle while evacuation was in train was even less pleasant for Wolff to contemplate than the complete destruction of his own ship which, without hope yet dutifully, he anticipated. He had seized all he could of the tactical initiative, and confirmed the impression he had given in the first battle of being a warrior in the very highest class.

'Full speed ahead and . . .'

Micklethwait of the *Eskimo* was of similar stature. Followed by the *Forester* he entered the outer Rombaksfjord at 1424 flying the signal, 'Enemy in sight ahead', which, though he could in fact see nothing through the German smoke, had the desired effect of inducing the *Hero*, *Bedouin* and *Icarus*, who were otherwise unoccupied, to follow him in that order. The smoke was so thick that the *Eskimo*'s speed had to be reduced to 15 knots, and she did not reach the narrows until 1445. Then, says Micklethwait:

'As the total destruction of the enemy could not be undertaken without running a certain amount of risk I proceeded straight through the narrow entrance, followed closely by the *Forester* and *Hero*, and accepted the risk of being torpedoed by a ship lying close to the entrance.'

Thus did an irresistible force encounter an immovable object.

At the moment of rounding the southern spit the *Eskimo* was alone against the two Germans who at once engaged. The range from the *Georg Thiele* was 5,000 yards which was known accurately from the chart, whereas the British had to find it in the normal painstaking way by rangefinder, trial and error. Nevertheless the German shooting was not good, the *Hans Lüdemann*'s guns being controlled from aft and the *Georg Thiele*'s fire control system having been irreparably damaged in the first battle. The opportunity, once allowed to slip, was not to be recovered for the *Eskimo*'s guns, under Lieutenant Duncan Ritchie, were very good indeed. He sighted first the *Hans Lüdemann* near the north shore and engaged her. Friedrichs took what was likely to be the last chance of firing his four torpedoes which sped accurately down the centre of the fjord, some surfaced, though the British could not yet see them. He was just in time, for very soon the after part of the ship was hit by one or two shells of a salvo which knocked out Nos 4 and 5 guns, killing or wounding their crews; since No 3 gun was also reported to him as having been damaged, he decided he could be of no further use and went ahead.

The *Forester* had pressed in as close to the *Eskimo* as Tancock could manoeuvre, yet the *Hans Lüdemann* was already further away than the *Georg Thiele* and soon vanished round the knuckle. Both British ships then closed the range to the one remaining enemy until it was down to 4,000 yards, and executed the sacrifice that Wolff had invited. The *Georg Thiele* was hit and hit again, yet it was a minor inconvenience of the British SAP shells that, bursting inside the target they could not always be seen to do so, and Micklethwait became impatient at the seeming lack of results from his guns and decided to fire his one remaining torpedo. He swung the ship to port with that intention just before the *Hans Lüdemann*'s four torpedoes were sighted approaching, and when they were he was already committed to the turn.

'... Damn the torpedoes!'

A master of the art of ship-handling, Micklethwait rang down for full ahead even though the ship was pointing at the north shore, only a short distance away. 44,000 horse-power, instantly developed, thrust her ahead of the tracks by a heart-flutter; then, accelerating fast and with the shore only 100 yards ahead, he reversed the engines and their braking effect was equally positive; shaking in every rivet she pulled up as the rocks vanished under the forecastle when viewed from the bridge, for her engine-room department was as efficient as her gunnery.

The *Forester* engaged continuously, and also fired a torpedo which does not seem to have hit though she thought it had. Then Biggs brought the *Hero* up, but when her fore part was through the entrance it did not seem to him as though there was enough room inside for three ships, so he stayed where he was, engaging with his foremost guns only. While there, a man in a rowing boat pulled over to the ship and asked the after guns' crews, "You sink the enemy?" "Yes," they replied. "Good!" he said. He was the schoolmaster and there, on the north shore, were the children skiing home.

The *Georg Thiele*, overwhelmed, fought on, and although her guns could claim no hits her enemies were distinctly reluctant to close and pass her. Two torpedoes remained, but one was tragically wasted when a man fell wounded on to the firing lever so that it ran wild and exploded on the shore; the other was the ship's last hope and the Torpedo Officer, Oberleutnant Sommer, stationed himself at the tube as Heppel had done in the *Hardy* and awaited his opportunity. As though ordained by a relenting fate there, suddenly, was the *Eskimo* beam-on and stopped, caught in a full ahead/full astern cycle from which there was no quick escape. Sommer fired, but must have groaned when the torpedo nosed and continued to run on the surface, indicating a depth-keeping fault and advertising its approach to the enemy. He could not yet know that he was lucky beyond belief; a submerged runner would almost certainly miss under the target, as one of the *Hans Lüdemann*'s was doing to the *Forester* at that very moment, wriggle as Tancock might. The *Georg Thiele*'s torpedo ran straight, that was the main thing, and because it was easily visible Sommer and his team watched its progress on tenterhooks, undistracted by the noise and carnage around them. Equally concerned, Brown circling overhead watched it too, and because he could not contact the *Eskimo* by radio, flashed, 'T–T–T–T', 'torpedo approaching!'

Micklethwait saw the torpedo at last but there was nothing he could do, for the ship was accelerating astern and any engine order would only have made matters worse. They were bad enough; the torpedo hit below No 1 gun and the bow collapsed from the stem to No 2 gun-deck, deprived of any structure to support it. No 1 gun vanished from sight, though it was still there hanging vertically from the upper deck now neatly folded downwards; the casualties can be imagined, few survived from the gun's crew and of course there was no chance for anyone in the magazine, shell-room, and the ammunition supply system below. 15 died at once, or were plunged into the water as the forecastle sank below them and were not recovered; ten were seriously wounded.

The *Hero* backed out through the narrows when the *Hans Lüdemann*'s torpedoes reached her, and Biggs watched them leap on to the low spit with their engines still running.

Heroics are conventional in such a narrative as this, and are often undeserved, overplayed, and make dull reading; but the *Eskimo*, *Georg Thiele* and their Captains were exceptional. It took the former's No 2 gun's crew precisely 30 seconds to shake themselves, look over their deck and wonder why there was water where there should have been ship, and fire the next round; Micklethwait, convinced that his ship would soon sink, continued the torpedo firing process by swinging her with a kick on the engines and the torpedo was duly fired when the sight came on, at 1452. It missed to the right.

The *Hero* now re-entered the fjord and the fight pressing in beyond the *Eskimo*, so that there was very little respite for the *Georg Thiele* who, with an anxious eye on her consorts which still seemed to be floating tantalisingly normally, fought on to the very end. Oberleutnant Fuchs, the Gunnery Officer, could still control his after group to some extent by telephone but had to shout over the front of the bridge to No 2 gun. Nos 3 and 4 fired irregularly as their ammunition hoists had been shot away and only the occasional round reached them. Then a hit near the bridge caused chaos and severe casualties both there and at No 2 gun; the Second-in-Command, Kapitänleutnant von Lepel, had just arrived to report the desperate state of the ship to his Captain and was mortally wounded, losing both legs and an arm. Fuchs was momentarily concussed but recovered himself, assessed the gunnery position and made his final report to Wolff, who received it prostrate and streaming with blood:

"Ich bekomme keine Munition mehr in die batterie."*

Heroics now would have been false ones. The wheel had turned full circle, for what the *Georg Thiele* had done to the *Hardy*'s bridge had now been done to hers. Himself wounded and virtually alone among the dead and unconscious, Wolff decided like Stanning to put his ship ashore and save what lives remained. Like him he gave the necessary orders and similarly there was no response, for the telegraphsman was dead, so he carried them out himself. Full ahead; and the remaining boilers delivered such a surge of power that the bow was lifted high over the narrow ledge at the waterside, while the forefoot crumpled inwards on the jagged rocks; the time was 1500.

* "I have no more ammunition for the guns."

Some men abandoned ship over the port side, and some lowered themselves from the forecastle directly on to dry land; meticulously Wolff ensured that all secret matter was sunk over the stern in deep water, as Stanning had done, and finally joined them. The ship was still being hit and more casualties were suffered on shore, but Wolff was astonished, like Stanning, to find so many of his people unharmed. Yet he had lost 14 men killed and 28 wounded as the price for delaying the British penetration. And delayed it was; so fierce and determined had been the *Georg Thiele*'s last fight that it seemed to deter the British even after her guns fell silent, and it was not until 40 minutes later that their first ship ventured round the knuckle.

And then there were None

The *Diether von Roeder* lay at the Post Pier silent and deserted, yet still in remarkably good shape as viewed from the *Cossack* and something would have to be done about her. In Narvik Harbour, Sherbrooke was indeed lord of all he surveyed, yet he was singularly ill-placed to exercise his sovereignty. At first he had an armed whaler lowered but then, wisely, thought better of the idea and ordered the *Foxhound* to enter and investigate.

Peters decided that this order was best obeyed by running alongside *Diether von Roeder*; 'Hands to boarding stations,' was piped and two groups of men appeared on the upper deck. The official party as detailed in the Watch and Quarter Bill was equipped by the Chief Gunner's Mate with rifles, pistols, cutlasses, webbing equipment and gaiters; Holtorf from his tunnel was particularly impressed by the gaiters, and who can blame him? The other collection resulted from the British sailor's uncontrollable urge to make a 'skylark' of any out of routine event, and tumbled up from below as swarthy, kerchiefed pirates with knives between their teeth.

As the *Foxhound* picked her way gingerly between the wrecks, her intention was amply clear to the Germans who realised that their last chance had come to inflict damage on the enemy, and Petty Officer Tietke in charge of the demolition squad was ordered to light the nine-minute delay fuzes to the two carefully placed depth charges. To Peters there was something sinister about this silent foe, not least the fact that, as he could now see, she appeared to be completely without blemish (all her damage in the first battle had been on the far, port side) and perfectly capable of rounding on him murderously. He ordered the teeming upper deck to be cleared, though that was not easily achieved, and then fired two or three 4.7in rounds which of course triggered no response.

Holtorf willed Peters to come on. He did so, but when the *Foxhound* was only 50 yards clear, Tietke and his two men jumped from their ship and ran for their lives, necessarily in full view. Peters stopped, and at once to Holtorf's dismay a hot rifle and machine-gun fire from houses along the waterfront raked the *Foxhound*'s decks, the soldiers and sailors responsible not having been told of the plot. The *Foxhound* was lucky to lose only one man killed, and also because, Peters immediately ordered full astern both to get clear of the firing and because it had quite convinced him that a trap was about to spring. The water churned, the ship gathered sternway, and then two colossal explosions rent the last of the German destroyers. When Peters' eyes had readjusted to normal after the blinding flashes and the smoke had drifted away, the *Diether von Roeder* was just not there.

So was the British aim achieved at 1520 on April 13th, 1940.

The Cease Fire

The game having been lost and won, the pieces left the board in various ways.

After the *Eskimo*'s torpedo hit and the *Georg Thiele*'s immolation, the *Warspite*'s aircraft sighted and reported the three German ships at the tip of the fjord, one of which lay at such an angle that her torpedo tubes bore down the waterway. Brown, no doubt wishing to jettison the bomb load before landing, asked permission to attack the ore railway; but that did not seem logical to the Admiral who ordered him to go for the destroyers. Brown told Rice who, surprisingly prudently, said, "Hang on a minute", when he saw that the width of the upper fjord was less than his turning circle, and that the only way to disengage after an attack would be upwards through the cloud; so that the problem of getting down again when blind promised to be hazardous if not impossible. They therefore had a shot at the already dead *Georg Thiele*, missed, and then landed alongside their ship in the outer Rombaksfjord on the very battlefield itself; surely a unique recovery.

Back on the bridge the aircrew astonished and delighted their seniors with the news of the *U64*'s sinking, and were congratulated on the whole of their four-hour flight. 'I doubt,' wrote the Admiral, 'if a ship-borne aircraft has ever been used to such good purpose'; and that record stood for a long time.

The *Warspite*'s great guns were sponged out and laid to rest, 'A' turret's crew proudly boasting of having fired 32 rounds from each barrel without a single delay or misfire. Caught with their blast bags off they were slightly groggy from 'B' turret's fumes and deafened by its noise, but were no doubt able to refresh themselves at last with a nice hot cup of tea. They in turn had wreaked havoc on the forecastle, their guns having been nearly horizontal in the final stages at close range. The deck was like a switchback, and damage below was pungently evident for many waste-pipes in the ship's company's heads were fractured—but perhaps the less said about the heads the better.

The whole gunnery system worked well, but it is not easy to understand why armour-piercing shells were used against destroyers throughout the action, assuming that thin-walled, high-explosive ones with instantaneous nose fuzes were on board, as they usually were; a hit by one of these on a lightly built destroyer would have been as catastrophic as a torpedo. Perhaps the spectre of armoured German cruisers was the cause.

From 1500, when the *Warspite* stopped in the outer Rombaksfjord, the Admiral awaited news from above the narrows with increasing impatience, but none came. For all he knew the three German ships at the end were prepared to sell their lives as dearly as had the *Georg Thiele*, but the *Hero*, *Forester*, *Bedouin* and *Icarus* were on the spot and presumably doing something about them without orders, as had been the hallmark of the British destroyers' behaviour until then. However their momentum had flagged since the *Eskimo*'s hit. At first she herself was an anxiety and the *Forester* stood by her, but then Micklethwait found that he could move her slowly astern; he eventually negotiated the narrows with great difficulty, pulling a great mass of tortured steel through the water from which an anchor had clearly let itself go for the ship twice pulled up short. As she was passed by other ships entering her crew cheered them on mightily as though, said Maud of the *Icarus*, she had just won the fleet regatta. Then McCoy considered whether to lead a final head-on assault, or whether there might be a less drastic solution to the problem such as indirect bombardment with aircraft spotting as had in fact been mooted in the *Warspite*. Nothing therefore happened.

The Admiral indicated his wishes fairly clearly at 1515, by ordering all available destroyers into Rombaksfjord. That produced the *Kimberley*; the *Punjabi* had already rejoined as enthusiastic as ever, with two boilers, three gun-mountings and all fires out. McCoy turned his problem over to his Admiral:

'One enemy aground out of action, two more round the corner out of sight. If they have torpedoes they are in a position of great advantage. *Hero*, *Bedouin* ammunition almost exhausted, *Bedouin*'s 'A' mounting out of action=1520'

He received no acknowledgement until 1535 when he was ordered to close to visual touch immediately and told privately but peremptorily:

'The torpedo menace must be accepted. Enemy must be destroyed without delay. Take *Kimberley*, *Forester*, *Hero*, *Punjabi* under your orders and organise attack sending most serviceable destroyers first. Ram or board if necessary=1545'

However, while the *Bedouin* was away with the Admiral, Biggs of the *Hero* decided to take matters into his own hands and led the *Icarus* and *Kimberley* round the last daunting bend, to a most satisfying anticlimax.

Up the Creek

That the three German destroyers who were the cause of this British concern had exacted such respect from their enemies must be to their, and Wolff's, great credit; but of course they had no means of fighting left in them. They had run their bows on to the narrow beach and landed the bulk of their ships' companies without difficulty, but demolition did not go smoothly and needed all and more of the time won by the *Georg Thiele*. The *Bernd von Arnim* in the centre was the first to finish; with her seacocks open, demolition charges exploded internally, and depth charges released over the stern, she took a list of 40° to starboard which increased until, at 1520, she keeled over beyond the horizontal. Her stern sank, but her bow rose piteously as though she strove to crawl the last few yards to shore.

On the north side the *Wolfgang Zenker* withdrew a little from the beach into deeper water, but similar demolition expedients had worryingly little effect. More and more depth charges were released, and finally three together which shook the ship violently and must have been dangerously uncomfortable for Bey and his small team; worse, they were still at it when the British arrived and opened fire.

They jumped into the motor boat whose engine providentially started, and it can be imagined with what relief they realised that they had done their work thoroughly when their ship turned right over at 1545, also watched by Biggs.

To the south the *Hans Lüdemann* grounded in unexpectedly shallow water and became firmly fixed. The same demolition measures were taken, and in addition a depth charge was positioned in the fire control room; when the fuze to this was lit the Captain and scuttling party abandoned the ship, but it seems unlikely that it exploded of a photograph taken later would hardly have showed a seemingly intact destroyer. When the British arrived she still looked menacing and they put several salvos into her, until it became quite clear that she had no fight left; then the *Hero* and *Icarus* sent armed whalers and boarded her. Ashes from a bonfire of secret documents were found on the bridge, a fire burnt aft, water rose slowly in the engine-room, and it was noticed that several 4.7in SAP shells had passed through the ship's structure without exploding. A badly wounded man lay hidden from his shipmates and was carefully moved to the *Hero*, but he could not be saved.

The *Hans Lüdemann* did not seem to be very firmly aground, and Biggs and Maud were keen to tow her away as a prize. The boarding party had taken the first step of hoisting the White Ensign above the Swastika, but then the *Bedouin* arrived and McCoy, urged by the Admiral to haste in view of threatening air attack, ordered her to be destroyed, and that was done by the *Hero* with a well-placed torpedo.

The British ships turned westward, and the silence of the tomb descended on Rombaken, grimmer even than before.

The Narvik Area

Peters took the *Foxhound* across the harbour to the *Cossack* and offered to tow her off, for she seemed to him to be stuck in a most unhealthy position. Sherbrooke however was not yet ready, though gratefully accepting the *Foxhound*'s doctor, and Peters left the harbour to pick up survivors from the *Erich Giese* as the Admiral had already ordered him to do. Most of those who were destined to reach land, after a nightmare swim of half a mile in ice-cold water that tested their endurance to the very limit, had done so. Many had perished, but the *Foxhound*'s whaler managed to intercept one raft before it reached the shore because it had no paddles and could move but slowly. Two officers and nine men were recovered, and when they

had been dried, warmed and plied with hot drinks, one of them—
'a very decent Pomeranian' as Peters thought of sufficient interest to
record—confided that there were U-Boats in the fjord. This Peters
reported, and taking the news seriously he established an anti-
submarine patrol to seaward of the *Warspite*.

The *Cossack* stayed firmly on Ankenes, shoring-up, tending
wounded and repairing damage, but feeling lonely and exposed.
The Germans ashore racked their brains for a means of getting at
her and their propaganda, making the best of a very bad job and
smarting from her earlier cutting out of the *Altmark*, anticipated
success. Mrs Sherbrooke recalls a disquieting broadcast by 'Lord
Haw-Haw':

'We said we would get the *Cossack* and we have. She is lying a
blazing wreck in Narvik Harbour and her Captain is dead on the
bridge.'

All that could be brought to bear however was a small weapon,
Gretton thought it was a howitzer or field gun though it seems more
likely to have been a heavy mortar, which opened fire deliberately
from somewhere up the mountain at 1700. Three shots fell at
diminishing distances, but when Gretton replied with a 4.7 they
ceased.

Oh, Sorry!

Also somewhat unnerving was a torpedo that had been fired by the
Hero at the *Erich Giese* by order of the Admiral. Having bypassed
its target it then narrowly missed the *Cossack* and exploded on the
beach near by, fortunately for her and perhaps also for Commander
Biggs.

Exeunt

The long anticipated air strike arrived, but on seeing the mass of
British warships dared not press home an attack. This diversion was
probably the reason for the *Erich Giese* being left afloat, burning,
listing and pitiable. She sank of her own accord in the early hours
of the next morning.

The Admiral did not withdraw the *Warspite* immediately the battle
was won, because the possibility of landing a force of Royal Marines
and seamen to seize the town while the Germans were demoralised
became suddenly very real. Sherbrooke of the grounded *Cossack*
urged it strongly. Whitworth decided against it, but although much

controversy had been generated by his decision it is not relevant to this narrative of the naval battles. The Admiral was given a task which he carried out to the letter, and there the matter will be allowed to rest.

On the other hand, the activities of the Warspite and the U-Boats after the surface battle are very relevant. At 1755 the Admiral had settled the question of landing and took his flagship westwards at 17 knots; at first he had only the *Foxhound* as antisubmarine protection, but soon the *Bedouin*, *Hero* and *Icarus* also joined. German aircraft were still in the area but did not attack the battleship, going for the *Ivanhoe* instead; the latter was quite alone, engaged in recovering the *Hardy*'s survivors and Captain Evans's merchant seamen, having entered the fjord after the main body to be of general use, but even so the bombing was half-hearted and did not trouble her.

Sherbrooke felt even more lonely on seeing this general exodus of his friends, particularly in view of the air raid warning he had been sent, and burnt his secret books; but the Admiral had not forgotten to leave him a helpmate, the *Kimberley*, while the *Punjabi* and *Forester* stood by the other cripple, *Eskimo*.

The *U51* was nursing her last supply of breatheable air in Ballangen Bay and saw nothing; but the *U25* had been making her way down Ofotfjord with the express object of catching the British on their way out, and did so in the narrows off Tjellebotn at 1840. Schütze was confident that he had penetrated the screen but the *Foxhound* had gained contact and Peters, made thoroughly U-Boat conscious by his Pomeranian, was certain the echo came from a submarine and counter attacked instantly. The depth charges exploded close alongside a matter of seconds before Schütze would have fired; the boat was shaken, minor damage was suffered and the attack thwarted. The Admiral signalled politely to the *Foxhound*:

'Hope you got it, thanks for your protection=1848' but whether he was really convinced that this was a U-Boat and a serious threat to the battleship must be doubted in view of his subsequent movements.

Schütze sought temporary refuge in a small bay, but half an hour later sighted a single destroyer, probably the *Ivanhoe*, and attacked her from 1,500 yards. He modestly admitted that his torpedo missed, but it was of course quite likely to have malfunctioned. The time would shortly come when the Germans would realise their torpedoes' shortcomings, but it had not yet done so. The *U25* then lay in

Tjellebotn Bay charging her batteries, and was spotted by the lighthouse keeper. Further down the fjord the *U46* was also waiting and duly sighted the force, but she was not favourably placed to attack.

When the *Warspite* was safely past Tranoy into the Vestfjord, the Admiral suddenly decided to return to Narvik and reversed course at 2050. This move seems so extraordinary that it is a pity his motives were not fully recorded, but it appears that they were largely chivalrous. He had left the *Cossack* aground in an enemy harbour, the *Eskimo* devastated and possibly sinking, and the *Punjabi* badly damaged, all with casualties who would be best cared for by the battleship's extensive sick berth facilities. He presumably hoped to be away again before air attack threatened in the morning, and he clearly apprehended no danger from submarines.

Although the *U46* had surfaced and was proceeding up Ofotfjord to try and find out what had happened at Narvik, she did not sight the *Warspite* returning. The *U25* did, and efficient and aggressive as ever Schütze took a quick surfaced shot from his charging position in Tjellebotn. He thought that the torpedo detonated short of the target on a shallow, and then that he was counter attacked, though the British record nothing. He stayed on the bottom where he was all the next day, afraid to move; the whole experience must have been dreadfully disheartening.*

All went well for the British. The *Kimberley* had tried to pull the *Cossack* off the shore in the evening, but she held fast and the wire parted. At 0300 on the 14th however, when the tide rose, she floated clear with only her own engines, and was found to be reasonably seaworthy and controllable if steamed stern first. She transferred her wounded to the *Warspite* and then made her way to Skjelfjord. The *Eskimo* overcame her difficulties most manfully and also reached sanctuary, in tow of the *Bedouin*.

That evening Skjelfjord harboured no fewer than five badly damaged British ships, the *Hotspur*, *Penelope*, *Eskimo*, *Cossack* and *Punjabi*. The German *Alster*, whom the British were surprised but delighted to find contained butter as well as armaments, was still there and was pressed into service, her heavy derricks being ideally suited for hoisting out the *Eskimo*'s forward gun mountings to lighten her for what, even so, promised to be a very chancy ocean passage. But it was the Lofoten islanders who helped the most, all available repair facilities and hospitals being put at British disposal,

* The *U25*'s last attack is not well documented.

and earned their guests' profound and lasting gratitude. Respect was indeed mutual, and when the ships left to fight again another day, which they were all eventually enabled to do, the Norwegians had learnt enough of the British spirit to be assured that they would one day come back, however long that might take.

When the *Warspite* took her second and final departure she was watched by the *U51* from Ballangen Bay but not attacked. The *U25* still lay bottomed at Tjellebotn and saw nothing. The *U46* started to attack two stopped destroyers, which may have been the *Bedouin* and *Eskimo* engaged in passing a tow, but then became aware of five more, probably the *Warspite*'s screen, and evaded. These three boats were understandably tired and dispirited, but the *U48* was comparatively fresh and Schülze, undeterred by his previous encounter with *Eskimo* and the rest, managed to penetrate the screen again, this time undetected. The position was southwest of Tranoy where the fjord was wide enough for the *Warspite* to zig-zag, and as luck would have it she turned just as Schülze was on the point of firing his four bow tubes. He managed to get off his stern torpedo at the battleship on her new course, but the track-angle was too fine. That was the last shot in the two naval battles of Narvik, the British having four times run a most hazardous gauntlet of which, fortunately for their peace of mind, they were entirely unaware.

CHAPTER SEVEN

Afterthoughts

Was the first battle necessary and who won it? Clearly it was less than necessary for the Germans, but did Warburton-Lee have to go in immediately and before there was any certain intelligence of the enemy? The advantages he seized by exploiting initiative and surprise have already been discussed but those were not reasons for fighting a battle. The answer depends on the British aim and that was never very clearly defined; certainly it was recognised that Narvik had to be recaptured from the moment the Germans were thought to be there, but Warburton-Lee could only have done that with his five platoons of sailors if there had proved to be negligible opposition from professional soldiers.

However the German destroyers were surely proper targets in themselves; in the first place because they were there, and might break out and escape; and in the second because they might stay and form part of a strong deterrent to a future assault, together with U-Boats, mines, shore batteries and above all a locally based air force. The Germans' intention was of course to break out, and their chances would have been good had their logistic plans matured. They would have done so that very night and, though the imagination reels at the thought of an encounter in the snow-shrouded narrows, it must therefore have been right to attack. If the British did not win, the Germans most certainly lost for after the first battle their aim was no longer possible of achievement. Perhaps there is no need to say any more on this topic than that Captain Warburton-Lee followed faithfully and very courageously in the Nelsonic tradition:

'No Captain can do wrong if he places his ship alongside that of an enemy.'

It is similarly unnecessary to labour the matter of Warburton-Lee's reinforcement, so clearly desirable now, so obscure then; but Heppel's and Ecclesiastes' precepts are apposite:

'Never fire torpedoes in penny numbers.'

'Whatsoever thy hand findeth to do, do it with thy might.'

Whether the British tactical aim in the second battle was well chosen is a matter of some interest. The strategic objective of the recapture of Narvik had been decided upon, and the German naval and military strength was known accurately enough for practical purposes; yet the problem of whether to combine a landing with the naval assault was not so easy of solution as much previous criticism has held. Unless it had proved practicable to tranship the Fleet's Royal Marines at sea, as it may well have done in those days before jackstay transfers were normal practice, several days would have elapsed before the main military force arrived. Always undesirable, delay could have been expected to allow the Germans to be reinforced with aircraft and submarines, and to refit their destroyers. Hindsight however highlights two important arguments in favour of a landing which were unforeseen before the battle. Firstly, the German troops reasonably thought they would be instantly attacked and largely abandoned the town; and secondly, the addition of the destroyer crews more than doubled General Dietl's force. He wrote: 'The carrying out of my task of holding Narvik was, I can openly say, only possible with the employment of such a strong naval force ashore.'

Further hindsight reveals, however, that when the British military force did arrive, its transports were not tactically stowed, and the General would not land until all was sorted out. It can be presumed that he would have been even more reluctant to commit his ill-equipped men to an assault as part, or hard on the heels of a naval battle. The reader must decide for himself whether landing should have been incorporated in the aim.

Was it right to send the *Warspite* in? The stark facts of the narrative say no; yet it is only fair to hear the other argument as told by the First Lord of the Admiralty, Mr Churchill, to the House of Commons:

'The craven and inept authorities at the Admiralty (laughter) took the risk and were very much relieved to find that there were no special traps of one kind or another in the fjords. . . . What would have been said if she had been sunk? "Who was the madman who sent one of our most valuable ships into congested waters where she could easily fall a prey?" If you dare and fail it is murder of your sailors. If you are prudent you are craven, cowardly, inept and timid.'

The risk was greater than anyone thought, but in war a course of action can only be called correct in the light of its results, for there are many too many factors in every situation for the human brain to apprehend beforehand. Logically the Germans should not have been able to seize and hold Narvik without air power, or Warburton-Lee to immobilise ten large destroyers with five small ones; yet both were done and the *Warspite* survived. Let the last word go to Admirals Micklethwait, Wolff and Captain Wright, all of whom said to me in nearly the same words: "Battles are for fighting." They practised what they preached (no hint of disrespect to the other Captains is remotely implied) and it seemed to work very well.

'For want of a nail—the battle was lost.' A lesson for all ages is to send fighting men into action with weapons that work. No development can be too thorough, no trials too exhaustive, to ensure that in those vital, fleeting moments when great issues are decided the means are worthy of the task. Capabilities and limitations must also be accurately known through actual performance, and never allowed to be exaggerated by enthusiastic proponents or to advance the status of some corps or service.

Finally, know your enemy. Whether differences in attitude between the British and German fighting sailors were inherent in the two races is a question for a psychologist, but observing that German soldiers are not noted for holding back when the odds are even or better, which is what their sailors tended to do in this and other battles, perhaps other causes should be sought. Since the reunification of Germany her fleet had been overshadowed by the Royal Navy, being always in a position of strategic and often of tactical inferiority. With good reason she expected to be beaten at sea, and consequently this often happened even when the tactical circumstances were not unfavourable, so that a tradition seems to have arisen which advocated caution in getting embroiled in a fight, but demanded resolute, not to say sacrificial resistance when cornered.

In the naval museum at Wilhelmshaven the highest honour is accorded to Captains who went down with their ships; the *Anton Schmitt* was named after a rating in the light cruiser *Frauenlob* at the Battle of Heligoland Bight, 1914, who, with the rest of the crew dead around him, continued to serve his gun until the ship sank.

Such deeds are certainly revered in the Royal Navy, but greater honour is reserved for those who achieve great results; Nelson is a national hero because he won his battles, not for the manner of his death; Dunkirk was an astonishing and gallant achievement, very properly enshrined in tradition, but no Briton is likely to be persuaded thereby that it was anything but a resounding defeat.

By contrast, great glory was given to the German destroyers at Narvik after their annihilation; a special medal was struck and replacement destroyers were known as the *Narvik* class. Fregattenkapitän Bey was promoted to Kommodore Destroyers and later to Admiral, when he went down with the *Scharnhorst* after the sort of indecisive performance that should have been expected had his abilities been objectively assessed after Narvik. He has been described as an impressive man and an excellent officer, whose main interest was technical; he had bad luck to be given the wrong employment, and perhaps that came about partly as the result of a slightly unbalanced tradition.

This theory may be strengthened by the fact that U-Boat Command in two Battles of the Atlantic was by no means strategically inferior, and its Captains behaved quite differently, taking every opportunity to attack. Now in 1973 when the world scene has changed, super-powers dominate the strategic horizon and freedom is overshadowed by the greatest threat it has ever known, the Royal and German Navies are only of account as two of many allies. It is devoutly to be hoped that the former's men will retain that will to win and their impudent belief in their ability to do so that has taken them and the cause of freedom so far; and that the latter, having embraced the same just cause, may expand in spirit as an equal. We can both take some comfort from one factor at least, that the Russian Navy, for all its massive strength, has no inspiring tradition at all.

APPENDIX 1

Ships and Senior Officers

British

Admiralty
First Lord, Rt Hon Winston Churchill.
First Sea Lord, Admiral of the Fleet Sir Dudley Pound KCB.

Home Fleet
Commander-in-Chief, Admiral Sir Charles Forbes KCB DSO.
Battlecruiser Squadron, Vice Admiral Jock Whitworth DSO (Short Title BC1).

Ships—First Battle
Hardy Captain B. A. W. Warburton-Lee, and Captain (D) 2nd Destroyer Flotilla (Short Title D2).
Flotilla Leader, 1,505 tons, completed 1936.
Complement 175. (It may be confidently assumed that the number of men actually borne exceeded the recorded complement in all ships.)
$337\frac{1}{2}$ by 34 by $8\frac{3}{4}$ feet.
Two shaft geared turbines, 3 boilers = 38,000hp = 36 knots trial speed. Service speed was about 31–32 knots.

Guns
Five 4.7in MkIX Quick-firing on MkXVI Mountings, single. 45 calibre, muzzle velocity 2,650ft/sec, hand operated, weight of shot 50 lbs, elevation 30° to 10° depression, ten rounds per minute, maximum range 16,900 yards (effective range was a fraction of this).
Eight 0.5in machine guns, AA in twin mountings.

Torpedoes
Eight Mark IX in quad mountings. (See Appendix 2.)

Hotspur   Commander H. F. N. Layman.
Hostile   Commander J. P. Wright.
Havock   Commander R. E. Courage.
Hunter   Lieutenant Commander L. de Villiers.
'H' Class destroyers, 1,340 tons, completed 1936/7.
Complement 145.
323 by $32\frac{1}{4}$ by $8\frac{1}{2}$ feet.
Two shaft geared turbines, three boilers = 34,000hp = $35\frac{1}{2}$ knots trial speed.
Four 4.7in guns. Other weapon details similar to *Hardy*.

Second Battle

Warspite   Captain V. A. C. Crutchley VC DSO. Flag of Vice Admiral Whitworth.
Queen Elizabeth Class battleship, 30,6000 tons, completed 1913.
Complement 1,124.
$639\frac{3}{4}$ by 104 by $30\frac{3}{4}$ feet.
Four shaft geared turbines, 80,000hp = 24 knots.
Armour: belt 4-13in, Decks $1\frac{1}{4}$-4in, Turrets 5-13in.
Guns
Eight 15in Mark I in twin turrets. 42 calibre, muzzle velocity 2,400ft/sec, hydraulically operated, weight of shot 1,920lbs, force of recoil 400 tons, elevation 30° to 5° depression, two rounds per minute, maximum range 32,200 yards.
Eight 6in mounted in the ship's sides.
Eight 4in AA.
Aircraft
Two hangars and athwartships catapult. Up to three Swordfish floatplanes or Walrus amphibious flying boats could be carried.

Bedouin   Commander J. A. McCoy.
Punjabi   Commander J. T. Lean.
Eskimo   Commander St J. A. Micklethwait.
Cossack   Commander R. St V. Sherbrooke.
Tribal Class destroyers, 1,959 tons, completed 1937/8.
Complement 190.
$377\frac{1}{2}$ by $36\frac{1}{2}$ by 13 feet.
Two shaft geared turbines, 3 boilers = 44,000hp = 36 knots trial speed.

Guns
Eight 4.7in Mark XII QF, on CP Mark XIX twin mountings. Hydraulically operated for laying, training and part-loading, muzzle velocity 2,650ft/sec, weight of shot 50lbs, elevation 40° to 10° depression, 10 rounds per minute. (A rate of fire of 8 rounds per minute was maintained by the *Bedouin* for a prolonged period.) This was an excellent system within the limits of the gunnery of 1940. Whereas exercises were carried out at 8,000 yards and over, effective hitting was not achieved in action at more than 4–5,000 yards.
Four-barrelled 2pdr multiple pom-pom AA.
Eight 0.5in machine guns in quad mountings, AA.
Torpedoes
Four MarkIX in quad mountings.

Hero Commander H. W. Biggs.
'H' Class destroyer.

Forester Lieutenant Commander E. B. Tancock.
Foxhound Lieutenant Commander G. H. Peters.
'F' Class destroyers, 1,350 tons, completed 1934.
Complement 145.
329 by $33\frac{1}{4}$ by $8\frac{3}{4}$ feet.
Two shaft geared turbines, 3 boilers=36,000hp=$35\frac{1}{2}$ knots trial speed.
Armament similar to 'H' Class.

Kimberley Lieutenant Commander R. G. K. Knowling.
'K' Class destroyer, 1,690 tons, completed 1939.
Complement 183.
$356\frac{1}{2}$ by $35\frac{3}{4}$ by 12 feet.
Two shaft geared turbines, two boilers=40,000hp=36 knots trial speed.
Guns
Six 4.7in similar to *Tribal* Class.
Four-barrelled multiple pom-pom AA.
Eight machine guns AA.
Torpedoes
Ten MarkIX in quin mountings.

Icarus Lieutenant Commander C. D. Maud.

'I' Class destroyer, 1,370 tons, completed 1936.
Complement 145.
323 by $32\frac{1}{4}$ by $8\frac{1}{2}$ feet.
3 boilers = 34,000hp = 36 knots trial speed. Two shaft geared turbines.
Armament for this operation, two 4.7in guns similar to 'H' Class, eight machine guns, and no torpedoes.

German

Commander-in-Chief German Navy, Grossadmiral Raeder.
Commander-in-Chief Fleet, Admiral Marschall.
Marinegruppenkommando West (Group West), at Wilhelmshaven, Admiral Saalwechter.
U-Boat Command, at Wilhelmshaven, Admiral Dönitz.
Senior Officer Afloat, Vice Admiral Lütjens in the *Gneisenau*.
Senior Officer Narvik Destroyer Force, Kommodore F. Bonte in the *Wilhelm Heidkamp*.
Senior Officer 4th Destroyer Flotilla, in *Wolfgang Zenker*, with *Bernd von Arnim*, *Erich Giese*, *Erich Koellner*, Fregattenkapitän E. Bey.
Senior Officer 3rd Destroyer Flotilla, in *Hans Lüdemann*, with *Hermann Künne*, *Diether von Roeder*, *Anton Schmitt*, Fregattenkapitän H-J. Gadow.
Senior Officer 1st Destroyer Flotilla, in *Georg Thiele*, Fregattenkapitän F. Berger.

Wilhelm Heidkamp	Korvettenkapitän H. Erdmenger.
Hans Lüdemann	Korvettenkapitän H. Friedrichs.
Hermann Künne	Korvettenkapitän Kothe.
Diether von Roeder	Korvettenkapitän E. Holtorf.
Anton Schmitt	Korvettenkapitän F. Böhme.

Diether von Roeder Class destroyers, 2,400 tons, completed 1939.
Complement 313.
384 by $38\frac{1}{2}$ by $9\frac{1}{2}$ feet.
Two shaft geared turbines, 6 boilers (of varying sizes) = 70,000hp = 38 knots trial speed.

Guns
Five 12.7cm (5in) single all handworked mountings, weight of shell $61\frac{1}{2}$lb, 10 rounds per gun per minute could be maintained for prolonged periods. Ammunition supply arrangements and the small allowance of 100 rounds per gun were criticised.

Six 3.7cm AA automatic; two twin, two single mountings. Twelve 20mm AA automatic; five twin, two single mountings. Both types of close range weapon performed extremely well and were most effective against aircraft and ships.
Torpedoes
Eight 21in Mark G7a in quad mountings. (See Appendix 2.)

Erich Koellner   Fregattenkapitän A. Schulze-Hinrichs.
Georg Thiele   Korvettenkapitän M-E Wolff.
Wolfgang Zenker   Korvettenkapitän G. Pönitz.
Bernd von Arnim   Korvettenkapitän C. Rechel.
Erich Giese   Korvettenkapitän K. Smidt.

Leberecht Maass Class destroyers, 2,2pp tons, completed 1937/8.
Complement 315.
374 by 37 by $9\frac{1}{2}$ feet.
Machinery, performance and armament were similar to the *Diether von Roeder* Class, except that four 3.7cm and six 20mm guns were carried.

U25 Korvettenkapitän Schütze.
Type IA, 862/983 tons, completed about 1935. This boat was one of the training flotilla pressed into operational service for the Norwegian campaign.
Complement 43.
$237\frac{1}{2}$ by $20\frac{1}{4}$ by 14 feet.
Two shaft diesel/electric = 2,800/1,000hp = $17\frac{3}{4}/8\frac{1}{4}$ knots.
Torpedoes
14; the main weapon was the G7e (electric) but some G7a (internal combustion) were usually carried as well. (See Appendix 2.)
Four bow, two stern tubes.
Guns
One 10.5cm (4.1in), one 20mm AA.

U46 Kapitänleutnant Sohler.
U48 Kapitänleutnant Schultze.
U51 Kapitänleutnant Knorr.
Type VIIB, 753/857 tons, completed 1938.
Complement 44.
218 by $20\frac{1}{4}$ by $15\frac{1}{2}$ feet.

Two shaft diesel/electric = 2,800/750hp = $17\frac{1}{4}$/8 knots.
Torpedoes
12; four bow, one stern tubes.
Guns
One 88mm (3.5in), one 20mm AA.

U64   Kapitänleutnant Schulz.
Type IXB, 1,051/1,178 tons. She was brand new and had her trials curtailed to take part in the Norwegian Operation.
Complement 48.
251 by $22\frac{1}{4}$ by 15 feet.
Two shaft diesel/electric = 4,400/1,000hp = $18\frac{1}{4}$/$7\frac{1}{4}$ knots.
Torpedoes
22; four bow, two stern tubes.
Guns
One 10.5cm, one 37mm, one 20mm.

Norwegian

Norge   Captain Askim.
Eidsvold   Captain Willoch.
Coast Defence Ships, 4,166 tons, completed 1900.
Complement 270.
301 by $50\frac{1}{2}$ by 18 feet.
15 knots.
Armour: 6in belt, 2in deck, 8in turrets.
Guns
Two 8.2in, six 5.9in, eight 3in, two 3pdr AA.

APPENDIX 2

Weapons

Torpedoes (See photo section)

Précis of German Staff Memorandum written in May 1940
'Torpedo failures during the Norwegian campaign have completely nullified the extremely favourable chances of success presented to our U-Boats. The decisively important employment of the U-Boat weapon achieved no success *at all*; the weapon failed. The facts show that if we had had a serviceable torpedo the events at Narvik could have developed very differently; the battles of April 10th and 13th, which led to the loss of ten of our modern destroyers could even have ended in a clear defeat of the enemy and with a much heavier loss to his fighting strength. One cannot at this stage assess how many U-Boats and their courageous crews were lost because torpedo failures not only robbed them of success but exposed them to pursuit. The failure of the torpedo weapon can only be described as a catastrophe.'

Analysis of Torpedo Failures between April 9th and 13th

When the above *cri de coeur* on behalf of the U-Boats is set alongside the known failures of the destroyers' torpedoes, the conclusion that the British might have been defeated, at any rate on the 10th, is seen to be not greatly exaggerated. And had the 2nd Destroyer Flotilla been annihilated the British must have thought twice about initiating the second battle, particularly because there would have been little or no intelligence from Narvik of how they had met their fate or the composition of the enemy.

Date	Firing Ship	Target	Results and Remarks
9th	BA	Norge	5 missed before two hit. One ran *under* a merchant ship drawing 7m when the torpedo was set to 2m.
10th	DR	2nd DF	Torpedoes ran *under* Hardy (2 or 3), *Havock* (1), *Hunter* (possibly 1); 2 ran on beach without exploding.
	HL	2nd DF	1 ran *under* Hostile; 1 or more ran surfaced.
	GT or BA	2nd DF	1 ran surfaced.
	U25	Bedouin, Eskimo	3 magnetic and 1 impact fired, depth set 5m. Two detonations within 100 yards of targets; evidently failure of magnetic pistols.
11th	U51	'H' Class destroyer	Range 600m; torpedo detonated 100m short of target. The CO, Knorr was 'furious, it should have been a certain hit'.
13th	WZ	Cossack	1 ran surfaced.
	BA	Cossack	1 ran *under*.
	HL	Eskimo, Forester	1 ran *under* Forester. 3 ran on spit without exploding.
	GT	Eskimo	1 ran surfaced at less than set speed; hit and exploded.

Only incidents where German torpedoes certainly, or almost certainly failed have been included in the above table. That they may have done so on more occasions will be clear from the narrative, but since the U-Boats' torpedoes were trackless there is no evidence from target ships of their running under.

There were three main causes of failure:

Magnetic Pistols

Theoretically simple to design and highly desirable for the greatly increased effect of a completely tamped explosion below the target, the practical snags to such a pistol were almost insuperable as the British also found. Movement of the torpedo in the earth's magnetic field (particularly in high latitudes), changes in the magnetism of the torpedo, and even the closing of relay contacts by vibration, could trigger the fuze at any time after the safety range had been run off. All these were discovered by the British through extensive trials, but the Germans had not done so to the same extent and certainly not in high latitudes. It is possible that they were inhibited by the need to keep their torpedo development completely secret. The British never used their magnetic pistol, knowing it to be unreliable.

Depth Keeping

Because magnetic pistols were to be used and torpedoes would normally be set to run under their targets, insufficient pains had been taken to ensure that the depth control gear functioned accurately. It certainly did not, causing torpedoes to run either surfaced or very deep. So although it was decided in the destroyers (and later in the U-Boats) not to rely on the magnetic pistol but to set torpedoes to run to hit, this could not be achieved and the only torpedo dangerous to a destroyer was a surfaced one.

Impact Pistols

Of less moment than the two major faults, the German torpedoes were nevertheless further handicapped by this pistol needing a very broad angle of strike to trigger. This was illustrated by the many torpedoes which ran up beaches without exploding.

Good Points

The German torpedoes advanced control system and the ability to 'angle' individual torpedoes at the last moment thus obviating the need to swing the ship to fire, were of course nullified by the faults.

British Torpedoes

The Mark IX destroyer torpedo emerged from a prolonged and very thorough development and trials period to become one of the most satisfactory weapons ever produced. No failures were reported in either battle, and a great number hit with drastic effect. So reliable was this simple, rugged torpedo that the submarine version was still in service in the Royal Navy until the 1970s.

Statistics

	British	German	
Mark	IX	G7a—Destroyer	G7e—U-Boat
Propulsion	Internal Combustion	Internal Combustion	Electric
Speed/Range (knots/yards)	35/11,000 30/14,000	40/8,200 30/13,700	30/5,000
Warhead (lbs)	750	660	660
Diameter (ins)	21	21	21

Gunnery

Notes on the British Destroyers' Fire Control System

In the director Control Tower above the bridge sat the Control Officer, the Rate Officer who was responsible for assessing the course and speed of the enemy, and the Director Layer and Trainer who kept their telescopes permanently sighted on the target. Above and abaft the DCT was the rangefinder. Data from all these was transmitted or telephoned to the Transmitting Station (referred to as the Fire Control Room in the narrative as being more descriptive) where it was transformed semi-automatically into gun bearing and elevation, and transmitted electrically to pointers at the guns. The Gun Layers and Trainers moved their weapons so as to bring their mechanical pointers into line with the electrical. When each gun was 'on' and loaded, a firing circuit switch was made and Gun Ready Lamps burned in the FCR and Director. When the former's crew was satisfied that the calculation was correct and spotting corrections applied, the Fire-Gong was rung. The guns could then be fired simultaneously by the Director Layer, usually a very experienced Chief or Petty Officer because it was a business of great skill.

Spotting was the concern of the Control Officer. Until a splash fell in line with the target it was impossible to tell whether it was over or short. To 'find' the target salvos were fired in groups of three, each with an arbitrary correction, first for line, and then in 'ladders' of 400 yard steps for range. Having bracketed the target, rapid salvos (half the armament) would be ordered if the range was long, or rapid broadsides if short.

The battleship system was no different in principle.

The German System

This was similar both in principle and in many details, except that the director was in the form of a pedestal around which stood the control officers and ratings, each with his own angled sight. A singular refinement was the firing switch in the form of a bulb, held between the teeth and actuated by biting.

APPENDIX 3

Casualties

Figures were not fully recorded by either side, but the numbers of dead are believed to be accurate except where indicated.

Ship	Dead	Wounded	Ship	Dead	Wounded
April 9th					
Eidsvold	262 approx.	?			
Norge	173 approx.	?			
April 10th					
Hunter	108	?	Wilhelm Heidkamp	81	?
Hotspur	20 approx.	25	Anton Schmitt	63	?
Hardy	19	12+	Georg Thiele	15	23
Hostile	Nil	Nil	Diether von Roeder	13	?
Havock	Nil	Nil	Hans Lüdemann	2	?
			Bernd von Arnim	2	?
			Hermann Künne		
			Wolfgang Zenker	Nil	Nil
			Erich Koellner		
			Erich Giese		
Total Dead	147		Total Dead	176	

Ship	Dead	Wounded	Ship	Dead	Wounded
April 13th					
Eskimo	15	10+	*Erich Giese*	83	Many, 9 captured.
Punjabi	14	28	*Erich Koellner*	31	40
Cossack	11	19	*Georg Thiele*	14	28
Foxhound	1	?	*U64*	12	
Forester		2	*Hans Lüdemann*	?	(casualties at Nos 4 & 5 guns)
Kimberley		1			
Warspite			*Wolfgang Zenker*		
Bedouin			*Hermann Künne*	Nil	Nil
Hero			*Bernd von Arnim*		
Icarus			*Diether von Roeder*		
Furious		The number of aircrew lost on 12th and 13th is not known.			
Total Dead	41		*Total Dead*	140+	

Overall Total   Norwegian 435: German 316+: British 188.

Bibliography

The War at Sea, S. W. Roskill. HMSO
Narvik, D. Macintyre. Pan
Die Deutsche Besetzung von Danemark und Norwegen 1940, W. Hubatsch. Musterschmidt
Admiral Dönitz Memoirs, Dönitz. Weidenfeld & Nicholson
Marine Rundschau 1972/8, H. Dehnert.
The Norwegian Campaign of 1940, J. L. Moulton. Eyre & Spottiswoode
Narvik, F. O. Busch. Bertelsmann
The Campaign in Norway, T. K. Derry. HMSO
Struggle for the Sea, G. Adm Raeder. William Kimber
Convoy Escort Commander, P. Gretton.
HMS Warspite, S. W. Roskill. Collins
The Tribals, Martin Brice. Ian Allan
Chronik des Seekrieges, J. Rohwer. Ian Allan
German Warships of World War II, J. C. Taylor. Ian Allan
The Mountains Wait, T. Broch. Michael Joseph
Winston is Back, A. Harder. Longman
Marder, Churchill & The Admiralty, S. W. Roskill. RYSI Journal, Dec. 1972

Index

Aachen, German ore-carrier: sunk 74

Abnett, Ordnance Artificer *Havock*: 91

Admiralty: 22, 25, 27, 29, 30, 41, 92, 98, takes charge of first attack 42–47, 54–56, second attack 100, 104, 108, 117, *Penelope* replies to 105, 106, Whitworth complains to 105

Air attacks, British: 108–111, 113, 121, 133

Air attacks, German: 100, 114, 129, 152

Air power: 13, 17, 100, 108, 110, 156, 158

Alster, German supply ship: 19, 20, sails 21, non-arrival 40, 92, 98, capture 105, 154

Altmark, German fleet auxiliary: 14, 152

Altona, German ore-carrier: sunk 74

Ankenes (Narvik harbour): *Bockenheim* grounds on 39, 52, 103, *Cossack* grounds on 141, 152, map 59

Anton Schmitt (*AS*), German destroyer: 18, 99, 163, rough weather 23, lands troops 36, on patrol 52, anchors 56, 60, sighted from *Hardy* 61, hit 63, sunk 64, 65, wreck 65, 74

AS—see *Anton Schmitt*

Asdic: use for navigation 54, 55, 57

Askim, Captain, CO *Norge* q.v.

'B', Force, British in 2nd Battle: 112, 118

BA—see *Bernd von Arnim*

Ballangen (Ofotfjord): German destroyers disperse to 51, 52, 76, 113, 116, 121, British survivors cared for at 102, 103, *U51* at 138, 153, 155, map 53

Bardu Foss, airfield: 101

Baroy Island (entrance to Ofotfjord): Germans pass 34, 36, *U25* patrols off 51, 54, 93, 98, 105, 2nd DF passes 54, *Rauenfels* passes 93, supposed fortification of 99, 106, 113, 116, 120, Force 'B' passes 119, 120, 123, map 53

Batteries—see Shore batteries

Battlecruiser action: 34–36, 41, map 26

BC1—see Whitworth

Bedouin, British destroyer: 47, 97, 140, 167, 172, with *Repulse* 51, attacked by *U25* 99, 104, patrolling 105–106, second battle 112, 118, 119, engages *HK* 124, engages *EK* 126–128, near-missed 132, engages *EG* and *DR* 135–137, enters Rombaksfjord 143, 149–151, leaves 153, tows *Eskimo* 154, 155, particulars 161

Beisfjord (Narvik harbour): 60, map 59

Bergen: 16, 41, 100, map 15

Berger, Fregattenkapitän, SO 1st DF: 18, 163

N.—M 173

Bernd von Arnim (BA), German destroyer: 18, 163, 167, 171–172, weather damage 23, action with *Glowworm* 24, first into Narvik 36–39, at Ballangen 52, 1st battle 76–89, damage to 100, 115, sails for 2nd battle 124, in Ofotfjord 128–134, enters Rombaksfjord 142, scuttled 142, 150, particulars 164

Bey (pronounced 'buy'), Fregattenkapitän E., SO 4th DF: 18, 128, surprises D2 74, first action in Ofotfjord 75–77, 82, 88–91, breaks off action 91–92, 95, assumes command 75–76, 99, break-out attempt 101, 103–104, 107, co-operation with U-Boats 106, order of battle 114–116, receives warning of attack 117, orders ship to sail 121, 124, orders retirement 134, 138, 142, scuttles *WZ* 150–151, subsequent career 159, 163

Biggs, Commander H. W., CO *Hero* q.v.

Birmingham, British cruiser: 22, 42

Blythmoor, British ore-carrier: 141, anchored in harbour entrance 39, 60, rounded by British 61, 63, 65, sunk 67, wreck of 73, map 59

Bockenheim, German ore-carrier: scuttles 39, wreck of 52, 60, 74, 141, map 59

Bodo: 106, map 45

Bogen Bay (Ofotfjord): 52, 121, map 53

Böhme, Frau: 40, 64

Böhme, Korvettenkapitän F., CO *Anton Schmitt* q.v.

Bonte, Kommodore F., SO German destroyers: 17, 18, leads into Vestfjord 32, enters Ofotfjord 34, arrives Narvik 36, sinks *Eidsvold* 37, appreciates situation 40, 50–52, asleep 60, killed 62, 76, errors of judgement 92, 95, success 95

Break-out of German destroyers: plan 16, difficulties 40, 101, attempt 103–104, further attempt impracticable 107

British Lady, fleet tanker: 118

Broch, T., Mayor of Narvik: 38, 39, 66

Brown, Lieutenant Commander W. L. M., Observer of *Warspite*'s aircraft q.v.

Bud, minefield off: 20, 29, map 15

Burch, Captain A. R., RM, *Furious*: leads air strike April 13th 133

Burfield, Lieutenant J. B., *Havock* torpedo control officer: 88, 90, sinks *AS* etc. 64, fires at *GT* 79, boards *Rauenfels* 93

Christiansen, Mrs: shelters *Hardy*'s survivors 102

Churchill, W. S., First Lord of the Admiralty: 160, initiates mine-laying operation 14, influence on operations 43, apologia 157

Clark, Lieutenant E. K. U. MVO, *Hardy*, flotilla gunnery officer: 44, 75

Communications, British tactical: bridge to bridge W/T 49, 123, 124, 145, insecurity of 55, 56, 57, air reconnaissance wave 120

Communications, German interception of British: 50–51, 55, 103, 117

Communications, German tactical: alarm signal 71, 75–76, 134, 138

Communications, U-Boats: 19, 106

Cope, Leading Seaman C., *Hardy*: 61, 62, 72

Cossack, British destroyer: 112, 128, 167, 172, leads port column 119, 132, engages 124, endangered by torpedoes 129, 133, 137, enters harbour and engages *DR* 140, aground 141–142, 147, 151–152, 154, particulars 161

Courage, Mrs Irene: 40

174

Courage, Lieutenant Commander R. E., CO *Havock* q.v.
Cripples Creek, Skjelfjord q.v.
Cross, Lieutenant C. P. W., *Hardy*, flotilla signal officer: 44
Cruisers, German, thought to be at Narvik: 75, 92, 98, 104, 111, 114, 149
Crutchley, Captain V. A. C., VC, DSC: CO *Warspite* q.v.
Currie, Commander R. A., *Renown* and *Warspite* staff officer operations to BC1: 34, 119

D2—Captain (D) 2nd British DF—see Warburton-Lee
Denmark, occupation planned: 14, 22
de Villiers, Lieutenant Commander L.: CO *Hunter* q.v.
DF—Destroyer Flotilla
Diether von Roeder (DR), German destroyer: 18, 36, 52, 140, 163, 167, 171–172, on patrol 56–58, anchors 60, engaged by 2nd DF 61, 62, 65–68, fires torpedoes 68–70, damaged 70, 99, as immobile battery 107, de-equipped 107, 111, 115, 2nd battle 135–136, duel with *Cossack* 140–142, abandoned 141, sets trap for *Foxhound* 147, blows up 148, particulars 163
Diether von Roeder Class, German destroyers: 17, 23, particulars 163
Dietl, General, German Army Commander at Narvik: 37, 51–52, 62, 123, lands 39, lack of supplies 40, need for air force 100–101, need for sailors to augment land force 107, 157
Djupvik Bay (Ofotfjord): 91, *EK* hides in 124, 126–128
Dönitz, Admiral Commanding U-Boats: plans 18, 19, 163, reinforces U-Boat force 98
DR—see *Diether von Roeder*

Eidsvold, Norwegian Coast Defence Ship: 56, 95, 171, by-passed by *BA* 37, sunk 37, 51, particulars 165
818 Squadron Fleet Air Arm: attacks 109, 110–111
EG—see *Erich Giese*
EK—see *Erich Koellner*
Elvegaardsmoen (Herjangsfjord): fall of 36, map 53
Emmenes (Obotfjord): 103, 134, 2nd DF's landfall at 58, map 53
Erdmenger, Korvettenkapitän H., CO *Wilhelm Heidkamp* q.v.
Erich Giese (EG), German destroyer: 18, 109, 133, 138, 140, 163, 171–172, loses touch on passage 24, 28–29, 32, 36, arrives 39, in Herjangsfjord 52, 56, engages 2nd DF 74, fires torpedoes 90, 91, 135, 137, low in fuel 74, 100, break-out attempt 101, 103–104, engine defect 115, 124, last fight 134–137, survivors 151, wreck sinks 152, particulars 164
Erich Koellner (EK), German destroyer: 18, 132, 134, 163, 171–172, in Herjangsfjord 52, engages 2nd DF 74, 91, 100, grounds 107–108, as immobile battery 115, sighted by aircraft 121, arrives Djupvik Bay 124, last fight 126–128, particulars 164
Esk, British destroyer: 20
Eskimo, British destroyer: 47, 112, 138, 167, 171, with *Repulse* 31, attacked by *U25* 99, 104, patrolling 105, tows *Penelope* 106, attacks *U48* 118, in starboard column 118, 119, engages *EK* 126–128, leads British force 132, chases *HK* 135, fight in Rombaksfjord 138, 143–146, 148, limps away 149, 153–155, particulars 161
Evans, Captain C., Master SS *North Cornwall*: 39, on board *Jan Wellem* 40, watches action 65, 70–71, 73, abandons ship 73,

175

escapes with British seamen 102–103, 153

First German Destroyer Flotilla: 18, 163

Forbes, Admiral Sir Charles, KCB, DSO, C-in-C Home Fleet: 43, 47, 92, 105, 108, 118, 160, efforts to intercept enemy 22, 25, 28, 29, 30, orders 2nd DF to Narvik 41, orders patrols 98, moves north 100, concentrates against Narvik 109, orders 2nd attack 112–114, 116

Forester, British destroyer: 112, 153, 167, 172, in port column 118, 132, follows *Eskimo* 138, in Rombaksfjord 143–145, 149–150, particulars 162

Foxhound, British destroyer: 112, 142, 172, as minesweeper 118, 125, 129, 132, in Narvik harbour 147–148, 151, picks up survivors 151, counter-attacks *U25* 153, particulars 162

Fourth German Destroyer Flotilla: 18, to Herjangsfjord 36, 52, action in Ofotfjord April 10th 74–91, 163

Framnes (Narvik): 38, battery on 43, 57, 58, 66, 73, 74, 135, 140, map 52

Freilinghaus, German ore-carrier: sunk 74

Friedrichs, Korvettenkapitän H., CO *Hans Ludemann* q.v.

Fuel, German shortage of: 40, 50, 101

Fuchs, Oberleutnant, *GT* GO: 78, 146

Furious, British aircraft carrier: with C-in-C 104, and see Air attacks, British

Gadow, Fregattenkapitän H-J., SO 3rd DF: 18, 163, sights *Glowworm* 24, organises patrols 52, 56

Gangelhoff, Oberbootsmaat, *EG* 137

Gardner, Lieutenant Commander H. H., *Furious*, CO 616 Sqn: 110

Garnett, Lieutenant I. G. H., *Bedouin* GO: 137

Georg Thiele (GT), German destroyer: 18, 148, 149, 163, 167, 171–172, arrives Narvik 36, 39, at Ballangen 52, attacks 2nd DF 76–90, damage to 100, 107, 115, 124, joins 2nd battle 129–133, enters Rombaksfjord 138, 142, last fight 142–147, particulars 164

German Force, main: 16–18, on passage 22–31

German Fleet: strategic inferiority 23, 100, 117, 158–159, possibility of Atlantic break-out 13, 16, 25, 28, 31

Gurkha, British destroyer: sunk 100

Glowworm, British destroyer: 42, on *Renown*'s screen 20, parts company 21–22, last fight 24–25, 28

Gneisenau, German battlecruiser: voyage north 16, 18, 31, 33, action with *Renown* 34–36, return to Germany 108, 163

Gordon-Smith, Lieutenant Commander R. C., *Hardy* Flotilla NO: 44, pilots flotilla to Narvik 54–58, rescued by Heppel 102

Gretton, Lieutenant P. W., DSC, *Cossack* 1st Lt: 141, 152

Greyhound, British destroyer: with *Renown* 20, 22, 25, 27, 42

Group West (Marinegruppenkommandowest), German HQ at Wilhelmshaven: 163, in command of naval operations 17, 51, 100, presses Bey to break out 101, 103, 107, warns of second attack 117

GT—see *Georg Thiele*

Gunnery: ineffective at medium ranges 24, 74, 110, 134, other aspects 35, 125–126, 149, 169–170

Hamnes/Hamnesholm (Ofotfjord):
no batteries at 36, passed by 2nd
DF 55, 56, 93, by Force 'B' 124
126, map 53

Hans Lüdemann (HL), German
destroyer: 18, 163, 167, 171–172,
rough weather 23, engages
Glowworm 24, at Narvik 36,
52, 60, action in harbour 65–71,
fires torpedoes 73, 77, damage to
65, 79, 99, 114, action in
Ofotfjord, April 13th 121, 124,
enters Rombaksfjord 142, fires
torpedoes 144–146, hit 144,
end of 151, particulars 163

Hardy, British flotilla leader: 113,
128, 133, 146, 167, 171, escort to
minelayers 20, battlecruiser
action 35–36, operation orders
48, passage to Ofotfjord 52–58,
action in harbour 60–62, action
outside harbour 66–69, third
attack 73, action in Ofotfjord
74–81, beached at Virek 90, 91,
101–102, boarded by HK 101,
refloats and grounds in
Skjomenfjord 103, 104,
survivors recovered 153,
particulars 160

Havock, British destroyer: 97, 167,
171, escorts minelayers 20,
operation orders 48, avoids land
55, waits 58, enters harbour
63–66, action outside harbour
66–70, third attack 73, action in
Ofotfjord 74, 77–79, leads line,
turns back 82, close action
86–88, rescues Hotspur 90–91,
deals with Rauenfels 93–94,
particulars 161

Hein Hoyer German ore-carrier:
sunk 74

Heppel, Lieutenant G. R., Hardy
Flotilla TO: 50, 72, 157, lands
at Tranoy 43–44, 58, torpedo
control problems 57, 60, fires
torpedoes 61, 62, 90, concurs in
beaching of Hardy 81, re-boards
Hardy 102

Herjangsfjord (Ofotfjord): 4th DF
arrives at 36, dispersal anchorage
51, 52, action in 74, British plans
113, 119, U64 in 114, 121,
Germans pressed into 133, 135,
138, map 53

Hermann Künne (HK), German
destroyer: 18, 163, 171–172, on
patrol 52, action in harbour
60–65, 68, 73, 79, state of readiness
100, 114, boards Hardy 101, 103,
escorts EK 117, sighted by
aircraft and sights British 120,
action in Ofotfjord 124–125, 132,
133, 135, beached and blown up
138, particulars 163

Hero, British destroyer: 172, lays
dummy minefield 20, 29, rescues
aircrew 110, operation orders
112, as minesweeper 118, 120,
125, 132, enters Rombaksfjord
143–146, 149, 150, leads up fjord
150, captures HL and sinks her
151, misses EG 152, particulars
162

Hipper, German heavy cruiser: 34
destined for Trondheim 18,
action with Glowworm 24–25,
British attempts to intercept 25,
28, 31, sighted by Hostile 42

Hitler: 14, 17, 22, 92

HK—see Hermann Künne

HL—see Hans Lüdemann

Holtorf, Korvettenkapitan E., CO
Diether von Roeder q.v.

Home Fleet: task to prevent German
break-out 13, 16, sails 22,
signals intercepted by enemy 50,
103, bombed 100, concentrates
against Narvik 108, lack of
aircraft carriers 134

Hostile, British destroyer: 69, 167,
171, sights Hipper 42, joins
Repulse 42, joins D2 44,
operation orders 48, loses touch
52, 56, rejoins 57, covering
patrol 58, 66, engages DR
66–68, third attack 72–74, 77,
rejoins flotilla 79, action in

Ofotfjord 80–88, rescues *Hotspur* 90–91, 95, to Skjelfjord 97, particulars 161

Hotspur, British destroyer: 92, 93, 95, 97, 171, escorts minelayers 20, sights *Renown* 29, battle-cruiser action 35, sights *Repulse* 42, operation orders 48, passage to Narvik 52, 55, 57, covering patrol 58, 66, action in harbour entrance 67–69, third attack 73, action in Ofotfjord 74, 79, 82–83, 86, hit 87, collides with *Hunter* 87, in peril 88–90, escapes 90–91, in Skjelfjord 97, 105, 154, particulars 161

Hughes-Hallett, Commander C. C., Staff Officer Operations to C-in-C: drafts orders for 2nd battle 112

Hunter, British destroyer: 167, 171, escorts minelayers 20, operation orders 48, passage to Narvik 55, 58, action in harbour 62–63, action outside harbour 66–71, third attack 73, action in Ofotfjord 74, 79, hit 82–86, rammed by *Hotspur* 87–88, sinks 91–92, particulars 161

Icarus, British destroyer: as minelayer 20, captures *Alster* 105, as minesweeper 112, 118, in action 124–133, enters Rombaksfjord 143, 150–151, captures HL 151, screens *Warspite* 153, 172, particulars 162

Iceland: possible German objective 28

Impulsive, British destroyer: as minelayer 20

Iron ore: strategic importance 13–14, 27, 41

Initiative, value in war: 51, 95–96, 156

Ivanhoe, British destroyer: as minelayer 20, attacked from air, recovers survivors of 1st battle, attacked by *U25* 153

Jan Wellem, German tanker: 124, 134, at Murmansk 19, 21, arrive Narvik 29, fuelling problems 40, British prisoners confined in 40, fuels destroyers 50, 56, 60, action in harbour 61, 63–65, 68, 70–71, Capt. Evans abducts prisoners from 71, 73, survives 103, refits destroyers 107, fuels *U51* 114

Kattegat, German tanker: 19, sails for Narvik 21, fails to arrive 40, 98, sunk 106

Kimberley, British destroyer: 172, screens *Repulse* 31, 42, 47, in Vestfjord 97, operation orders 112, in port column 118, in action 125, 132, 140, assists *Cossack* 142, 153, 154, enters Rombaksfjord 150, particulars 162

Knorr, Kapitänleutnant, CO *U51* q.v.

Knowling, Lieutenant Commander R. G. K., CO *Kimberley* q.v.

Kothe, Korvettenkapitän, CO *Hermann Künne* q.v.

Kristiansand: German landing 16

Landing parties, British: 43, Admiralty proposes 42, operation orders 48, possibility of using 58, 72, 156–157, not ordered in 2nd battle 108–109, 152

Layman, Commander H. F. H., CO *Hotspur* q.v.

Leads (Norwegian coastal waterways): strategic importance 14, German supply ships in 21, 106

Lean, Commander J. T., CO *Punjabi* q.v.

Leberecht Maass Class, German destroyers: 18, poor sea-keeping qualities 23, 24, reported by British 98, 110, 113, particulars 164

Lepel, Kapitänleutnant von, *GT* 2nd-in-command: killed 146

Lighthouses extinguished: 33
Lilandsgrund (Ofotfjord): *U25* patrols off 114, 129, *EK* passes 121, map 122
Lippe, German ore-carrier: 103
Lofoten Islands: Whitworth arrives off 22, patrols west of 28, German opportunity to dominate area 35-36, Home Fleet off 103, 109, assistance of islanders 154-155, map 45
Lulea (Swedish Baltic port): iron ore shipped from 14, map 15
Lütjens, Vice Admiral commanding battlecruisers: 16, 163, leaves destroyers and turns seawards 30-31, opportunity to overwhelm *Renown* and dominate Lofoten area 35

McCoy, Commander J. A., CO *Bedouin* q.v.: 31, 161, reports Baroy fortified 99, SO destroyers in 2nd battle 118-119, 138, 140, leads starboard division ahead 126, 128, appreciates situation in Rombaksfjord 149, orders sinking of *HL* 151
Mandalka, A., *GT*, Bootsmann and Director Layer 78
Mansell, Lieutenant Commander V. G. D., *Hardy* 1st Lt 90
Marinegruppenkommandowest—see Group West
Marines, Royal: supernumeries in 2nd DF 20, 65, 80, not landed after 2nd battle 109, 157
Marschall, Admiral, C-in-C German Fleet 163
Martha Hendrik Fisser, German ore-carrier: sunk 74
Maud, Lieutenant Commander C. D., CO *Icarus* q.v.
Merchant seamen, British: confined in *Jan Wellem* 40, escape of 71, 73, 102-103, 153
Merchant ships at Narvik: 29, 37-39, 40, 58, 65, British ordered to sink 42, 48, 54, 63, 68, suffer in 1st battle 61-74

Mersington Court, British ore-carrier: 103
Micklethwait, Commander St J. A., CO *Eskimo* q.v.: precept 158
Millns, Mr F. L., *Havock* Gunner (T): 63, 94
Minefields, British: 97, plan to lay 14, 20, operation 21-22, *Hero* patrols 29, hazard to German destroyers 32, map 15
Minefields, German: thought by British to exist 17, 44, 98, 99, 111, 113-114, 156
Minelaying destroyers, British: 20, 21, detached to lay 22, half armament removed 20, 30, 118, join *Renown* 29, off Vestfjord 42
Minesweeping—see Paravanes
Moskenes (Lofotens): *Furious* launches air strike off 109, map 26, and see Skjelfjord
Mountain troops, German: embark in destroyers 17, 22-23, land at Narvik 36, 38-39
Murmansk: *Jan Wellem* at 19, 21, 28

Narvik Class, German destroyers: 159
Narvik harbour: Germans arrive 36-40, action in 60-74, 2nd attack 134-136, *EG* leaves 136, *U51* leaves 137, *Cossack* engages *DR* in 140-142, *Foxhound* enters 147, *DR* blows up in 148, *Cossack* aground in 151-152, 154, map 59
Neuenfels, German ore-carrier: sunk 74
Norge, Norwegian coast defence ship: 37, 56, 95, 167, 171, sunk 38, 74, particulars 165
North Cornwall, British ore-carrier: 39, 65, spared by *Havock* 68, survives 103
Norway: strategic importance of 13-16, 27, invasion of 16-20, 21, 22-33, 36-39

Ofotfjord (leads to Narvik): German
destroyers enter 34, shore
batteries believed to command
36, 43, 111, 113, 124, 2nd DF in
54-94, British patrols in 98-99,
U-Boats in 51, 54, 56, 93, 94,
99, 104, 105, 106, 114, 121, 123,
129, 137, 152-155, German
patrols—see Patrols, German
break-out attempt through 104,
Force 'B' in 120-155, map 53

Ore Quay (Narvik harbour): 38,
48, 70, 110, 124, map 59

Osborne, Lieutenant Commander
(E) J. A., *Hotspur* EO: 88, keeps
engines going 89

Oslo: German attack 16, 41

Pacey, Leading Airman, M.,
Telegraphist Air Gunner,
Warspite's aircraft q.v.

Paravanes, British destroyer
minesweeps: 112, 118, 125, 132

Patrols, British: off minefields 20,
29, 97, in Vestfjord and Ofotfjord
36, 41, 98-99, 104-106, 114, 118

Patrols, German destroyers off
Narvik: 51, 52, 56-58, 92, map 53

Penelope, British light cruiser: with
Repulse 42, ordered to Narvik
and cancelled 47, meets 2nd DF
after 1st battle 97, sighted by
Bey 104, permissive order to
attack Narvik 104-105, decides
against 106, grounds 106, in
Skjelfjord damaged 106, 154

Peters, Lieutenant Commander
G. H., CO *Foxhound* q.v.

Piening, Gunnery Artificer, *EG*:
137

Plans, British: minelaying 14-16,
20, D2's 43-49, to recapture
Narvik 100, to attack Germans
at Narvik 104-106, 108-109,
112-114, 116, 119

Plans, German: to invade Norway
14-20, Bonte's to defend Narvik
50-52, Bey's to break out 101,
103, to fight to the end 117

Pönitz, Fregattenkapitän G., CO
Wolfgang Zenker q.v.

Post Pier (Narvik Harbour): troops
landed at 36-38, *DR* anchors
near 60, drags anchor to 70,
DR stays at 115, 140, 147, hit
by torpedoes 135, destroyers
berthed at 110

Pound, Admiral of the Fleet Sir
Dudley, KCB, First Sea Lord: 160

Punjabi, British destroyer: 47, 171,
with *Repulse* 31, operation orders
112, fuels 118, in starboard
column 118, in action 124,
engages *EK* 126-128, splinter
damage 132, engages enemy in
harbour 135, hard hit 135-137,
rejoins 150, stands by *Eskimo*
153, in Skjelfjord 154, particulars
161

Raeder, Grossadmiral: initiates
operation 14, 163

Ramnes (Ofotfjord): Germans land
at 36, batteries believed to exist
at—see Shore Batteries, D2
ordered to patrol east of 47,
U46 off 51, 56, 93, 98, 104, 114,
HK patrols to 52, air attack
ordered on 113, Force 'B'
approaches 124, maps 53, 122

Ramsund channel (Ofotfjord): 98,
map 53

Rauenfels, German ammunition
ship: 19, sails for Narvik 21,
non-arrival 40, 92, attacked by
U25 93, intercepted, boarded
and blown up 93-94, 98, wreck
sighted by Bey 104

Reardon, Petty Officer, *Warspite*:
129

Rechel, Korvettenkapitän C., CO
Bernd von Arnim q.v.

Reid, Lieutenant Commander (E)
A. G., *Hunter* EO: 87

Renown, British battlecruiser, flagship
of BC1: 42, Operation Wilfrid
20, 21, patrols off Skomvaer 22,
movements to intercept German
force 25-32, 33, action 34-36,

180

41, *Repulse* joins 103, flag transferred to *Warspite* 114
Repulse, British battlecruiser: detached to assist *Glowworm* 25, 28, ordered to join *Renown* 31, 41, 103, to Vestfjord 41, 42
Rice, Petty Officer Airman F. C., pilot of *Warspite*'s aircraft q.v.
Ritchie, Lieutenant R. D., *Eskimo* GO: 144
Rodney, British battleship: 100, 104
Rombaksfjord/Rombaken: 139, Germans retire to 134, 136, 138, British follow 138, action in 142-147, 148, 149-151, map 53
Roope, Lieutenant Commander G. B., CO *Glowworm* q.v.
Russian Navy: tradition 159

Saalwechter, Admiral Commanding Group West q.v.
Scandinavia: British trade with 27, map 15
Scharnhorst, German battlecruiser—see *Gneisenau*
Schultze, Kapitänleutnant H., CO *U48* q.v.
Schulz, Kapitänleutnant, CO *U64* q.v.
Schulze-Hinrichs, Fregattenkapitän A., CO *Erich Koellner* q.v.
Schütze, Korvettenkapitän, CO *U25* q.v.
Second British Destroyer Flotilla: 98, 160, 166, 167, commanded by Warburton-Lee 13, escort to minelayers 20, battlecruiser action 35, ordered to Narvik 41, 42, staff officers 44, reinforcement of considered 46-47, 76, 92, 156-157, sighted by *U51* 50, 51, 1st battle 52-96, surviving ships retire 97-98
Shells: 4.7in semi-armour-piercing (SAP) 82, 84, 85, 144, 151, 15in armour-piercing 128, 136, 149, 12.7cm high-explosive 73, 78, 81, 84, 85, 132, 135-137, 141
Sherbrooke, Commander R. St V., CO *Cossack* q.v.

Sherbrooke, Mrs: 152
Shore batteries: believed to exist, Germans attack 36, D2 informed of 42-43, ordered to report 54, British sensitivity to 99, 112-114, 120, 124, 156, DR thought to be 140, salvaged AA weapons as 109, 111
616 Squadron Fleet Air Arm, *Furious*: abortive strike 110
Skagerrak: German force off 22, 28, map 15
Skjelfjord (Moskenes Island, Lofotens): emergency base 97, 105, 106, 118, 119, 121, 154, map 45
Skjomgrund Shoal (Ofotfjord): *Bedouin* and *Punjabi* pass inshore 132, map 130
Skjomnes/Skjomenfjord (Ofotfjord): merchant seamen cross 103, *Hardy* re-grounds in 103, aircraft reconnoitres 121, map 53
Skomvaer (tip of Lofotens): *Renown* off 22, 28, 41, map 26
Skredneset (Ofotfjord): *Hardy* aims to pass close to 48, not sighted 56, torpedoes explode on 129, map 53
Smale, Able Seaman, *Hardy*: takes wheel 81
Smidt, Korvettenkapitän K., CO *Erich Giese* q.v.
Smith, F., Telegraphist Air Gunner, *Furious* and *Hero*: 120, abortive strike 110
Smoke screen, British in 1st battle: D2 orders 75, adverse effect of 76-80, 82
Sohler, Kapitänleutnant, CO *U46* q.v.
Sommer, Oberleutnant, *GT* TO: hits *Eskimo* with torpedo 145
Spooner, Captain E. J., DSO, CO *Repulse* q.v.
Stanning, Paymaster Lieutenant G. H., *Hardy*, Secretary to D2: 35, 49, 78, 102, 146, lands at Tranoy 43-44, first council of war 44-46, observes harbour

181

action 58–62, 69, second council 72, identifies *GT* and *BA* 76, assumes command 80–81, beaches *Hardy* 90

Stavanger: Germans approach 41, map 15

Stewart, Able Seaman N., *Hunter*: saves Stuart-Menteth 91

Straumen Narrows (Rombaksfjord): Germans pass 142, *Eskimo* and *Forester* pass 143, *Hero* in 144–145, German torpedoes run onto spit 146, *Eskimo* retires through 149, map 139

Stuart-Menteth, Lieutenant H. A., *Hunter* 1st Lt: collision 87, trapped 88, saved 91, captured 92

Supply ships, German: plans 17, 19, sail 21, Bonte's lack of concern for 50, 92

Sweden: iron mines 14, to be left alone 22, map 15

Swordfish, British torpedo/spotter/reconnaissance carrier and catapult aircraft: strike against Trondheim 108, against Narvik 109–111, 133–134, and see *Warspite*'s aircraft

Sydney-Turner, Lieutenant Commander P. G. O., *Furious*, CO 818 Sqn q.v.

Taarstad (Ofotfjord): *EK* ordered to 115–116, 117, 128, map 122

Tancock, Lieutenant Commander E. B., CO *Forester* q.v.

Third German Destroyer Flotilla: 18, 163, in harbour during 1st battle 52

Thomas, Marine D., *Hotspur* 89

Tietke, Petty Officer, *DR*: in charge demolition 147–148

Tillie, Sub Lieutenant L. J., *Hotspur*: 89

Tjeldoy (Ofotfjord): 2nd DF passes 54, map 53

Tjellebotn (Ofotfjord): *HK* off 120, *U25* attacks *Warspite* off 153, and again 154, bottoms in 155, map 53

Tjelsund Channel (Ofotfjord): 98, map 53

Torpedoes, British Mark IX: 2nd DF policy 48, control details 57, effective weapon 168, particulars 169, ship outfits App. 1 Fired by: *Hardy* 61–62, 67, 90, *Hunter* 62–63, 67, 68, *Havock* 64, 67, 79, *Hotspur* 67, 87, *Hostile* 73, 80, 82, *Bedouin* 128, 135, *Punjabi* 128, 135, *Eskimo* 128, 138, 144, 146, *Forester* 138, 144, *Hero* 151, 152

Torpedoes, German Mark G7a/G7e: particulars 19, 169, angling of 57, 69, 168, failure as weapon 39, 99, 153, 166–168, malfunctioned 38–39, 69–70, 77, 91, 93, 99, 105, 129, 133, 137, 145, 167, redistribution of 107, 115–116, tracks visible from air 140, 145, ship outfits App. 1, Fired by: *BA* 38–39, 79, 133, *WH* 37, *DR* 68–70, *HL* 73, 77, 144–146, *GT* 78, 86, 132, 145, *EG* 90, 91, 135, 137, *EK* 128, *WZ* 128, 129, *HK* 132, *U25* 93, 99, 129, 153, 154, *U51* 105, *U48* 155

Tranoy Island (Vestfjord): D2 seeks information at pilot station 43–44, 58, 2nd DF passes 54, *U51* patrols off 98, 105, *U48* patrols off 114, 118, *Warspite* passes and returns 154, *U48* attacks *Warspite* off 155, map 26

Tribal Class, British destroyers: 42, 97, 132, particulars 31, 161, ability to shoot ahead 125

Trollvik (Herjangsfjord): *HK* beaches 138, map 130

Trondheim: capture of 16, 18, 28, 41, British air attack 108, map 15

Troop movements, British: 100, 108–109, 157

U-Boat Command: plans 17, 18–19, 159, 163, communications 19

U-Boats, general: 98, 114, 121, dispositions 51, one seen to pass Tranoy 44, Bonte's reliance on 51, operations in narrow waters 19, 106, poor liaison with surface forces 93, 103, 106, British disregard of 98, 108, 113–114, 118, 153–155, 157, torpedo failures—see Torpedoes, German

U25: plans 19, off Baroy 51, fails to sight 2nd DF entering 54, attacks *Rauenfels* 93, sights 2nd DF leaving 94, attacks *Bedouin* and *Eskimo* 98–99, sights German destroyers 104, sights British destroyers 105, moves to Lilandsgrund 114, sights aircraft 121, attacks port column and moves down fjord 129, attacks *Warspite* 153, and again 154, bottomed at Tjellebotn 154, 155, particulars 164

U46: plans 19, off Ramnes 51, 98, fails to sight 2nd DF entering 56, sights 2nd DF leaving 93, 94, ordered to Narvik 103, 106, between Baroy and Ramnes 114, attacks *Warspite* 123, sights British leaving 154, 155, particulars 164

U48: ordered to Vestfjord 98, off Tranoy 114, attacked by *Eskimo* 118, attacks *Warspite* 155, particulars 164

U51: plans 19, sights 2nd DF in Vestfjord 50, 51, attacked by destroyers 98, attacks destroyers 105, fuels at Narvik 114, bottoms in harbour 124, escapes to Ballangen 137–138, 153, sights *Warspite* 155, particulars 164

U64: plans 19, 172, ordered into Vestfjord 98, anchored in Herjangsfjord 114, sunk by *Warspite*'s aircraft 121–122, 148, particulars 165

Valiant, British battleship: 104
Vestfjord (outer approach to Narvik): 9, U-Boats stationed in 19, 51, 113–114, 118, 155, British minefield in 20, 32, *Renown* joins destroyers at entrance 27, 29–30, Germans enter 32, *Repulse* proceeds to 41–42, 2nd DF in 42, 52–54, 97, British patrols in 36, 41–42, 97–99, 104, 105, 114, 118, Germans break out into 101, 104, *Furious* aircraft overfly 109–110, report mines in 111, Force 'B' in 116–120, 154–155, map 45
Victoria Cross: Roope 25, Warburton-Lee 13, 46
Villiers—see *Hunter*
Virek: *Hardy* grounds at 90, 101–102, map 83

Warburton-Lee, Captain B. A. W., CO *Hardy* and Captain (D) 2nd DF: 160, wins VC 13, 46, escorts minelayers 16, 20, joins *Renown* 27, 29, 30, 35, returns to Vestfjord 41, ordered to Narvik 41, 42, seeks information at Tranoy 43, decision to attack 44–47, 49, 105, 117, is not reinforced 47, 49, issues orders 48–49, seizes and loses initiative 51, 58, 75, 95–96, 156, passage to Narvik 53–58, not helped by Admiralty 54, 56, action in harbour 60–62, orders continuation of action 67–68, 71, decides to attack again 72–73, sights 4th DF 74, orders retirement and smoke 75, reports enemy cruiser 75, action with *GT* and *BA* 76–78, mortally wounded 78, 80, 102, as leader 46–47, 49, 78, 102, 119, 156

Warspite, British battleship: 172, with Home Fleet 104, operation orders 112, hoists flag of BC1 114, enters Vestfjord 116, warning to Bey of 117, passage up fjords 118–148, opens fire 125–126, sinks *EK* 128, general engagement 129–132, engages *DR* and *EG* 136, 140, enters

Rombaksfjord 148, withdraws 153, returns to Narvik 154, withdraws finally 155, threat from U-Boats 113, 118, 123, 152–155, 157–158, gunnery problems 125–126, 129, 149, particulars 161

Warspite's aircraft: 161, launched 119–120, sights *HK* 120, sights *EK* and *HL* 121, sinks *U64* 121, scouts ahead of force 123, warns of *EK* in ambush 124, 126, remains in Narvik area 140, reports *DR* 140, reports torpedo tracks 140, 145, lands 148

Watling, Leading Seaman, *Hotspur*: 35, 89

Weserübung, Operation: see Norway, invasion of

WH—see Wilhelm Heidkamp

Whitworth, Vice Admiral W. J., CB, DSO, Commanding Battlecruiser Squadron (BC1): 161, in command minelaying operation 20–22, appreciates situation 25–28, meets destroyers at Vestfjord and proceeds seawards 29–32, followed by German battlecruisers 31, 33, action 34–36, sends destroyers to Vestfjord 36, orders D2 to rejoin 41, considers reinforcing D2 47, 76, 92, orders patrols in Vestfjord 98, complains about conflicting orders 105, commands Force 'B' 112–113, transfers to *Warspite* 114, issues tactical orders 116, briefs aircrew 119, no need to give orders 132, tactical signals 140, 141, orders aircraft to bomb destroyers 148, orders action in Rombaksfjord 150–151, orders *EG* to be sunk 152, decides not to land and retires 152–153, returns Narvik 154, disregards U-Boats 118, 153–155

Wilfrid, Operation: see Minefields, British

Wilhelm Heidkamp (*WH*), German destroyer: 163, 171, Bonte's leader 17, bad weather 23, sinks *Eidsvold* 37, lands Dietl and troops 39, remains in harbour 51–52, 60, sighted by *Hardy* 61, hit by torpedo 62, 63, 65, weapons, etc. salvaged 99, 107, 111, 115, sinks 107, particulars 163

Willoch, Captain, CO *Eidsvold* q.v.

Wimpel, large German pendant: 76, 88

Wolff, Korvettenkapitän M-E, CO *Georg Thiele* q.v.: 163, 167, 171–172, precept 158

Wolfgang Zenker (*WZ*), German destroyer: 18, bad weather 23, in Herjangsfjord 52, engages 2nd DF 74, engages *Hardy* 91, state of readiness 100, 114, 115, break-out attempt 101, 103–104, grounds and damages propeller 107, 114–115, joins 2nd battle 124–125, fires torpedoes 128, 129, enters Rombaksfjord 134, 142, scuttled 150–151, particulars 164

Wright, Commander J. P., CO *Hostile* q.v.: 161, reports 1st action 92, 97–98, assumes command of 2nd DF 93, encounters *Rauenfels* 93–94, wishes to return to Narvik 97, precept 158

WZ—see Wolfgang Zenker